*A story from the heart:
How one head-driven person
learned to live in faith not fear*

JOURNEY
to the
IDEAL

Michelle Bain

JOURNEY
to the
IDEAL

By Michelle Bain

www.michelle-bain.com

Copyright 2015 by Michelle Bain
Revised Edition 2017 by Michelle Bain

ISBN 978-0-9962154-0-4

*To the many voices
of love and support who made this book possible:
Karen, Chris, Mom & Dad, Sunny & Lesa, Meg*

and

*To the One Voice
that makes all things possible*

Introduction

I am a runner. I simply love to run . . . and run . . . and run. I burn through a pair of tennis shoes at least every three months as I cover miles of outdoor terrain. Sometimes, it may only be for a quick mile or two, but usually not a day goes by without my shoes hitting the pavement.

Because of my passion for running, it is automatic for me to parallel my entire life to "one good long run." Like any physical run, this run called *life* presents my every footstep with mental and physical challenges, while it constantly tests my endurance as I leap to avoid obstacles big and small.

With real and metaphorical runs, there are also mixtures of sunshine and gray skies, sandy beaches and barren fields, times with partners and times alone. I gather experience with each passing mile. At the end, both have helped build me into a stronger person than I was before I started.

While I learn incredible lessons from each lap of life (how I like to label time periods or series of events) physical running has one distinct advantage: it helps release me from the grip of my overactive mind. A run is a short period of freedom from the constrictive, fear-based mental reality I tend to create on a daily basis. When I run, I peacefully soak up the scenery and temporarily set myself free from the constant volley of thoughts which bounce around inside my head.

If it sounds like I might be a head-case, there's no doubt that I am. My head "runneth over" as it over-thinks, over-plans and over-analyzes. Although my mind is exceptional at many things (such as business), a head full of racing thoughts is usually not the most constructive place for me to be. My brain hardly ever rests. It is on a never-ending mission to figure out why events happen in my life, or it is busy devising some plan to change things to be the way it thinks they should be.

Another exhaustive trait my head possesses is the desire to know all the answers in advance. Constantly in seeker mode, I spend many hours searching for the meaning of life, my ultimate purpose and the reason for the existence of all things. If I were ever to create my own board game, it would be called *The Relentless Search for Meaning*.

These few things I mention about me (runner, head-case and seeker) lead us to the book you hold in your hand, *Journey to the Ideal*. It is a story about four significant laps in my life which span eight years and 45,000 miles. During these laps, a major transformation takes place as I transition from old-self to ideal-self.

The first lap is the largest, both geographically and in quantity of experiences. Each lap that follows is a smaller distance, then smaller, until there are only a few inches to travel in Lap Four. As distances decrease, the experiences become more profound. Every page is honest and true. I won't spoil the ending, but I will tell you that a fear-based head no longer directs my life.

As you can imagine, on a run this long there are many opportunities for me to trip over some large cracks in the sidewalk. I do get a few skinned knees in this book. That's life though, right? You pick up, dust off and keep on running.

So, my friend, it's time to throw on our running shoes so we can get started on this journey together. Remember, the way I view life is that the experiences of one are there to benefit the many. If you find a special pebble or a little flower along the way that might help you or another, pick it up and take it with you.

Okay, here we go . . .

LAP I

THE WORLD SHOWS ME THE WAY

Chapter 1:
Letting Go—My Box

No, not now—please, please don't let this happen right now. Not while I'm trapped in my car with no way to move or breathe—no way to escape. Please, pleeeease have mercy on me this time. Do not start your vicious attack on my nerves, you deadly little microbes of mental destruction.

Not today, when I'm late, hot, confined and defenseless. This will be too much for my already frenzied mind to handle. I'll lose control and get into an accident. Please pass up just this <u>one</u> stressful situation instead of pushing me over the edge into insanity. Please, please, pleeeease!

It is too late. The invisible microbes have already been released and their attack on my nerves is in painful motion. The tiny particles ride the river of my blood intent on one thing—complete body infiltration.

As they flow, their jagged little arms reach out and latch on to my dangling nerve endings. Quickly, they scurry up toward the skin surface where they break free. Every disturbed nerve in my body ignites in anger at this violation, yet the microbes continue on their mission.

They crawl on my skin, over my body and up the back of my neck. Within seconds, hundreds of imaginary little bugs creep across my scalp. My entire head starts to itch uncontrollably. My skin is covered by a layer of a thousand inescapable pin pricks.

I . . . . can't breathe . . . . I'm going . . . . to suffocate . . . . There's no air . . . . in here . . . .

My lungs are so tight, air can't get in. The air is hot and thick, like black sludge—globs of it. I can't suck it in through my mouth or nose without choking.

No way . . . . to get . . . . air in . . . . I have . . . . to get out . . . . I . . . . need air . . . . I have . . . . to escape!

While every nerve in my body continues to explode, I hyperventilate in silent hysteria, unable to stop the episode. As I sit trapped inside my SUV, in sweltering heat, surrounded by hundreds of honking cars, my anxiety attack continues to consume me to the point of delirium.

I look around for some possible way to escape. Morning rush hour traffic is at a dead stand-still on the Los Angeles 405 freeway. Bumper to bumper, solid lines of cars extend for miles before me, beside me, all around me. There is no way to break free from the hell I am in. Claustrophobia sets in further and the sludgy air in my car thickens to tar.

If I . . . . can just get . . . . fresh air . . . . I'll be . . . . okay.

I crack the window a fraction. Hot, smoggy air bursts at my face like flames raging through the broken window of a burning building. Quickly, I close the window and crank the air conditioning to maximum capacity. My lungs ache for breath as I gasp and wheeze, but there is *not enough* air.

I yank off the seatbelt, but it doesn't help. Trapped behind the steering wheel, I can't move enough to escape and I still cannot breathe.

"I'm in hell," I cry in agony. "What if I die during this experience? What if I die right here in the hell of 405 traffic, stuck in an SUV?"

How did this happen? How did I let myself get to this point of crippling, consuming anxiety again? How? How? How?

Negative thoughts. Negative thoughts initiated this entire episode of mental and physical horror. Negative thoughts that started out small, which quickly grew and gained momentum as they globbed on to one another; eventually morphing into an enormous black sludge that contaminates my air to the point of suffocation.

Depression, despair, anger, discouragement and other vile emotions pushed these thoughts together and molded them into a ball of darkness. A ball that grew so huge, it exploded and set free the hundreds of microscopic pin pricks which assault my every nerve.

Welcome to the mind of Michelle Bain . . . my own personal torture chamber.

# # # #

Flashing back to ten minutes before the attack—I sit helplessly in my car as I inch along in traffic. It is hot outside today, a typical sunny summer day in Southern California. In spite of the air conditioner, I start to feel little beads of perspiration form along my hairline. My car thermostat reads ninety-five degrees outside.

"The smog from all this traffic mixed with this heat is disgusting," I complain to the empty car. "I wish I could open the window and breathe some fresh air."

As my body heat continues to rise, the nylon lining of my pantsuit starts to grow damp and begins to stick like Saran Wrap to my thighs. I press my face up to the air vent of the SUV, suck in a breath and attempt to overcome the first small waves of claustrophobia that wash over me.

"Stop pushing the brake pedal!" my throbbing toes—crammed into narrow, uncomfortable dress shoes—seem to scream up at me as I brake for the hundredth time after rolling forward a few-inches.

I slump forward in misery and rest my head on the steering wheel in defeat. A horn blasts next to me and jolts me back to reality.

"What good does honking do, you idiot, when no one is able to move?" I cuss at the driver, glaring at him in disgust.

Glancing at the car's clock, my heart beat accelerates. Even though I planned an extra thirty minutes for traffic, there is no way possible I will make it to my meeting on time. It is *not* going to happen. At this rate, it will take me another twenty minutes to travel the quarter-mile to my appointment.

"Lovely. I have to call and tell them I'll be late," I fume. "This is just great. I planned extra time for traffic. How can this be happening?"

Tears of frustration well up in my eyes as I realize it has taken over an hour to go less than fifteen miles. The lining of my pants seems to grow smaller and the air in the car hotter. Anxious thoughts start to swirl around in my mind.

"You will not cry over this!" the voice in my head bellows. "You watched *A League of Their Own* and know the rule: There's no crying in baseball. You are a Professional Business Woman who does not have time for tears. You do not have time to redo makeup. You do *not* have time for a silly thing like emotion!"

Sweat trickles down the center of my back, like my body is determined to mock me and prove that while I may be able to control tears, it will find another release.

Is this really my life? This captivity; this misery? Is this my choice for daily existence? To sit, day after day, in painful shoes and an uncomfortable suit, stuck in bumper to bumper traffic on a freeway filled with angry drivers, while I attempt to sell product that I have little interest in?

Where's the joy in this? Does the joy come from "the stuff" I'm able to buy from the money I earn? Is this my ideal self? Someone who sacrifices joy for hours of misery each day, so that I hit some made-up personal goal that revolves around ego and material possessions? As a thirty-five year old woman, am I happy with this life?

More important, am I happy with who I am?

There it is. The hidden question which lurks in the back of my mind, camouflaged by denial and self-deception. It springs out of hiding and starts to shoot round after round of self-judging thoughts at lightning speed. *Splat! Splat! Splat! Splat! Splat!* The thoughts stick like paint ball splats to the dark ball of negativity that has formed. As each splat builds upon the next, the glob quickly grows until this ball of darkness finally reaches maximum capacity and explodes.

My mind pushes over the edge out of control, and I fall head first into the pit of anxiety and the full attack begins . . .

# # # #

I survive the anxiety attack without dying in a car accident. At my destination, I run straight to the restroom to perform damage repair—even though I'm already fifteen minutes late.

"My head looks like a tornado hit it," I think as I attempt to smooth down the mess my scalp scratching caused. Then I move over to the electric hand dryer to dry the noticeable sweat creases in my pants.

Back at the mirror, I stare at my reflection for a few long seconds. Snapping out of my daze, I plaster on my best fake smile, swing open the door and stride out as the Professional Business Woman I pride myself to be. Hopefully, they will buy it.

"'Never let them see you sweat,' they say. If these people I meet with each day only knew. If they only knew that many times, this smiling face is just a façade and that sometimes I'm only hanging on to some form of sanity by a thread, I'm sure they would cancel all together," I confess to myself.

But I don't let them know that *this* is what hides behind my smiling face because I am a Professional Business Woman—one they trust to get the job done. *That* is who I am and *that* is what is expected so *that* is what I deliver. The woman I am today shoves down emotion and puts on a happy, got-it-together face for the world.

Sometime during the course of life, my sense of self, or *who I am*, was replaced by *who I am is what I do* so that my self-value is now defined by what I accomplish as a business professional, instead of by my character attributes. I have lost sight of my true self completely and today I only know *who I am* by the title I carry on a business card. It's the bright, shiny label that tells the current make and model of Michelle the Business Machine.

Is this who you really are though, Michelle? Someone so afraid to break out of the role she has assigned herself that she is forced to act like someone she's not? Someone who parades a façade of happiness but really has no idea what happiness truly is? Is this who you want to be?

No it is not. This is not who I want to be, nor is this the life I want to lead. I want more than a head constantly filled with negative, fear-based thoughts; a head that bombards me with expectations about how I must act and what I must be and do.

*I want joy and happiness! I want escape from this constrictive world I have compressed myself into so that I can figure out who I really am behind the façade. I want freedom—from my anxiety, from my structured life, from my too-busy head, from my old restrictive self—and in this very important moment, I am **finally** ready to do whatever it takes to gain this freedom!*

As I step onto the escalator, I reach into my computer bag for my cell phone and dial my best friend, Chris. Something big is happening within me right now and I need her to be part of it.

Chris and I met four years ago at a different company and it was an instant friendship. I don't remember this, but she says that after a few conversations between us, I declared, "You're going to be my best friend," to which she replied, "Okay."

Regardless how it started, we have been inseparable ever since and have shared many times of laughter, tears, joy and pain. She is someone I trust, who is like me in many ways: physically since both of us like to hike, bike and surf; professionally since we are both in sales in the same industry; and spiritually because we both strive for personal growth.

Yet Chris is vastly different than me because she is capable of identifying and feeling her emotions. She doesn't turn them off like I do. She's an energetic, positive woman who is also selfless, thoughtful and really in touch with her heart. Chris would stop a moving train to save a wounded bird or would give you her last dollar if you needed it. Things I would never think to do. She comes from a place of love and connection, whereas I am driven by my head.

Even though she's only a few years older than me, I always joke, "Chris, I want to be like you when I grow up," because she has mastered the faith-not-fear and heart-not-head thing. She always jokes back, "Don't worry. You'll get there some day."

She is forever my cheerleader, always there with an encouraging "You can do it!" and as I ride up the escalator, I need her supportive voice more than ever. Why? Because in the short space between restroom and escalator a divine moment of clarity found its way into my consciousness. I am now ready to make one of the most substantial decisions of my entire life.

"Chris," I say into the phone, "I'm through with unhappiness and anxiety attacks. I will no longer define myself as some business role instead of knowing who I really am. No more! I just decided I'm going to make the gigantic leap and run with The Idea. I am GOING FOR IT!" I say with total determination.

"Good for you!" she responds enthusiastically, like she had prayed for this exact call and her wish finally came true. "Life is about happiness, especially self-happiness, Michelle. You need to go for it. Let me know what I can do to help make it happen."

I love my best friend. I swear, sometimes Chris knows me better than I know myself. She sounded so ready for my news, she probably had the phone in her hand when I called.

So on this hot summer day, filled with breakdowns and breakthroughs, The Idea moves from fantasy into reality and Michelle's Great Adventure is born.

# # # #

The Idea. The Idea is a crazy dream that has been brewing for the last few months. What initially sparks The Idea is something so simple—a coffee mug. Yes, a $7.95 black ceramic mug stamped with white words changes the entire course of my life.

The ironic part? I don't even drink coffee. I bought the mug for a friend, but the question it asks is so intriguing I decide to keep it to use as a pen holder.

"What would you attempt to do if you knew you could not fail?" is the captivating question the mug asks me each day from its place on my desk; to which my daily response is, "I don't know!"

Some people may have an instant answer to this question and others may have lists of things they would attempt. My answer is a complete blank. I have no clue what I would do if I knew I could not fail. My entire life is so motivated by the drive to succeed and the terrorizing fear of failing that I plow forward through life on no-fail auto-pilot.

"Do whatever it takes to succeed," the ego-driven voice in my head orders as it relentlessly pushes me toward my ever-elusive bar of perfection with its cattle prods of tough-love and self-judgment. "Self-acceptance is only allowed when you reach the top. Until then, you are someone who *hasn't got there yet* so keep moving! Be more, do more, win more, buy more, say more—and do it all perfectly!"

So this is what I do, like a machine someone has turned ON: Michelle the Machine. For decades, the critical voice in my head has commanded me to succeed and for decades I have followed this no-fail order. The result of functioning on auto-pilot mode for so many years is that I am no longer able to see possibilities that exist outside my present reality. Instead, I live trapped inside a restrictive, structured mental space—my Box.

In my Box, there are only carefully calculated decisions, detailed sets of plans and an obsessive need for control over work, life, relationships, emotions, each path or turn, all decisions, and all outcomes. There is no room for spontaneity or flexibility. This rigid control system is designed to do one thing: prevent the wretched *unknown* from causing chaos or failure in my life.

"Baby, why are you so afraid of the unknown?" my dear friend, Karen, asks me on a regular basis.

"Because the unknown is too unpredictable. What if the outcome is bad? Then what? Too big of a risk. I haven't come this far to risk moving backward. If I stay in control and always have a solid plan, then my chances are much better for avoiding both failure and hardship." This is my standard reply.

"But isn't that mentally exhausting? Don't you believe that God is capable of handling things? Do you realize that you would survive and still be loved if you failed?" she always questions further.

"God might be capable, but testing that theory is a risk I'm not willing to take. The stakes are too high with potential failure looming out there somewhere. I will continue to handle it—all of it," I respond with confidence.

Karen is another voice of reason in my life. As an unconditionally loving mentor/sister/friend figure, I deeply value her. She has this caring way about her, always calling me "Baby" and endearing names. She sees my positive qualities and wants the best for me, which is a good thing since I don't often acknowledge these aspects of myself.

Like Chris, Karen is honest enough to say, "I don't think you are seeing things accurately," or, "I think you are heading down the wrong path," which I love and respect about her, especially since she's usually right. A woman of grace and dignity whom I admire and aspire to be like, she puts others first and has a ton of wisdom and life experiences to draw from. Karen has wise eyes that see deep into an issue and I trust her viewpoint.

Since I am often preoccupied with following the orders bellowed by my head, there are many times I feel like God communicates loving words of wisdom to me through Karen and Chris. Because of this, I take heed and listen to these women with sincerity. They both come from a place I haven't quite tapped into—somewhere so far outside my structured mind, I don't know how to find my way to it. It is a faith-filled place where love and God prevail, where life seems much easier. Until I am able to find it, I continue to listen to the voices of those who live there.

With regard to my need for control and my unrelenting drive for success at all cost, God has been feeding me the message "You are off path about this" via both Karen and Chris for years. Unfortunately, my own voice of command still overrides in these areas with its logical, machine-like response, "Information Not Deemed Valid—Proceed as Instructed."

Lately however, *something* inside me feels a sadness, like I should listen to them instead of my old programmed thoughts. It is the same *something* that whispers, "It's okay to stop being a well-structured 'human doing' machine. Let go, feel and dream a little. Things will be okay." This whisper seems to have grown louder since I bought that silly coffee mug!

Maybe I should listen to the whisper. What's the worst that can happen if I go beyond my normal view of life and dream a little? I don't have to take action on anything I come up with.

Backed by the strength of the whisper, I decide to step past my old established boundaries a little—just a little, of course. I stop asking myself the mug question at my desk, where logical Business Michelle sits to take actions toward success. Instead, I bounce the question around during my early morning beach runs, when my mind feels more light and free.

"What would I attempt to do if I knew I could not fail?" I ask as I jog along the beach path before sunrise. "Ocean waves, do you know the answer? Morning sun, will your rays shine the answer upon me?" I throw the question out to these elements but get no response. It appears they do not have the answer I seek.

After many mornings, something inside me starts to soften in the dark silence right before dawn. Small fantasies from my childhood begin to play like soundless movies across the dark morning sky. I remember my daydreams as a young girl about castles that stand proudly atop tall hills, sandy beaches with roaring waves, meadows of green grass and beautiful museums loaded with treasures. These images dance across the sky, along with fantasies about horseback rides through vineyards, camel rides through deserts and deep-water swims with colorful fish in the ocean.

Excitement quickens my footsteps as these scenes become clearly visible, like they were when I was a child. I forgot about my old internal treasure chest labeled *Childhood Dreams!* I buried that chest almost three decades ago under piles and piles of *Life*. It seems almost impossible that this chest filled with exciting fantasies and dreams could still exist inside me!

As I continue my morning runs, other visions begin to unfold and parade across the sky, only these scenes consist of real memories, not fantasies. Memories from age ten, when I sat on the floor next to my great-grandmother in her old wooden chair and stared at her in wonder. My great-grandmother, Josephine, was from Czechoslovakia and she seemed exotic to me. She came from somewhere on the other side of the world and spoke a language I couldn't understand. Everything about her fascinated me.

When she talked to my grandpa in her native tongue, my young mind would race, fantasizing about the unknown wonders of foreign lands and languages. She was proof to me that the world was a vast place and I vowed as a child to explore the world someday.

As I grew older and became laser focused on success, I buried this vow deep within me instead of fulfilling it. With the release of the fantasies and memories, the vow has managed to work its way back to the surface and has brought with it the answer to the question on the mug.

What would I attempt to do if I knew I could not fail? *I would* *travel all over the world!*

At last, I have the answer! My heart skips a beat as a surge of happiness bolts through me. Overwhelmed, I pause my run for a minute and turn to stare out at the ocean.

What's on the other side of all that water? What would it be like to find out? Could I summon enough courage to do something like that?

The siren mounted at the door of my safe, secure Box starts wailing, "Red Alert, Red Alert!" Mechanical arms of fear snake out and try to grasp onto me and pull me back inside. As preservation mode kicks into high gear, my head is quickly flooded with a tidal wave of visions of bad outcomes. The mechanical arms flail around and attempt to erase my fantasies and memories from the sky.

"You will fail," the voice in my head roars. "You will end up penniless and lose everything if you do something like this. You might even *die*," it threatens. The mechanical arms hiss like whips as they reach out and try to pull me back into my comfort zone and slam the door shut.

The stable structure of my entire life is in jeopardy because of this new dream and my logical head is determined it will not lose. For many days, whenever the dream surfaces, negativity is immediately there to smash it down with examples of how wrong things could go. Fear wins—I remain locked inside.

But then, I find a window in my Box that I never noticed before. I happen across it when I listen to advice from Chris and begin to meditate each evening. It takes me many nights of battling head chatter to finally reach moments of quiet, but eventually my perseverance pays off. In the silence, I feel an incredible peace. It is in this state that the hidden window is revealed, cracked open ever so slightly—just enough for me to hear the soft whispering voice say, "You could travel the world, Michelle, and it could be an amazing adventure. Dreams *do* come true."

I love the message of this whispering voice, so full of encouragement and faith.

"I know live voices who speak similar messages—Karen and Chris!" I remember aloud. I call both women individually and tell them about The Idea. They are receptive and supportive.

"I think it sounds like a fabulous idea! You should do it," Chris encourages. "Baby, if anyone can do this, you can. You are the most capable person I know," Karen confirms in a voice filled with confidence.

"I might be capable, but does that mean I will be successful at it? Am I willing to give up everything I've worked for—a job that pays well, my ocean view apartment, the convertible, the SUV, the motorcycle—all my stuff and most importantly, my reputation as a success—and risk total failure for the unknown?" I say to Chris.

"These are all replaceable, Michelle," Chris counters as I rattle off the list. "You can always get another job. You have a great reputation and track record in the industry. There are other apartments, vehicles and stuff. What you *can't* replace is happiness and peace of mind—neither of which you have."

She's right, but can I replace lost pride if I fail? What if I give up everything, flop on my face and have to come crawling back with my tail between my legs after a few weeks? Could I survive that? If I only knew I would succeed at this!

The roots of my fears run too deep. I'm not willing to make this big of a gamble, even if happiness is the grand prize. Instead, I stay trapped by my old fears for many more days and sadly listen as the soft voice continues to whisper through the window.

That is, until an anxiety attack during a traffic jam and a moment of awareness come together one sunny Los Angeles day. On this day, Michelle the Machine breaks down and I finally acknowledge, Michelle the Human Being—a woman who wants happiness more than anything else.

I will risk it all to find happiness. I will pull off my old label. I will listen to the voices of others who have faith in me instead of listening to the commanding voice in my head. I will break free, face fear and walk into the unknown. And maybe, when I am free, I will find out who I really am.

# # # #

"When something is meant to be, it will happen effortlessly."
I don't remember which resource provides this gem of advice but it is a valuable lesson I experience firsthand when I start to make arrangements for my trip. Once the big decision is made, everything else falls into place at astonishing speed. The ease of how things flow for the next few months is a miracle to me, something that starts my faith-ball rolling at a healthy pace.

The very day I declare my commitment aloud to Chris, I start to take action by getting specific about what I intend to do and see. The final decision is to leave in less than two months and to travel one complete lap around the globe over a span of six months. I will visit thirteen countries as extensively as time allows, which should include stops at approximately seventy cities. Planes, trains and buses will be involved. Everything in California will be sold or stored beforehand.

In spite of the constant opportunity for complications to arise, a majority of my tasks go smoothly, almost without a hitch. There is definitely a lot of footwork and decision making involved but the flow with which things happen is quite effortless, which makes me feel like this trip is meant to be.

The lease on my apartment ends so I throw furnishings and clothing into storage and sleep at a friend's house with my packed bag. The SUV lease ends so I downsize to one vehicle. A good friend offers to pay half the convertible payment so she can enjoy a top down experience at a reduced rate. The motorcycle sells the first day it is advertised to the first buyer at asking price. My employer is able to fill my position with a coworker who has recently been released due to downsizing and I am able to train him before I leave. A friend introduces me to around-the-world flight travel, saving me thousands of dollars on airfare.

Soon, all flights are booked, followed by train passes for Europe. I discover an amazing website that allows reservations at hotels the day of arrival. Vaccine and visa deadlines for India are met with only a day to spare. I build my personal website almost overnight and research the thirteen countries and seventy cities I want to see within a four day period. The agenda for the entire six months is posted online before I leave so that my family and friends can track me.

Effortless. I need to continue to use this idea "When something is meant to be, it will happen effortlessly."

This is an entirely new concept. Before this, the control freak in me would never have stopped to consider if something was "meant to be." If I want something to take place—like a job, a relationship or a purchase—I usually just force it to happen. All signs are ignored as I persist with as much effort as possible. Like swimming upstream, it is exhausting, but it has always been my way.

From now on, I need to stop ignoring the signs. If something takes extreme effort and the path is filled with obstacles, it is probably not meant to be. Quit forcing things to happen. This way is so much easier!

While smooth flow moves things along, there is one big issue that takes place shortly before I resign from my job. A major account is suddenly denied funding on a deal that I have worked for over a year and a half, which shorts me a large commission that is already factored into my trip financials. My travel budget is instantly cut in half.

Besides money, there is also an ego dilemma about walking away from one of the largest sales the company has ever experienced for this particular product. I am set to be hailed a superstar for this win.

The account anticipates funding within a few months and I now face a big decision. Do I postpone the trip in hopes that the account will eventually get funding or do I follow my dream and have faith that it will all work out somehow in the end?

The voice in my Box screams out the door at me, "You are an idiot if you don't stay! So much work, so much money! You're going to be deemed a superstar and you're thinking about walking away? That's just stupid! Get logical!" The mechanical arms flail around again as they reach out farther to try to pull me back in. I feel their familiar grip take hold of me.

"I can't give it up," I blurt out to Chris. "I have to stay!"

"It will all work out," Chris says. "Other opportunities will be there," Karen confirms. "Have faith," the soft voice whispers in the quiet of meditation.

I take a big leap and follow faith instead of logic and make a different choice than I would have made in the past. I let go of ego and embrace trust instead.

This feeling is so exhilarating!

"I'll cut back on souvenirs and eating out and will stay at lower end hotels. I have to believe that if I hand this deal over to someone else, it will come back to me in some good karmic way, right Chris?" I say into the phone with a bit more confidence than I feel.

"Keep the faith, Michelle. Faith is your new path. It will all work out," Chris replies with her normal sureness, because she believes this to be true.

I continue to stick with my faith-based decision, in spite of the argumentative voice of my ego. Although my head is busy with plans, tasks and actions—a comfort zone it thrives in—it still finds plenty of time to bellow out about potential financial disaster. I stay out of the reach of ego and fear by listening to those I trust instead.

My two best defenses from being lured back into old thinking become silence and the voices of others. Maintaining a solid meditation practice is essential so that I connect with the quiet voice that encourages me onward. It speaks less with words now and is present more as a feeling of peace and calm within the storm, which I value. I also call Chris, Karen, my family and other friends for live support.

Chris and Karen have obviously been on board with The Idea since the beginning so we talk almost daily as departure time draws near. My sisters, Sunny (six years younger than me) and Lesa (eight years younger than me) are both active backers of their big sister and wish they could come too. My dad is also supportive, although my mom takes a bit of convincing. Once she sees I'm determined, she throws in the towel and climbs onboard as well, although she requests that I update the website daily so she can keep tabs on me. My other friends promise to email and track me, as do many of my accounts and co-workers.

All this positive energy and support fuels my commitment to let go and live in faith instead of fear. I embrace myself as Michelle Bain: jobless, homeless, income-less and begin to experience a small sense of freedom from my stripped down existence.

One mechanical arm manages to snake out and attach on to me though. It holds a steadfast vision of myself as physically flawless for the trip.

"If I only have one bag of stuff to get by on for six months, I want to look good carrying it! The right shade of blonde hair and the ideal weight are essential. Then I will be ready to conquer the world alone! I will be the thinnest, most beautiful me I can possibly be for my adventure," I declare.

As I attempt to control and force physical perfection, mass catastrophe follows.

It starts with my hair, which is already blonde but not the *perfect* shade of light blonde. After wandering the aisles of Rite-Aid for nearly a half an hour, I finally select the ideal color and rush home to apply it. It turns my hair dark, almost brown. Rushing back to Rite-Aid, I buy highlight cream and then fly back home and apply it. The result: orange, brassy hair. Another trip to Rite-Aid for yet another shade of blonde leaves me with orange roots and the rest has an odd bluish tint. In horror, I head back to Rite-Aid for more highlighting cream, after which I am left with orange roots and bluish hair streaked with blonde chunks that have a slightly greenish hue. After all this, it gets worse. My hair starts to break off in large six inch chunks from over-processing.

"Karen, what am I going to do?" I cry in despair when I show up on her doorstep in tears over the disaster I have created on my head.

"We need a professional," she replies and immediately dials the phone. The professional hairdresser turns my hair a boring shade of mouse brown and then proceeds to cut it off so it is short and spikey. That's all she can do. With each snip, my visions of gracing the world with flowing blonde hair fall to the floor to be swept up into a dustpan and tossed into the trash.

Now comes the body issue. Seeking comfort in food, I eat chocolate like a madwoman and gain ten pounds in less than two weeks. I weigh more than I have ever weighed in my life. As I unpack my carefully arranged duffle bag and proceed to try on each meticulously selected article of clothing, half of the clothes are too tight.

From a physical perspective, I am about as far from my initial vision of flawless as I can handle. I have two choices at this point: I can listen to the judgmental voice in my head that mentally beats me up when I fail to achieve, or I can break free from the mechanical arm of perfection by choosing to accept what I look like and proceed with what is.

I accept that this is my appearance. I will not let self-judging thoughts about hair and weight ruin my trip. That is something the old me back in my Box would do. I am not her. I am Michelle, of Michelle's Great Adventure. I move on!

# # # #

I am spending my last night in California with Karen and her husband Bill so that Karen can take me to the airport the next day. This is exactly what I need. Last words of wisdom and moral support are essential before I take off on my big adventure tomorrow.

Right now though, I am downstairs alone in the spare bedroom. Well, not completely alone. There always seems to be one other *element* with me wherever I go. An element I desperately hope to leave behind—my Box.

"There's no denying it. As much as I like to think I have escaped, the demanding voice rattling in my skull is still so loud it's deafening sometimes. I'm a bona fide head-case struggling to stay free," I think to myself as I lie in bed in the darkness and stare up at the ceiling. "Everyone always jokes with me about how into my head I am, but my mind is seriously out-of-control." I shudder as I remember the anxiety attacks.

"I am too fresh out of my old habitual mindset and haven't developed solid new thought processes yet. Usually, I call Karen or Chris when my over-active mind starts to spin so I can hear alternative views. They are my conduits of God! What am I going to do when I can't call them? What if I can't fend off fear and negativity?

"I have to come up with a plan. I leave tomorrow and I sure can't take them with me!

"Hmmm, or can I? If I get into a sticky situation and ask 'What would Karen or Chris advise me to do?' and tell myself to take that action, can I keep my thoughts on a positive path?

"If I do that, is it schizophrenic? I don't think so. After all, they are real people. More important, who cares? My goal is to stay free from my old thoughts and to escape being driven by fear so that I can experience a new way. I am willing to give up everything to pursue a dream out there. I have to be willing to do anything that might help me stay out of my chaotic mindset as well.

"It's settled—I'm going to try this plan. If I feel too crazy telling myself what to do in a Karen or Chris voice, I can always visualize them standing in front of me. It's worth a shot, especially when I know the alternative. No anxiety attacks allowed on Michelle's Great Adventure. The only ones invited on this journey are God, my newly freed self, and now some loving, make-believe voices.

"Gosh, if I do discover myself, I hope the ideal-me isn't so exhausting!" I say as I roll over, tucked snugly into bed by my new solution.

Chapter 2:
First Steps of Faith—Seat 24A

"You can do this, Michelle, just get on the plane," I assure myself, in my best make-believe Chris voice. "One foot in front of the other, you know how this works. Your legs carry you forward, one step at a time, toward the first destination on Michelle's Great Adventure... seat 24A. No more anticipation, no more planning. You are on your way.

"Right now, in this moment, only one simple action is required to start the entire next journey of your life, and that is to keep moving your back foot forward past your front foot, as many times as necessary to reach seat 24A. Take a deep breath, Michelle, and lift that back foot up and begin your dream," I instruct.

My feet weigh ten thousand pounds each. They will not move. My chest feels like an invisible vacuum has been plugged into my lungs which is sucking out every ounce of air. I am stuck and about to suffocate from anxiety. The mechanical arms of my Box are everywhere—grabbing and pinching my consciousness with statements of fear.

"You're all alone. You have no security, no job, no home and no money to come back to. What the heck are you doing? There's no logic to this!" the thoughts cry out.

I look around at the other passengers. No one else seems to have an issue moving to their seat. Only me—the anxiety freak—who is being attacked by her out-of-control mind.

"Stop feeding negativity before it turns into a glob! Take a breath and pull yourself together, Michelle. Move forward NOW!" I command in a make-believe Karen voice.

I stagger forward another few rows, tripping over my own feet in the process, only to run into the back of the person in front of me. There is a traffic jam of people and I am stuck at row 10.

"This has to be some cruel joke," I think with a dry laugh. "A traffic jam *and* an anxiety attack. What is this, déjà vu? Great, now I have a ridiculously slow *fourteen row battle!*"

The insane thoughts continue to fly around, "What if the plane crashes? What if you run out of money? What if people think you dress weird? What if you can't understand what anyone says? What if you gain more weight? What if you have to come home with your tail between your legs after only a few weeks because you're not strong enough to cut it? What if you get stranded somewhere and die all alone, far away from everyone you love? Worse yet, what if you get back and can't get another job?"

Splat! Splat! Splat! Splat! Splat! Splat! Splat! Splat! The paint ball gun starts to fire destructive thoughts at a round per second. The dark glob grows and begins to eclipse the emotions of excitement and glory I recently felt. Beads of sweat start to form at the base of my neck and trickle down my back. Nerve endings ignite. I know what is next.

I inhale deep and close my eyes. The desire to take off my jacket loses to my insecurity about releasing my death grip on Seat 10C.

If I let go, I will run.

"Keep your grip on the seat and get a grip on your thoughts," I instruct myself in my Karen voice. "What you feed will grow, so feed the positive thoughts instead. Do *not* get sucked in! Get out of those thoughts! Have faith and stay out!"

The young mother that sits in 10C glances up at me with caution as the panic in my grip vibrates down her seat. She instinctively looks from me to the child next to her, as she contemplates if she needs to take action to protect her daughter or not.

Never releasing my grip, I crank my head around toward the front of the plane and eye the exit—my opportunity for escape. Escape from all of it—the plane . . . and the entire dream.

"It's not too late, there's still time to run. Maybe you can get your old job back. Maybe they haven't rented your apartment to someone else yet. Maybe there's a loophole in the system and you can cancel all the flights you booked and they will give you your money back. There has to be some Chicken Exit Clause," my thoughts cry.

The mother in 10C continues to look at me warily. I take another shaky step forward toward Seat 24A.

"Feed the positive, not the negative. Deep breaths, no anxiety attacks. Move one foot in front of the other. Simple steps forward. Don't let fear suck you in and make you its prisoner again. Control your thoughts," I continue to advise myself, the same way Karen might.

"Focus forward and grasp on to that surge of excitement you felt when you arrived at the airport today, only a few short hours ago. This excitement is the tip of the iceberg for the thrills yet to come. You are about to travel the world! This is the opportunity of a lifetime as well as the first step toward embracing the unknown. Think of it as a game: a fun, new life-changing game of living in faith instead of fear," I encourage myself, like Chris would. "Move forward, Michelle! Seat 24A and the adventure of a lifetime await you!"

I step . . . and continue to step—both down the aisle and back into freedom. After many steps, I look up and realize I'm standing at row 24.

I have reached my first destination!

Sighing with relief, I squeeze past my elderly neighbor and sink gratefully into my window seat and the soft fabric of 24A. I smile a shaky smile at her. She smiles back before she reaches into a leather bag tucked under her seat and pulls out a book.

I release another relieved sigh and sink further into my seat, comforted by the worn fabric and the valve above my head which disperses air to my strained lungs. The silence of my seat companion gives me the quiet I need to review what just happened.

This plan I came up with last night might actually work!

God, once again, talked words of wisdom to me through the voices of Karen and Chris, only since they weren't really present, I parroted their voices and told myself what to do instead.

Basically, God talked to me, through them, through me. That's a lot of players on the field, but I don't care for now. I only care that the encouraging voice won over the anxiety-based voice, and that I made it to my seat. Oh, and that God was there somewhere directing the episode.

Now, I need to just pray that this entire team of players shows up every time I need them! Someday, maybe I will cut out a few of the middle men, but for the time being I'm going to stick with what just worked. As long as that final positive voice wins out and I stay free, I don't care how many other people and voices are involved!

With my seatbelt securely fastened, I glance at the many passengers filling the empty seats. Did any of them detect the effort and teamwork it took to get me to Seat 24A? Probably not. Especially since, for most, the basic act of stepping onto a plane and finding an assigned seat does not involve an excruciating twenty-three row mental struggle.

I lean my head against the airplane window and enjoy how the cool glass comforts my forehead. The large plane soon flies through the air, leaving my old world behind. Looking out the window, I stare down at the bright lights of Los Angeles as they fade into the distance. The lights span for miles in a golden glow against the darkness of the night. Soon, the glow changes to a distant shimmer, and then there is only black.

As the blackness intensifies, the weight of the darkness presses against me and my mood of victory begins to fade. Sullen thoughts drift into my consciousness and I feel my back muscles start to tighten.

Obviously, my Box is still on the plane and is determined to be part of the journey. I still have a shot at leaving it behind; if I can just manage to stay clear of those old thoughts!

I relive my parting conversation with Karen so that my focus stays away from anxiety provoking thoughts.

"Baby, a few things are going to take place whether you like it or not," I remember her warning me. "The first is that, no matter how well you plan this trip, things will never go exactly as you planned. The sooner you accept this and become flexible, the less pain you will experience. As much as your ego likes to think so, the universe does not revolve around you and your meticulous plans. You have been fighting this fact far too long already. Use this trip as an opportunity to learn to go with the flow of life. When the going gets tough, turn to God and trust that you will be provided with everything necessary to help you through it."

"Second," Karen continued, "you will need the help of others. You must learn to accept this help, not just on this trip but in life! You have made it this far on independence but it is time for you to learn that you need people and that people need you. You can't always go it alone. Alone is an ego word. People want to help because it feels good to give and help others. It's your duty to accept this help but to also give back and help others in return. Remember, sometimes you give by receiving."

"Finally, if you get out there and run out of money or even decide that you don't like to travel, come home. No big deal. Don't let your ego cause you to tough things out when it might be better if you come home," she wisely advised.

"As for what you pack, just wear that beautiful smile of yours every day and that is all you will need. Trust me."

I am so lucky to have this much wisdom, love and support in my life. I only hope that someday I will be the person giving advice like this to others. Such amazing people whose minds are filled with positive thoughts and whose hearts are filled with faith and love!

I have a small journal with me and I quickly pull it out of my jacket pocket and write <u>My Trip Vows</u>:

    1. I will start each day with the thought 'things will go perfectly today' and no matter what happens, I will have

faith that things are going exactly as they should.
2. I will embrace the unknown and will wake up each day excited and ask, "Okay, God—what's in store for me today?" instead of constantly expecting things to go according to my plans.
3. I will accept and give help.
4. I will do my best to live in Faith not in Fear.
5. I will remember that I am never alone. God is more powerful than my fear and will be there to guide my way.

In this moment, instead of invisible microbes of destruction, I feel faith coursing through my veins. Calm and peace surround me.

I place my hand on my heart and feel the soft *thump, thump*. It has a gentle movement and a quiet, soothing sound, versus the *splat, splat* of bad thoughts.

In the background, I hear the imaginary squeak of an old rusty hinge as the door of my Box shuts behind me. Closing my journal, I hug it tightly and fall into a peaceful sleep with the knowledge that, for the moment, I am free.

Chapter 3:
My True Calling Revealed—Spain

"We will be landing momentarily in Bilbao, Spain. Please make sure your seatbelts are fastened and that you remain seated until the captain has turned off the seatbelt sign," the flight attendant instructs over the intercom.

The plane touches down and I barely notice the bounce of the tires as they meet the runway because I am too distracted by the butterflies fluttering around in my stomach in nervous excitement. A few seem to fly up my trachea toward my throat and I have to swallow hard a couple of times to get air flowing again.

Glancing down at the small blue stone Karen gave me, I read the golden words stamped across it: "Let Go and Let God." As my fingers rub the smooth stone, a little sigh of relief escapes me and the butterflies calm down slightly.

I am not alone.

While I may not be alone spiritually, I am definitely alone physically. As I stand in the airport baggage claim, it occurs to me that what I could use right now is a set of very real hands to help unload my sixty-five pound bag off the luggage carousel.

Yes, sixty-five pounds. Sometime during my flawless-flip out-phase, my ego snuck in the false idea that Europe would not be equipped to handle my basic needs and that the safest plan would be to pack for every season and haul it with me. Because of this, I am lugging around winter boots and a wool jacket in ninety-seven degree temperatures in Spain.

"Oh, but it is so much smarter to be prepared than to fail due to negligent planning. Better safe than sorry!" is the ingenious philosophy behind the thoughts that controlled my packing. The word *smart* and hauling around boots in sweltering heat suddenly do not jive when old logic meets new reality.

As I struggle to lift my bag off the carousel, I realize with brutal honesty that although I might have accepted that there was nothing I could do about the hair/weight situation, I definitely had *not* accepted my appearance.

At least two-thirds of my bag is filled with material junk intended to sooth my chubby body, short-hair, and damaged ego. More clothes, accessories, shoes, beauty products, hair dryer, hair straightener (ironic since I have no hair) were all piled in last minute when I declared with indignation, "I look bad enough already. I flat out refuse to look like a backpacker on top of it!"

My inability to accept my appearance and my lack of faith that my needs will be met have both dealt very heavy hands. About thirty pounds heavier than I can manage!

During my flip-out, I also decided "experience will never be enough" and that self-help/spiritual books were essential for me to develop a new enlightened mental state. So eight books went into the bag. I packed so many self-help books, there was only room to squeeze in one travel book—and here I am on a trip around the world!

How enlightened do I need to be to realize that sixty-five pounds of crap is about sixty-four pounds too much in ninety-seven degree heat?

It only takes about ten seconds after landing to realize, with all the many books I brought, I neglected to pack the most important book of all—an English to Spanish phrasebook.

Well, if I was able to talk myself down the airplane aisle by convincing myself to look at this trip as some "life-changing game" about living in faith, then I guess I sure let the games begin with this first curveball!

"Okay, find the tourism office. They will speak English," I say to myself. I ask fifteen people for directions; in return, I received two shoulder shrugs, about eight blank stares, and at least five "no entiendo" . . . whatever that means. Obviously, communication is going to be an issue.

I feel my vows to maintain the thoughts "Things always go perfectly" and "Embrace the unknown" about to fly right out the window. Thoughts like "I should have started in Scotland where they speak English" and "I should have listened to my *Learn Spanish in an Hour* recording instead of sleeping on the plane" take over instead.

Too late now.

At the tourist office, I grab a city map but can't pinpoint the road for my hotel. "How did getting to my hotel suddenly become the most difficult thing for me to achieve? I guess my choices are walk, bus or taxi. Taxi would be easiest—since I have no clue how to get there—but I have to consider potential cost since I'm on a budget," I say as I bounce around my options.

"What if the hotel is really far and a taxi costs me an arm and a leg? What if I spend all my money on cabs in the first country? I wish I had an extra arm and leg right now. An added arm to help carry my bag and a leg to kick myself in the butt for not mapping the distance from airport to hotel ahead of time!" The long tentacles of the mechanical arms stretch and wave around me all the way from the plane.

I could use a good sign right now that faith is the surest answer. One small sign would work wonders to keep me pointed in the faith direction.

"Hi, you look like you could use a bit of help. What can I do?" asks a clean cut guy in a business suit—in flawless English—who has walked back toward me.

I stare at him in utter shock and amazement.

Is he real? How did that happen so fast?

"I'm sorry—I thought you looked English or American. Do you not speak English?" he questions, since I had not yet replied to his offer of help. I quickly snap back to reality and explain to Sam, who I later find out is a yacht race promoter from England, my predicament about the unknown distance to my hotel and the tight finance situation.

"Come on. I'll grab us a cab. We can drop you off first so my company can pick up the full fare," Sam suggests.

A moment of suspicion about this being "too good to be true" flitters through my head and then the sound of Karen's voice rings out, "People want to help you and you need to let them."

Well, no time like the present to put this idea to the test!

After a twenty minute hunt for my hotel and a $50 dollar taxi fair, I wave goodbye to Sam as I stand safely at the doorsteps of my first hotel. Off he goes, never to be heard from again. A random person who appears out of nowhere to do a good deed for another, with no expectations in return.

My bag suddenly feels a few pounds lighter as I head up the steps, as if Sam's kindness is still there helping fuel my muscles.

This first night, I lie in bed with my hand on my heart. As I feel the comfort of its rhythmic beat, I ponder the concept of giving and receiving help. I have never been willing to fully participate in this exchange because my ego says, "Needing help shows weakness. If you admit you need help, people will think you're not capable. Plus, if you accept help, then you owe someone something in return. Better to struggle and owe nothing, than to accept help and then feel obligated to someone. It's much easier to function as an independent unit."

Memories flash of the many times I risked serious physical injury while lifting things like sofas and TVs which weighed ridiculous amounts, instead of calling a friend or a neighbor for help. I felt pride in myself but suffered backaches for weeks.

Really, how sane was that thinking? Maybe my one-sided view of giving and receiving has been off-base. Maybe there is another reason to help and be helped like Karen explained when she said, "People want to help you because it feels good." Maybe it's an emotional, feel-good heart thing. Sam helped me because he saw someone in need, not because he saw something to gain.

It's the first night of my trip and I already find myself face-to-face with truths about my old beliefs. As I factor in painful memories about the times I battled depression alone, unwilling to get support and help, my faith in that old message dwindles even more. "So many years of life spent suffering in silence! All because my ego said, 'You can do it alone. You don't need anyone's help,'" I think with regret.

"Pride and ego, masked as independence, have run much of my life at my own expense," I acknowledge. "Not only did I make life harder for myself, but independence is a *lonely* place to be. Like a lone wolf, I needed no one!"

But this isn't true! I obviously need Karen, Chris, my family and other friends. What is glaringly obvious is that I need a <u>new me</u>! A new me who is willing to change and grow toward the woman she is meant to be. This all starts with overriding old, ingrained beliefs that have run my show for far too long. It's time to start some major reprogramming, Michelle, and to let new concepts take over!

I decide right then and there to add a new affirmation to my life. I pull out my pocket journal, flip to <u>My Trip Vows</u> and add: "6. People of the world are good. They want to help me."

Karen always says that although I'm a head-case, my perfectionist issue does have one advantage: it pushes me to evolve past most personal issues quicker than anyone she has ever met. Over-achievement may be the cause, but I am starting to believe that another undiscovered part of me has been ready and eagerly waiting to evolve past my old ways. Accepting and giving help is a step in this direction.

As I lie there in the darkness, the hairs on my arms rise in goose bumps and a huge, genuine smile spreads across my face as I realize that it is only my very first night and I already feel different. I giggle a little, I can't contain all the joy I suddenly feel.

An old saying pops into my head: "Today is the first day of the rest of your life."

Yes, Michelle, it is!

# # # #

I have never seen so many people over the age of seventy gathered in one city. There are hundreds of them in Burgos. This group monopolizes every square, walkway and park and it is very clear this is *their town*. "I love it!" I exclaim in joy. "I feel like I struck some type of elderly goldmine."

The city has a beautiful, picturesque park. Rows of tall, leafy trees shade park benches that flank each side of a long central path. Every fifteen feet or so, there is a pause in the path for a sculptured water fountain or blooming flower garden.

In theory, it is the ideal place for the citizens of Burgos to socialize or relax while they enjoy some protection from the hot sun. In reality, the seniors own this entire strip and it is impossible to get a seat on a bench unless one possesses gray hair or a cane.

I watch this never-ending game of musical benches in total amusement from my seat on the ground by a tree. The second one person stands up, another dives in at remarkable speed to take the vacant spot. All places are filled, as if to prevent "unwanted visitors."

Each evening, activity shifts away from the park and into town, so that the city center transforms into elderly happy hour. Around 8 p.m., the elderly men and women begin to arrive in small groups to claim their places on the city center benches, all dressed for evening social time. Then, they gossip and visit until 1 a.m. in the morning.

"Such a different lifestyle from the older people I know back in the States, who are in bed by 8 p.m. and live a life of solitude filled with hours of television," I say with admiration. "These people are alive!" It demonstrates an entirely new aspect of life-after-seventy to me and I love it.

The curious tourist in me decides to test the strength of the elderly cartel and so I head to the park one morning to scope out an opportunity to participate in the game of musical benches. After about an hour of wandering, I see it—an open spot at the end of a bench! I rush over and sit down, triumphantly radiating how impressed I am with myself for outsmarting the others with my quickness and laser sharp eye. The huge grin on my face clearly says, "I got you this time!"

As I sit and gloat, out of the corner of my eye, I notice the old man next to me as he slides a few inches in my direction. The hair on my neck raises a little, but he smiles and says something in Spanish. I brush it off and assume he's being friendly.

He slides a few inches closer as he talks. I smile—since I can't communicate back—but my hand instinctively grabs my purse. My personal space has been violated, but I rationalize, "I'm in a foreign country. Perhaps they don't recognize personal space here!"

I go with it, until he moves even closer. He now sits right next to me. Alarms start to go off. Suddenly, he leans over and grabs my boob with his bony hand and honks it like a bike horn, in full view of all the other benches!

I yelp with surprise, shoot up off the bench like a rocket and sprint for the safety of the park edge. When I look back, sure enough, my spot has already been filled by another wrinkled old man and together these two are laughing up a storm.

I don't know if this is a common territory tactic employed by all members of the cartel, but it sure is an effective strategy in my case. He wiped that "I got you" look right off my face in one second flat.

The elderly of Burgos reign once again. My lesson? Age and experience trump speed and agility when it comes to the race of the benches.

# # # #

After living such a structured life, I expect a long adjustment period in order to feel comfortable outside the safe life I had built. In contrast, I soak up the freedom and adapt with ease after only a few short weeks. My body especially accepts the change. Tight neck muscles—which barely allowed me to turn my head before—are soon non-existent and my daily tension headaches are completely gone.

Even though I weigh more, without the pressure of success, striving and structure, I actually feel lighter than I have in decades. This minimalist lifestyle seems to fit more comfortably than my old one and the shock of this leads me to feel a bit disappointed.

How could I have spent so many years working toward what I thought was an ideal life, only to find out that it doesn't really fit me? That I am happy to have no home, live out of a bag, and rely on local transportation?

As I watch the countryside pass by from my comfortable seat on the train, I notice the occasional small town and wonder about the lives of its people. "Why did they chose to live there? Because their family was born there? Because it is small and quaint? What do they do for a living? Own a little corner grocery? Do they eat dinner as a family every night? Are there scandals that rock the small town or is it a place built on brotherly love?" I ask myself. The entire train ride experience becomes a fun *Michelle Foreign Film Opportunity* as I create scenarios based off of my imagined answers. The mysterious question "What story does the next town hold?" keeps the rides exciting.

The ever-changing scenery also makes for a beautiful experience. Orange groves stretch for miles and some of the most spectacular sites I see are from the windows of trains as I travel from one city to the next.

These quiet, peaceful rides offer me time to reflect on recent experiences or, in some instances, to ponder my entire existence. As I gaze out the window, I often listen to inspirational audiobooks on my iPod, such as Dr. Wayne Dyer's *Inspiration: Your Ultimate Calling* and *Manifest Your Destiny*, or Law of Attraction books by Esther and Jerry Hicks.

"What is *my* destiny? I have always pigeonholed myself into sales and marketing because of my degree but is this really my future? What am I supposed to do with my life? What is my true calling? Will I ever recognize it?

"I want the joy others experience each day while doing something they love. What would bring me that joy? How do I attract what I want in life? And what if my only want is to be the ideal me? Is that enough? I wish I knew the answers. The harder I search, in books and assessments, the more elusive the answers remain."

As my true calling continues to hide from me, I feel comforted when I acknowledge how little I miss many aspects of my old life. One thing I do miss though is my label. I might not be a perfectionist, success-driven, control-freak trapped inside a demented mental world at the moment, but after so many years of living life on auto-pilot, there are some messages that feel permanently welded to my being. Professional identity is one of them.

"I don't feel capable of letting go of the old instilled belief *who I am is what I do* because I haven't discovered who else I am yet," I recognize in silence. "I feel naked and exposed gallivanting around the world without any type of label. I need to come up with some temporary title before I fade right off into nothingness in Spain."

I sort this out in my next email home when I automatically sign the email: Michelle Bain—Professional Tourist/World Traveler.

"Ah, I'm a Professional Somebody again. Albeit a self-proclaimed one, but it sounds legitimate and feels like a good fit. I'm keeping it!" I exclaim to myself, relieved to have a title again.

The other characteristic I actually miss from my old world is an element of structure, but I for sure do not want the rigid, inflexible structure of the past. I want new, loose structure.

Am I capable of modifying old ways, or will I end up sending myself home in my Box? I have to give it a try or else I will never know if I can create positive changes. How about if I start small?

I begin by making a simple daily agenda, since it will aid me in my new role as non-paid Professional Tourist:

- 7:00am — Alarm goes off
- 7:15am — Meditate
- 7:30am — Visualize
- 8:00am — Get dressed and eat fruit
- 8:15am — Review proposed site visits for the day
- 8:30am — Head to "work"
- 7:00pm — Return home after dinner
- 7:30pm — Complete travel journal and download photos to website.
- 9:00pm — Read or watch TV or go to Central Square and people watch
- 11:00pm — Go to sleep

"Okay, now I have a label, a job and a daily agenda. That's quite a few old concepts moving forward into my new reality. Will things get out-of-control again?" I ask myself with concern.

Don't worry about your ability to control old extreme tendencies, just embrace this new experience and have faith, Michelle. Remember, let go and let God.

I let go of worry and fully dive into the awareness that, for the first time in my life, I have a job that causes me to jump out of bed with excitement every morning. Instead of crying, "Please don't make me do this again!" I joyfully ask, "What's in store for me today?" No dread about the day — only enthusiasm.

No more standing in front of a closet in frustration as I try to decide which boring suit to wear. Now, I put on the same clothes from the day before and head out the door.

Precious hours wasted in traffic jams? No way! Now, I leisurely stroll through a city, or a park, or watch the countryside pass by from the comfortable seat on a train.

Instead of accounts and product, I spend each day soaking up the culture of this glorious world at museums, cathedrals and other historical attractions and learn things that truly fascinate me and feed my soul. As I meander through a random park, my heart beats the rhythm "joy, joy . . . joy, joy."

Most importantly, when I smile, it is a smile of genuine

happiness that extends up into my eyes before flowing out to others like a soft mist of positive energy—not some false smile that attempts to mask internal agony. I smile at everyone with such enthusiasm, they immediately smile back. The life energy that surges through my body is so different from the tired stagnation I felt back in California. Back then, I survived days versus enjoyed them!

Even my senses are more alive. A simple sandwich sends my taste buds into a frenzy as the exotic cheese and fresh baked bread combine into a delicious duo on my tongue. At the park, the flowers are saturated in vibrant shades of red, fuchsia, violet and yellow. Paintings dance out of their frames. Birds chirp and sing a happy chorus. It's like my abilities to see, hear and taste were dormant until now and with this new freedom from stress, they have become extra-sensory.

Is this how others always live, in this state of joy? If so, my life has been so miserably off mark. My Box might have contained elements to create a false sense of happiness, but now I see with new eyes of wonder how joyful life can be. The unknown is not a place of terror. It is actually exciting!

My new Utopia has one small glitch—the language barrier. Living without words is rough, especially for someone from a marketing and sales background where the ability to talk is a requirement. Lack of communication causes me intense discomfort.

I try talking louder and enunciating slower but nothing seems to work. In frustration, I realize no matter how many times I repeat something, if a person does not understand my language, they are all wasted words. This is the first time since infancy I am unable to achieve simple verbal communication and it makes me feel like a helpless child, which is more than I can handle.

I become obsessed with finding a translation book and go from bookstore to bookstore in those first cities in Spain, but have no luck. My anxiety grows and soon I convince myself that I cannot survive without words. I finally break down and ask Chris to FedEx a translation book to me from the States, confident that there is no other way.

"I know I am to blame because I'm the one that neglected to pack a translation book, but why is it so remarkably hard to find one here? It's like they don't exist!" I complain into the phone during my S.O.S. call home.

"Good question, Michelle. There is always a reason. Everything always happens perfectly, remember?" Chris reminds me. "Relax and move on. The book will be there in a few days. I promise."

Now that a solution is in motion, I relax and let go. In the weeklong gap before the book arrives, I allow faith and God to step in again. *Poof!* Like a magic trick, there are suddenly many ways to communicate that are revealed to me—no words required.

Same people, same language barrier, but now that I have released the feeling of helplessness, I find that I am able to get exactly what I need without a word. Hand gestures, pointing at maps or books and drawings seem to work just as well in most cases.

Actually, I notice that these non-verbal methods work better than words because it requires me to pay closer attention. I am so focused, I see each individual on a more personal level. The option to grab the words and rush off to my destination does not exist. Gestures and expressions are needed to complete the picture. Sometimes no words are exchanged at all, only looks, and I understand.

Wordless communication transitions into something fun. Situations I dreaded before become opportunities to prove the goodness of people. Like when a man in the drugstore walks me almost half a mile across town to show me where the hardware store is. He knows I will not understand his directions so he simply leads the way. We cannot understand each other but our smiles seem to fill the void as we walk along in silence to our destination.

Upon arrival, I explain with hand gestures and drawings that I am looking for an adaptor. The man from the drugstore, the hardware store clerk and I have a good time as we attempt to figure out my drawings. We laugh even more when the clerk takes my current adaptor into his hands, rotates the prongs forty-five degrees and *poof*—I have the exact adaptor I searched the city to find. Bonding over a simple adaptor would never have happened if I relied on a translation book.

People of the world are good and want to help me. Ask for help and receive it!

Both of these ideas become obviously clear with one particular situation. As I get off a subway, I almost cry when I see the forty or so stairs I have to climb with my heavy bag. A rough looking guy rushes by me as I stand there pondering what to do. About ten steps up, he stops suddenly, turns around, comes back down, picks up my bag, carries it to the top of the staircase, leaves it and then rushes off without even a backward glance. Not a word is exchanged, yet this Good Samaritan with his rough exterior, saves me without even expecting a thank you in return.

It sinks in that there is a bigger, universal language that connects us all. One which takes place without effort and communicates sometimes better than words ever can. This connection stems from desire—the desire of two people to share an experience or resolve a situation and it comes from the heart, not the head. This universal language of the heart knows no boundaries of countries and cultures and it is beautiful. It is a language that I never would have discovered if I had not experienced it personally through the helpfulness of others, in the absence of words.

This shift in my awareness causes me to appreciate silence more than ever before. Silence holds a certain power and when I am alone in meditation, I feel this power. Now, I realize it reaches beyond my own silence to link the space between people as well. It is the silent power of creation—the language of God—and it is profound.

The more time I spend in silence, the clearer the message of the soft, quiet voice becomes. No longer a whisper through the crack in a window, I now find it coming from somewhere deep within me. Because of the peace and clarity it brings to me, I add a silent session to my evenings in addition to my morning meditation.

My nightly pattern is to head back to my hotel shortly after dark, both for safety reasons and because I have a tight budget and want to minimize how often I eat at restaurants. Instead of television, I read or sit in silence and contemplate life and my future. This time is when I reflect on the wonderful qualities of people currently in my life, as well as visualize what ideal qualities I desire to have.

My friend had given me a DVD called *The Secret* as a going away present. One evening, I pop it into my laptop and instantly fall in love with the Law of Attraction concept and the ideas expressed in the movie. After this, I watch the DVD almost every night.

If repetition firmly ingrains an idea so that it takes root, then I am going to take advantage of my evenings to plant positive ideas. I want to live by this law! Plus, it's fun to experiment with the Law of Attraction while I'm out in the world each day and to connect with feelings of joy when I visualize each morning!

Each night, after I watch the movie and before I go to sleep, I sit for half an hour in meditation; free from all thought.

Freedom. That is what silence holds. In the freedom, I connect with God. I realize that, for me, the answers will always be found in the silence.

# # # #

It's in Madrid, my fourth city, that I recognize my natural travel ability to know exactly where I am, where all major attractions are, and how to get almost anywhere within minutes of arriving to any city. This is a pretty big deal for a woman who can't get to the local grocery store back home without relying on a Garmin navigation system. Geography seems natural for me as a Professional Tourist.

I am only in Madrid for about half an hour when a couple walks up and asks for directions so I show them where we are on the map and point them in the direction they need to go. Then I stop for a minute and look around. In this popular tourist city, I see couples and families standing on all corners staring at maps in confusion.

"What a great opportunity to help!" I declare. Later that day, I guide a young couple all the way to the train station because they are in a panic about missing their train. Afterwards, I have a flashback of when the drugstore clerk walked me across town to the hardware store.

It does feel great to help others. I think I'm starting to catch on!

I search for different ways to help. Since I am relatively young and strong, it is easy for me to lift luggage onto trains for elderly people and families with kids. The look of relief on their faces is so uplifting. Many times I cannot understand their words, but their expressions clearly communicate their gratitude. I know exactly how they feel as I remember the teen that carried my heavy bag up that huge flight of subway stairs.

I like helping others! My heart feels full every time I help someone and I find that I am not focused at all on me, only them. It is definitely a trait I am going to keep as part of the ideal me!

# # # #

After exploring Seville for a few days, I head further south to Cordoba and Granada and then return by express train to Madrid. This means I have pretty much covered the entire length of Spain in three weeks.

While in Madrid, I make the executive decision to unburden myself of twenty-five pounds of clothes and books, including all eight self-help/spiritual books. I am confident Europe has what I need, including spiritual growth experiences. I have a few recordings on my iPod for trains and such, if I want to connect with some key messages while I watch the scenery.

I am excited about my last region of Spain, when I go from Madrid to Valencia and Barcelona in the northeast, because I consider this part a brief vacation. While immensely rewarding, I am a Professional Tourist who has clocked fourteen hour workdays for many weeks straight. It's time for a quick ocean break from site-seeing and adventure—which Valencia offers—so that I can put my toes in the sand and *be* versus *do* for a few days.

These are the types of awareness which help me separate from my old ways and to forge new paths. Before, I would never have recognized the need to *be* in my non-stop state of *doing*. This might seem like a small step to someone else, but it is a huge step in a new direction for me.

While traveling east toward Valencia, I hit play on one of my favorite audiobooks by Dr. Wayne Dyer. His message is so good that I have already listened to this book at least four times. After listening over and over, his voice has become almost hypnotic to me, like soft music playing in the background during meditation. In a peaceful haze, I daydream about all the possibilities for myself and for life.

As the train approaches Valencia, I put my iPod away and look at the small beach city with excitement. "Ah, I can smell the ocean!" I sigh. "Nothing says vacation like the smell of the ocean and the taste of salt in the air! I am not going to do *anything* but sit on the beach and listen to the ocean for two days."

I rush strait from the train station to a cab which takes me to the beach. After checking in to the cheapest ocean view hotel, I throw my things on the bed and run down to the sand, as giddy as a little kid. The sand feels so cool and soft as I roll around in it, still fully clothed.

Sitting on my towel, I stare out at the ocean as the waves gently lap the edge of the shore. The soft sound is like a magical melody vibrating through all the space that surrounds me. I visualize each wave washing over me, collecting any tension in my body and then carrying it away into the ocean. With each set of waves, I feel lighter and even more at peace.

I am in a state of total relaxed bliss.

I gaze up into the cloudless sky and watch with fondness as recent memories from Spain dance across this blank screen and play before me like a silent movie, much like my fantasies once did in the dark morning Californian sky.

In my second city, Salamanca, I unexpectedly caught the festival of Santa Maria. Hours of fireworks burst in celebration over the city center as the festival at the Cathedral danced below.

Then, a few weeks later in Granada, I walked right into the Procession of the Madonna where thousands of women holding white candles walked for miles in single file lines. Marching bands delivered sounds of celebration as the procession carried the Madonna statue throughout the entire city, back to her respected alter at the town church. The coming together of so many in adoration of the Madonna touched me with its aura of spirituality, faith and devotion.

Memories like this float across the sky, mixed with visions of beautiful cathedrals and museums I toured.

What a wonderful trip already! My eyes have witnessed such ornate architecture, historic culture and enchanting works of art!

What captures my heart the most though are the people I meet each day. After all the experiences with universal language and giving and receiving, I am finally starting to feel the truth that we are all one. We are bound together by something powerful, which I experience as God.

People of the world are so good. Their helpfulness and generosity continues to warm my heart on a daily basis. I want to bring joy to others and give back on a grander scale, but how?

More importantly, what can I do to maintain this feeling of happiness in my heart forever? Is it possible to travel for the rest of my life? Probably not, but maybe I can build a life where there's enough freedom to travel often.

"All of this always comes back around to my never-ending quest to discover my true calling. I wish I could finally figure this out,"

I think with slight frustration. "Some type of career which allows me to use my best talents and to give back to this great world. Something that brings me joy and bliss, since I know first-hand that these are real, achievable facets of life now—not just fantasies."

I have to stop thinking about this again before I get stuck in the spin cycle of what/where/how/when and end up wasting this beautiful relaxing day at the beach attempting to figure out something I have tried to figure out a thousand times before. Enough with thoughts!

Instead, I tap my iPod ON button and listen to the soothing tone of Dr. Wayne Dyer's voice as the words from *Inspiration: Your Ultimate Calling* flow into my ears. His calm voice caresses me into a tranquil state again.

"Inspiration shows up right before our eyes, even when we may have stopped thinking about it. Our purpose manifests in many ways and won't be limited to a career slot. In fact, it's often something that requires us to leave a particular kind of employment to pursue something we never even considered before," Dr. Dyer conveys.

Hmm, leave a particular kind of employment. I wouldn't have thought it possible in the past, but since I actually did quit, I know I can definitely do that!

"Anything that excites us is a clue that we have the ability to pursue it," and "Anything that is causing excitement within us is evidence of a spirit message that is saying, 'You can do this. Yes, you can!'" he continues.

What causes me excitement? Well, travel obviously, but what else? My newfound love of helping and communicating with people definitely excites me. I also like to captivate people through my energy. I absolutely loooooove to write and read. Honestly, I would write and read all day long, every day, if given the chance. You wouldn't even have to pay me!

I sit up fast, like someone yanked both my arms. My stomach feels like a lightning bolt shot down from the sky and zapped a thousand watts of electricity into it. The electric energy flies up my spine and electrocutes my tongue, forcing the words "I WANT TO

WRITE" to shoot out of my mouth.

What the heck just happened to me? My body feels like I really did get zapped by lightning. Even my throat still feels like it is vibrating!

A writer? None of my past analysis or assessments ever came close to any creative ideas like writing! All the tests suggested more logical roles that fit my business skillsets. Where did this random, crazy idea come from?

It came from the same place as the coffee mug answer—that place where I store *Childhood Dreams*. For a brief second, when I included *honesty* into the equation, factual information was brushed aside and the truth released itself from my heart. Relief, peace, acceptance, joy and gratitude swirl around in my soul with such intensity. I don't know what to do, so I start to cry.

My heart feels like it is about to explode it is so full of joy!

The avalanche of memories and ideas which follow in the next few minutes causes me to run from the beach in search of a notepad. So many flashbacks from my youth and so many concepts fly at me, I feel like I am going to trip over them as I race up the stairs.

Fun memories of stories and poetry I wrote in early years dance in my head. At the same time, I remember all the positive messages I received about my poems, essays, papers, and speeches throughout high school and college. I think about all the joy I experience when I read countless books and then use the information to help myself and others.

I want to write books like that and I want to write books for kids too!

"I need to write all this down!" I say to my empty room, and then giggle. "Of course, I want to write about it, because I AM A WRITER and I know it with all my heart."

After a few hours of continuous typing, I already have six of the children's books written, ideas outlined for a child and adult series and a vision page completed for my career as a writer.

I can't seem to turn off the flow of words!

"Maybe it's best if I shelf my newfound calling until I return since there is quite a journey ahead of me still," I think, after realizing the number of hours which have already flown by since I first started typing. "There will be plenty of time to write later."

For now, I will let the flame of discovery and excitement of knowing burn brightly inside me as I continue to explore the world.

Chapter 4:
Intuition—Portugal

As I depart from the overnight train I had taken from Spain for my brief weeklong stay in Lisbon, I have a strange sense of déjà vu.

"I feel like I've been here before," my memory says, "but I know I've never visited Portugal until today. There's no way I could have mistakenly taken that twelve hour train ride and not remembered it! No, I'm sure this is my first time in Portugal."

So why does it feel so intimately familiar to me? Like I'm finally returning home after being away for many ages, possibly even lifetimes?

There is an amazing sense of peace and serenity that instantly settles over me when I step off the train and touch foot on Portuguese soil, like I am encircled by some wonderful non-confrontational vibration.

A small country on the coastal edge of the continent, Portugal once excelled at world exploration. It seems to be filled with peaceful seaward people and is a dramatic contrast to the Los Angeles vibration of frantic pace, rat race, traffic jams and materialism.

Be it a past memory or some form of intuition, my instinct says, "I will return here someday and it will be to stay." I can't explain how, but I know it instantly.

After leaving the train station in a taxi, I ask to be dropped in the historic district. As I meander the cobblestone roads, I admire the beauty of the trademark Portuguese tile walls that cover the exteriors of buildings from base to roof. Every building supports a unique pattern, all hand painted and crafted with care. There are hundreds of tiles per building.

How much time it must have taken to complete each of these, and there are roads full of these buildings! What admirable craftsmanship to possess as a country. Each building looks like a work of art!

Ahead, a woman skillfully balances a tall bundle of laundry on her head. She makes her way past me and slowly climbs up the steep hill in the direction of an ancient castle. The sun peaks over the castle, casting a shadow on the cobblestone road, as if attempting to help make her journey a little easier. In this picturesque scene, time appears to have stopped many centuries ago.

Off in the distance, an old electric trolley struggles to make it up a hill and it again feels like someone has turned back the hands of time. To me, life in this older section of town suggests simplicity; a concept I too often forget. I soak up every minute with appreciation.

# # # #

So far on this trip, I have managed to do everything possible to avoid taking buses. One time in Spain, I walked hours out of my way because a bus was the only available alternative. I do not understand the numbering system and I'm afraid I'll end up on the wrong bus heading in the wrong direction, so I simply refuse to take them. Instead, I walk, take a taxi or choose the metro, where I can clearly see the name of the various stops.

Not to say that I am at all metro savvy. My only real experience with the metro was in New York once and a few times in Spain. I think I have a decent grasp on how metros work though, especially when compared to buses, so I decide to use the Lisbon metro to get to my hotel.

I jump on and quickly realize I chose the wrong direction (since the next stop is the last on the line). "I've never been to the last stop. I assume the train must loop back around or something so that it can head the other way, right? If I stay where I am and ride out this process, then eventually I will get to where I want to go, yes?" is my logical thinking. So I sit there, with my big bag, and wait for the metro to continue onward and loop around so it can take me in the direction I want to go.

Within seconds, I find myself alone. The noisy group of teens, the elderly couple, the businessman, and the mother with her two children all exit the car, while I sit there; hands folded in my lap, expectant look on my face.

The teens reappear outside the car. They speak Portuguese, with quite a bit of animation, and I watch them in amusement as I wait for the car to pull away. Finally, they decide there is no other choice but to take action, so two of the teens jump back on. One grabs my bag and heads for the door, while the other grabs me by the jacket sleeve, pulls me to my feet, and rushes us both off the metro as the doors start to close.

As I follow them meekly up the stairs while they laugh about "The American", I feel humbled by the experience but also feel grateful that "Teen people of the world are good!"

Since my ego is already bruised, right now seems like as good a time as any to tackle the whole bus-phobia issue. I make my way over to the nearest bus stop, walk up to another potential passenger, point to my end destination on the map and then smile my best smile.

"Twenty-three red," is all he replies in faulty English and points toward the bottom of the hill, where in the distance I see another bus stop. I drag my bag down the hill to the bus stop and wait for the bus to arrive.

About fifteen minutes later, a bus marked '23' in a red circle arrives. I struggle my way up the bus steps and point out my hotel location on the map to the bus driver. He nods his head and I take a seat. As we approach, he notifies me, "This is you," and off the bus I climb.

This is what I was so freaked out about?

I am so glad I faced my dread of buses early on. Lisbon is

known as *The City of Seven Hills* and my legs would have taken a brutal beating if I walked everywhere. Buses are simple if I am willing to rely—yet again—on the help of others.

####

American tour groups are so fun for me! I run into a few in Lisbon, and it is so relaxing to have conversations in English again. Plus, senior citizen groups are so sweet. They are protective of me, like I am instantly one of their grandkids. They all seem to share the common opinion that I am slightly insane, which they express aloud.

"Honey, you can't do this all by yourself!" one man from Kansas declares.

"You gave up everything and took off? What are you going to do when you get back? You can't just pick up and leave like that!" a lady from Missouri points out to me.

My favorite one is, "I wish my grandson would find a neat little gal like you with all that spunk! Here, honey, let me buy you an ice cream cone." That comment made me smile for days.

Even though we only recently met, it is nice to feel their concern for me. It makes me think of all the people back home who care about me too.

Not only does this group of travelers demonstrate to me that happiness can be experienced at any time in life but also that it is never too late to live out a dream.

In the short time it takes for me to assist someone up a flight of stairs, I have heard all about their own personal dreams and desires, as well as what they have achieved and which ones they missed. The missed dreams are often due to physical limitations and I am so grateful that I am traveling while I am young.

When I hear the common statement, "If only I would have,"

my eyes fill with tears of gratitude as I realize, "I am."

####

Hopping off the beaten path in Lisbon, I head to the outskirts of town. There is a cathedral I really want to see that is a bit out of the way, so I saved it for this last day.

I can't really explain why my desire to visit this particular cathedral is so intense, but I'm willing to take four modes of transportation to see it. After I take the metro, then a bus, then an electric trolley, I walk up the hill to where Basilica da Estrela stands.

"This better be worth it," my mind complains as I trudge up the last part of the block, but I quickly shake off this thought. There she stands: pure white with a large dome and two matching bell towers which flank her entrance. I walk through one of the doors, into a world of marble and statues.

Call me odd, but cathedrals as well as many churches always present themselves as live women to me. I am fascinated by them, which is why I seek them out as must-see locations for every city I visit. To some people, these are only buildings made of glass, wood and stone. To me, they are unique individuals ready to tell me their personal story through their many characteristics. Elements such as materials, lighting and décor all give me hints as to who a cathedral is.

For example, some stone interiors convey a slightly standoffish vibe; as if her cool, hard interior says, "I'm here for the long haul, but I am not concerned with providing a soft, comforting place for you to conjoin." Other times, I walk into a white marble cathedral where bright light shines through beautiful stained glass windows and she cries out, "Come and bask in the beauty of my divine grace!"

Many times, a church made predominantly of wood carries a sturdy warmth, like a grandmother inviting me to join her for a bedtime book. Sometimes a wood interior with exposed beams will have too many sharp edges for me, like an uptight teacher with a severe bun who is ready to slap my wrist with a ruler.

Then there is the actual décor of a church or cathedral, which speaks a tremendous amount about her personality. Some cathedrals are simple, wearing only their stained glass windows for jewelry. Others not only wear stained glass, but have beautiful wrought iron gates and silver candelabras as accessories as well. Some have ornate clothes made of richly textured draperies and colorful tapestries. Still others have cosmetic makeup in the form of brilliantly painted murals and domes filled with faux trompe l'oeil that deceives the eye.

Like I would describe a real woman, I use adjectives such as "charming", "striking", "pretty", "plain", "homely", "ostentatious" and "exquisite" to describe these women made of wood and stone.

As individual as their structures and interiors are, each cathedral's energy is also unique. After enjoying the many characteristics of a cathedral, I always sit with my eyes closed for some length of time and attempt to connect with the *essence* of who the cathedral really is. Like a live woman, there is the exterior she presents to the world, and then behind all that there is the real self she also possesses, discovered in the silence, when the external is stripped away and only her energy remains.

With my eyes closed off to surrounding elements, I attempt to connect with that essence. Sometimes it comes to me quickly in a live, physical way. My ears will start ringing loudly or my body will feel the heaviness or lightness of the space around me. Other times, I feel no connection and I leave in sadness because while I am able to witness the beauty of the exterior and interior, this individual will not open up enough to let me know who she really is. I know part of the sadness is because it mirrors my old ways—as a woman who portrayed a certain image to the world but hid her real self.

Basilica da Estrela in Lisbon boasts a Baroque style which makes her a bit elaborate. The marble is extensive, covering the floor in geometric patterns, as well as all the walls and ceiling. She has a young Southern belle feel to me because all the marble is in shades of grey, pink and yellow and she has graceful rounded curves instead of sharp angles.

There are statues along the sides leading up to the altar with beautiful paintings scattered in between. A large tomb dominates the right transept where I read that it is Queen Mary I who built the Basilica. About a hundred rows of wooden pews with a long, narrow center aisle make up the mid-portion. The curved ceiling spans high above with the same hues of pink and grey.

Although the colors are relatively light in shade, there is still a darkness about the Basilica, with only a limited amount of natural light seeping in from the clear windows many feet above. No other light is visible, which lends a slight air of mystery.

"What is she trying to hide?" I wonder to myself as I wander around, almost squinting to view paintings and statues. Spotting a pew by the outer edge, I walk over and take a seat. There, I begin to relax and allow the energy of the cathedral to embrace me.

"Who are you, Miss Estrela?" I ask in silence. "For you seem to be a Miss to me with all of your pink tones and curves and air of mystery. Appearances aside, who are you really?" Closing my eyes, I sit in the silence. Soon, I'm absorbed by the cathedral as her blanket of serenity wraps warmly around my shoulders.

A tap on my right shoulder jolts me out of my daze. Opening my eyes, I turn to see who has reached out to me, a little surprised that someone would physically touch me while I sat there alone with my eyes closed.

An elderly man stands a few feet off to my right, smiling and motioning for me to follow him. After a second of hesitation, I remember that I'm in a church, so I rise and follow him to a thick wood door with massive iron hinges. He unlocks the door with an old skeleton key, walks inside, turns to me again and beckons for me to follow. Once we enter, there is a soft click from the latch as the door firmly locks behind us.

We are inside a small room, almost like a study or den. Long sashes of thick brocade fabric hang over the windows so that only a few pale glimpses of light sneak in. As my eyes adjust to the dimness, I see that the walls are covered with paintings depicting beautiful scenes from the Bible. Heavy pieces of ornately carved wood furniture are scattered around the perimeter, making the room appear even smaller.

"Wow," I say to the man as I wander around observing the furniture and murals, which are much more elaborate than the ones present in the cathedral. "This must be a very important room."

He doesn't understand me but smiles as I walk around admiring the artwork and furniture. His smile is almost teasing, as if hinting, "Wait, there's more!" He motions toward another closed door which is partially covered by a long sash of red velvet fabric.

Again, the man produces another skeleton key and unlocks this hidden door. I follow him onward, wondering with nervous anticipation what's in store for me in the next room. I gasp aloud—dumbstruck by what is revealed.

Towering before me is the most magnificent miniature nativity scene ever created.

This is simply spectacular! So much activity is happening in this scene, I don't know where to start!

I glance at the man in delight. His smile is now so full I can't even see his eyes. Reaching over, I hug him and say, "Obrigada!" which means thank you. "Thank you!" I repeat in English, as my eyes fill with tears. He joyfully laughs at my reaction and ushers me to the left so that I can walk around the glass encasement so as to view this creation from every angle.

My breath is taken away by the amount of activity and detail portrayed in this twelve-by-twelve foot encased diorama. The artist creates levels of dimension by varying figure sizes: the figures near the top are small so that they appear off in the distance whereas the figures close to the glass are much larger. The depth and movement this creates is unbelievable, as if the scene extends for miles out into the distance as well as straight up into heaven.

The scene unfolds across mountains and valleys, through the bustling village filled with shops and houses. People work and play, animals eat and roam. Then it continues upward past the town, toward the nativity which bears the infant in the manger surrounded by Mary, Joseph and three wise men, and extends up into clouds filled with the angels of heaven who watch over all from above.

The elaborate detail is so intricate—no feature is missed. Even the facial expressions of every figure look captured in reality. I look over at the man again with tears in my eyes and he grins back with a smile that says, "See, I told you!"

For half an hour, I travel along all the little roads and peak into the windows of the village shops. Food that looks so real it could be eaten sits on the tabletops inside. I admire the way the artist portrays themes of good versus evil throughout the village. Pickpockets get caught in the act as little devils linger close by. It is a small area to convey such extensive visual information especially since the maximum figure size is only about twelve inches.

I later learn that the entire scene was created back in the early 1800s by Joaquim Machado de Castro, contains 500 figures and is carved out of cork and terra cotta; the two products of Portugal. It took him almost forty years to complete the scene.

"This is a magnificent jewel hidden away from the rest of the world which I have been given the privilege to witness." This realization brings another tear to my eye as my heart brims with gratitude.

As we depart, I thank the elderly man profusely for this wonderful gift he has bestowed upon me, which will be etched in my memory forever. He gently picks up my hand and holds it to his heart, looks deep into my eyes for a few seconds and then smiles. I feel his message as clear as if he has said it to me with words. It is a lesson I will always remember:

Behind every door lies a beautiful unknown and it will be shown to you . . . if you just have faith.

This experience of hidden magnificence ends my week in Portugal. It is time to move on to see what other doors will open and what other gifts of faith will cross my path.

I should be disappointed about leaving this country I instantly love after so little time, but instead I feel incredible happiness. My instincts already told me upon arrival what I need to know.

I will return here someday.

Chapter 5:
Self-Love—Italy

The warm golden sun glitters across the water at the horizon's edge and casts a glowing reflection over the city. The water in the canal seems to dance in this last glimpse of light, in anticipation of the darkness of night. As the final rays of the sun disappear, quiet settles in and the only sound is the soft *pat pat* as the dark water gently laps against the cement wall of the canal.

As I stand on the old stone bridge and look down into the black water, I hear the distant sound of music floating toward me. The music grows louder and I identify the vibration of a familiar tune as it blows from an accordion, "When the moon hits your eyes like a big pizza pie, that's Amore!"

Ah, the adopted national anthem of Italy. I should have known.

As if aware that his beautiful music has announced his arrival, the accordion player makes an entrance into my sunset scene. He plays his instrument while posed comfortably in the nose of the gondola which has revealed itself from behind an old building. As it turns the corner, I see the gondolier navigate the boat from the tail. Nestled in the comfortable midsection are a man and a woman.

The boat moves toward my bridge and I gaze at the young couple snuggled affectionately in each other's arms. They stare into one another's eyes and share a soft kiss as the gondola glides along in the canal below me.

Lights twinkle off in the distance from the many candles which adorn the café tables; signals that evening has officially arrived. I watch from my isolated perch on the bridge as they sparkle, almost like little stars on land.

Venice is the most romantic city in the entire world, and here I am—alone.

"I will not survive a month in this country unless I find a way to overcome my grief about being alone amidst all this **love**. I have to accept that Italy is a country known for romance, so it is going to show up everywhere," I tell myself. "No more cringing each time I hear 'That's Amore' as it blasts out of every speaker in the entire country. No more eye rolling every time I pass a couple kissing. I have to accept that this is the honeymoon capital of the world and there are about a hundred honeymooners on every street."

As I see it, I have a few options: 1) I can join the masses, fall in love with the first guy I meet and then drag him all across Italy with me for a month or 2) I can work on a long avoided project: learning to actually love myself unconditionally.

How crazy that sounds! I can hear the conversations when I get home. "So, you went to Italy for a month. Did you fall in love?" someone will ask. "As a matter of fact, I did . . . with myself!" will be my corny reply.

Who knows, maybe with all this love in the air, I might actually win my never-ending battle with perfectionism and self-judgment this time. It's worth a shot. The energy here definitely supports success with love.

"Option number two it is—I start <u>Project Love</u> immediately!" I declare.

I have to really prepare for battle with this issue. The voice in my Box has drilled me with a million loud messages for the past thirty years on how perfection is the only acceptable standard so this idea is deeply imbedded. I am still a woman who looks in the mirror and only sees what's not right, just like I never remember all my huge business wins, only the losses. Fear and tough love are still my primary motivators and my bar remains unreasonably high.

In Spain, I discovered my true calling is to write. Here in Italy, it is time for me to overcome self-destructive thought patterns and to replace them with love and acceptance for myself.

JOURNEY TO THE IDEAL

This project is going to require me to venture into unknown territory . . . my heart. To go there, I will need one remarkable plan!

That night in Venice, I formulate the plan for Project Love and jot it down in my pocket journal. Immediately thoughts like, "It's not good enough. It's too simple," spring up. I reread the tasks and instead of revising any, I say a little prayer of "Let go and let God" with my blue stone in my hand.

As I lay there in my small, single bed, I giggle with nervous anticipation about what tomorrow holds, like it's the first day of a new school year. I feel positive energy already because normally, I would work many additional hours on any idea or plan I did not consider faultless instead of letting things rest.

I am already choosing new action. Hope is on the horizon!

The next morning, after I sit in silent meditation for fifteen minutes, I reread the list and know it is just right, no revisions required. It might be simple, but less is more in this case. The less I have to do, the less there is to judge, which means less opportunity for critique and more chance for it to work in my favor.

I am still too much of a realist to think that I can wake up in the morning, flick on some switch and *poof* my change will be complete. Not with all the mindset adjustments and habitual thought patterns I need to revamp. Like I said before, some of those old mechanical arm messages have left pretty deep brands on me, but a good thirty days of practicing contrary action in Italy should get me moving in the right direction.

Project Love—Every day for my entire stay in Italy, I will:
1. Look in the mirror in the morning, stare into my eyes, then smile and say, "Michelle, I love you so much" four times.
2. Write a list of five positive things about myself each morning, and a list of ten general things I am grateful for.
3. Exercise for a half hour every day, besides only walking.
4. Help at least two people per day in some way.

5. Thank someone if they complement me and then make my head agree with what they say.

That's all there is to the entire plan. I ponder how ridiculously easy these five things might seem to most people, but I'm not most people. I'm someone who has been driven by a negative, judgmental mindset for three decades.

Okay, take a deep breath. Time for more new action!

I sit on the floor, in front of the long mirror mounted on the closet door, so that I can complete Task #1—where I look into the mirror, stare into my own eyes, smile and say, "Michelle, I love you so much" four times.

I attempt to look into my eyes but my focus immediately diverts upward to my hair, and there I am—quick as ever—back into judgment instead. I critique how short my hair is, before I move lower to analyze how uneven my eyebrows are, before I zero in on the pores of my nose.

Three critiques in three seconds. Record breaking even for me. This is going to be even more difficult than I imagined.

I grit my teeth and growl, "NO MORE!" and again look into the mirror. This time, I keep a steady gaze and only let myself look at my eyes. I don't let my focus stray as I stare directly into my eyes for many minutes.

At first, I take notice of their color—how intensely blue they are. As I continue to stare into them, my attention slowly begins to shift as I recognize something else working its way forward in the eyes staring back at me. I feel a flame start to burn in the pit of my stomach, a growing anger.

Rising to the surface of those blue eyes is sadness . . . a blue sea of sadness. A sadness that runs so deep, it reaches all the way down to the depths of her scarred soul. An overwhelming sadness caused by heartache and pain that reveals a heart that has been broken over and over again. Like an abused child, one who craves love and happiness but only receives constant rejection. Those are the eyes that stare back at me.

The flame of my anger grows as I admit . . . *I* am her abuser. The judgmental thoughts in my Box and the unrealistic expectations they hold caused the thirty years of pain and sadness that reflect back at me.

How could I have let my broken thoughts get so out-of-control? How could I let a non-stop barrage of judgmental, critical thoughts steal all the love and happiness from this beautiful soul in the mirror?

I continue to stare into those eyes of sadness for many minutes as I allow my past errors to fully sink in. I was wrong and I know it. It was wrong to let perfection rule my life, wrong to set unrealistic expectations and wrong to withhold love. All of it was wrong.

"Michelle, I love you so much," I quietly whisper. It is so hard to say. I choke on every word. I see tears well up in the eyes in the mirror. This woman with these amazing blue eyes *is* beautiful and she *is* enough.

How could I have been so blinded by broken thinking to not see this before?

"Michelle, I *love you* so much," I say again a bit louder and with more persuasion. The woman in the mirror jumps a little, as if surprised that she would hear these words from me again.

This time, I lean closer and look more deeply into her eyes, and say with as much conviction as possible, "Michelle, I love you *so much*." Tears start to stream from her eyes and down her cheeks as she stares back at me and my heart is suddenly flooded with a compassion like I have never felt before.

"I do, Michelle, I love you so much, I am *so sorry*," I sob as the dam of my heart breaks open further. "I am sorry for all the years I kept you trapped inside a Box of suffering. You did not deserve those mean comments or harsh judgments that were relentlessly hurled at you day after day, or the horrible way I treated you for so many years. You are a beautiful soul who deserves much more."

"You deserve more, Michelle! You deserve love and I promise to love you and to fix my broken thinking and to never abuse you again," I vow as years of pain and sadness wrack my body in heaving sobs.

As I speak these words, I realize I mean what I say with all of my heart, my entire heart. I never want to look into these eyes and see that amount of pain and heartache again. I will do whatever it takes to change, even if it means reworking every single broken thought pattern in my entire head. I won't return to a prison of destructive, fear-based thoughts which kill happiness and love.

As if to confirm her faith in me and my words, the woman in the mirror smiles at me—a genuine smile that emanates from the soul. I smile back at her with a matching smile, one full of a soulful determination to change.

We are on the path to a new beginning, Michelle.

# # # #

I stick with this daily ritual as I travel south by train from Venice. Thankfully, the morning portion becomes easier in the days that follow.

Another breakdown, I suppose, so that I could break through to a new way of being.

That first mirror experience was very powerful and has a lingering affect. Whenever I feel the urge to skip out, the haunting visions of sadness, as well as the memory of the compassion that I felt from my first experience, drift into my thoughts and I take action instead.

Soon, I begin to have fun with it. I wink and mix in fun statements like, "Sugar, you're so hot, you could set a building on fire!" and "Boy, that tee-shirt looks great on you for the third day in a row!"

The continuous positive thoughts and comments feel like soothing balm on my old branded scar. Saying it aloud is immensely helpful. Not only is there more conviction to what I say, but it also makes me feel like I'm talking to a close friend who I love, which is the new relationship I hope to construct with myself.

For Task #2, I write the five positive things about myself every morning and make sure to include physical, mental and spiritual attributes. I begin to read my Positive Attribute list aloud, as well as my ten daily gratitude items. Verbalizing these give me strength too.

I start to bring my journal with me everywhere so I can pull it out and re-read both of my growing lists in the quietness of a church or park to deeply appreciate each item. That powerful silence really catapults me to another level because I know God is there to receive it.

For Task #3, I figure out how to do an entire Pilates workout on a single-sized bed since sometimes the floors of my budget hotels leave a little to be desired. It is amazing what is physically possible in a small space.

For Task #4, I also help two people a day, no matter what, and find myself saying, "Good job Michelle," in recognition. Little confirmations and words of encouragement like this start to make a difference. I like being a self-supporter of the emotional variety instead of only being a self-supporter of the financial variety. It brings me a new happiness to treat myself with love, encouragement and kindness.

The gorgeous men of Italy continuously help me with Task #5: accepting compliments. One day as I approach a museum, a random man walks up to me, takes my hand and says, "Senora, I have to tell you how beautiful you are . . . bellissima!" My old head immediately objects with the thought, "No way. I have short hair and wear this same tee-shirt every day!" I stick to the plan and respond, "Thank you!" and smile. To squash my old thoughts, I make sure to point out the truth: that even in a tee-shirt with short hair, I am beautiful.

Another handsome man in a suit stops me at a crosswalk and

exclaims, "Senora, your smile! I think, I think I love you!" and I reply, "Well, thank you very much!" before I give him a wink and then practically skip across the road.

It appears that Karen may be correct. All I really do need is my smile!

As my heart fills with more self-love each day, I feel a surge of newfound hope. Something inside me is changing in a major way.

If I can just manage to keep up this new pattern for the rest of my life somehow, I know my life will always contain happiness.

I spend more time in meditation in my room, in my beloved churches and cathedrals, and soon in parks. It is so important to me to take a few minutes to acknowledge my good fortunes and connect to God through silent gratitude. In the silence, I have this complete sense of faith and peace that translates into, "Don't be afraid, you are not alone. I will show you the way." It's incredible to travel completely alone and feel safer than I ever have in my entire life. My trust expands with each passing day.

I watch *The Secret* almost every night still. This idea of "What you think about, you bring about" goes hand-in-hand with Karen's expression "What you feed will grow." They both really make me realize how imperative it is that I feed positive thoughts.

In my Box, all that was fed were damaging ideas so my fears escalated to paralyzing proportions. I spent a majority of each day struggling to swim upstream against a raging current of anxiety, negativity, judgment and control. When I look back, I see that many times when something bad happened, I focused relentlessly on it and saw it happening in my mind. Based on the Law, it makes sense that this bad thing would become a reality.

So that I am able to start reprogramming these thought patterns in the present moment, I decide to red-flag myself by saying "buoy" whenever I go to thoughts of what I DON'T want to happen. This word refers to my extremely simple, yet textbook example, of "What you think about, you bring about."

A few years ago I was on a camping trip and two of us decided to take a jet ski out for a spin. It was my first time ever steering a jet ski. There were no other boats around and nothing else in the water except for one red and white buoy surrounded by a fifty yard radius of open water in every direction.

"Don't hit the buoy," my friend joked since it would be almost impossible for this to happen. I kept focusing on not *hitting the buoy* with such intensity that it was like there was a magnet connected to it! We were going so slow it was ridiculous and I still kept inching closer and closer straight toward the buoy until I finally ran smack into it and sent us both swimming.

I never felt like such a complete idiot in my life, but it proves "What I think about, I bring about" and so I decide to use the word "buoy" as my wrong-thought red-flag.

I also start to review my work-hard mentality and how effective this has or has not been. I think everything, especially a job, requires extensive effort; which is why I am a complete eighty-hour-a-week workaholic. I come from hard working parents so some of this is learned but a majority of it comes from my own experience. I listen to the voice screaming in my head about success and decide that if I work hard, I won't fail. I succeed, which proves the theory, and soon I have another exhausting belief pattern branded into me.

Now, every night, I watch a video with a completely different message. Experts in the movie say that if I visualize the end result, get into a feeling place of it happening, let go of the *how* and the results, that what I visualize can materialize.

"But that is too easy!" my old belief protests.

Maybe I'm ready for easy. Maybe I'm tired of believing that <u>life is hard</u> or that I have to <u>work really hard to make something happen</u> and consider that there might be another way beyond the old ideas of my Box.

I have watched this movie many times by now, but something clicks with me in Italy. I decide to put more effort into the practice of visualizing, asking and receiving so that I can test the power of it. The movie suggests starting with simple visualizations to build faith in the process.

One Tuesday morning in Florence, I decide to visualize a red rubber band around my wrist since this seems simple. I walk out the door, step onto the sidewalk and my left foot lands smack on a red rubber band. That's all the proof I need. The 7:30 a.m. Visualizing Sessions on my <u>Daily Work Agenda</u> take on a whole new meaning from that day forward.

Some mornings, I picture myself as I sit at a desk happily writing novels while other mornings I envision myself trekking across new countries. One morning, I imagine myself on horseback next to the love of my life as we gallop across a green field. The entire process adds a positive vibration to the start of each day.

What I think, I create . . . so I better make sure God has a hand in my thinking!

# # # #

"What is another dream that has been buried for years that can come true in Italy?" I ask myself with excitement. "How about exploring the countryside on horseback? Remember those childhood fantasies of cantering along on a beautiful black stallion with my hair blowing in the wind? Ahhh . . ."

So I don't have hair that blows in the wind, nor do I have a beautiful black stallion. What I come across, by way of a flyer while in Sienna, is the opportunity to join an organized horseback riding trip through the vineyards of Tuscany. I ride a brown mare instead of a black stallion and I am with a group of happy American travelers, but the green valleys are there and I am surrounded by luscious grapes and olives.

We eat lunch at a medieval village and have a sensational day. I enjoy every minute of it, especially the part where a fantasy comes true. Everyone keeps repeating a common message: "You should write a book about this someday."

Interesting, since a book about my trip has never crossed my mind, nor was it listed on my original brainstorm of writing ideas.

One member of the group recommends I visit Cinque Terre, which is a series of five small harbor towns located along the Italian Riviera. A nine mile walking trail runs along the cliff edge and winds its way through each of the towns. This is not on my initial trip list, but my new American friends say I cannot miss it, so I decide to be flexible and go with the flow, shaving a few days off visits to other cities to squeeze in Cinque Terre.

I arrive by train to the first city, Riomaggiore, and find a beautiful hotel room by the water for very little money. "All good signs," I decide.

I left my larger bag locked up at a train stop by Pisa, so I only have my small backpack, which I toss on the bed. I lock the door and run out to catch the train going to the far end of the nine-mile trail. My intention is to hike the trail back to Riomaggiore. It's already about one o'clock and I want to squeeze the hike in today because there is talk of rain heading toward the coast.

"This is so beautiful with all of the winding cliff trails that weave through small vineyards," are my admiring thoughts as I walk alone for many miles. I climb up huge rock formations and hike through dense vegetation, all while the ocean crashes into the cliff walls below. "How fortunate am I to have this trail almost to myself?" I say as I hike, grateful for the chance to be present in the moment versus distracted by idle conversation.

I pass the first city and can see the next city off in the distance. It starts to rain, lightly at first. By the time I reach town, the rain cascades in a steady stream of droplets.

"Well, it appears they were right about the rain," I think as I head up the cobblestone road. The main reason I live in Southern California is because one of my primary life rules is that I don't do rain—it is too messy and I avoid it at all cost. "This hike is so beautiful though," I admit. "Should I buy a poncho and continue, or should I catch the train back and skip the rest of the trail?" It is a big decision for an anti-rain person like me.

Out of nowhere, *Forrest Gump* pops into my head. That part where he is running across the United States and keeps going and going. "Forrest Gump wouldn't stop because of some little thing like rain!" I declare, so I buy a plastic poncho and keep going.

Everyone else hopped off the trail, so I have the path completely to myself now. "This is the most pleasant walk I ever remember having in the rain," I decide. As I meander along, admiring the beauty, I talk aloud to myself, since there is no one around to hear. Usually I only talk to myself in silence, so I conclude that this is temporary insanity due to the rain.

While walking, I review how well <u>Project Love</u> works and how glad I am that I kept it simple. When I started, I felt so separated from the woman reflecting back at me in the mirror—like she was a stranger, but now when I look into the mirror, I feel an integrated wholeness and self-love. The verbal gratitude lists alter my outlook so that I am more appreciative of myself and of everything in life.

As I walk, I run through a fun list of all the things I am grateful for right in this moment. "Thank you for my shoes which are soaked but have solid soles and thank you for my healthy body that is able to walk this trail. Thank you for that little tiny purple flower I just passed because it is so delicate and small but still alive and beautiful." Things flow from my lips to God as I mosey along the trail with a smile on my face despite the rain.

I create a little rain song as I walk, including new objects I discover along the way. It is totally silly, but as I sing aloud in my off-key voice, it dawns on me that I actually find myself pretty entertaining company! In the past, I was too busy critiquing myself to relax and enjoy the true me.

There are some slippery places by the stone staircases, and

more than once I get slapped in the face by a wet tree branch, but this rainy walk with myself turns out to be a good time.

Eventually, I meet up with an Australian couple and we walk and talk for a bit in the rain. A few miles before the end of the trail, we are forced to stop due to a mudslide. After all that trudging in the rain, we have to take the train the rest of the way because the trail is totally blocked. Completely drenched and freezing, I am more than willing to end my hike.

The Australian couple's hotel is in the opposite direction so we are waiting for different trains. Local trains in Cinque Terre are infamous for being late, and we all sit in the rain for at least half an hour before we finally hear a whistle blow. It is the train traveling toward Riomaggiore, my town.

"Bye you two and safe travels! There is no way I am missing this train!" I yell over my shoulder as I rush toward the compartment in front of me and yank the doors open with all my strength. I am determined to stay true to my words and to escape the downpour.

Okay, my first sign that something is not quite right should have been the neon orange piece of paper taped to the window at eye level, but I am too busy enforcing my will to notice this as I pry my way into the compartment.

If I was a tiny bit more patient, my second sign about a potential issue would have been how hard I have to yank the compartment doors to get them to open. I am too anxious and distracted to register that normal entry does not require this much strain and effort.

What finally triggers an alarm in my head is when I look up and notice that it is completely dark inside my car and that I am the only person in it.

I struggle to pull the doors back open but they are completely locked tight. I yank on the pass-thru door but it is locked also. I can see people far away in a distant car and I bang on the window, but there is another entirely empty, dark car between us and they can't hear or see me. I look toward the door at the other end of my compartment and spot a distant light.

"Head into the light, Michelle, head into the light," I joke with myself as I walk toward the source. All the pass-thru doors are unlocked, so I sprint across the next dark car, and then also through the final dark car to the door at the end. It is locked. I am at the end of the train. There are no people, only a bright light.

My mind starts to race to the next possible solution as my heart starts to beat faster.

"Head back the other way so you are at least close to people," is my next logical thought. I take off again, barreling through the dark cars this time like a crazed animal looking for an escape. I make it back to my original car in time to watch the sign for my town become a thing of the past. I couldn't have got off anyway, because I am still stuck in a car with side doors that won't open.

Panic grips my stomach. I start to pull every lever and push any button I can reach, but it is useless.

What am I going to do? I can't let this growing panic build. I need to stop it before it escalates into an anxiety attack. It's time to call in reinforcements.

"You are going to calm down, that is what you are going to do," I tell myself in my best Karen voice. "There's another town in fifteen minutes or so. The one where you locked up your big bag and computer. You will be able to get off there. It's all fine, you're fine."

Minutes later, I spot the town of La Spezia in the distance and a wave of relief washes through me.

Slight detour, that's all. No big deal. Everything's fine.

The train pulls into the station and I bang on the window and try to capture the attention of people farther down who are waiting to ride the train. Two men see me and dash over and begin to yank on the doors. As hard as the men struggle, the doors will not open.

To my horror, the train starts to pull away again. I pound on the doors as the men stand helplessly outside. One man runs alongside the train and gives me an "I'll call someone" signal with his hand. He attempts to reassure me with his gesture as he watches my panic-stricken, grease-streaked, rain-drenched face fade off into the distance as I continue to pound and pull on the doors.

"Okay, this is it, Michelle. This is a test of faith. Things have gone really well with all your self-love efforts, but you can't forget that your biggest obstacle is always fear," I remind myself like Karen would. "See how quickly it can regain control and throw you back off track? There are bound to be more tests this trip so just relax and trust. You know that your trust always grows stronger each time you feed proof to the idea that good prevails. This is only an experience to add proof!"

I take a deep breath, go back to one of the dark cars and sit down in a seat. I review my situation and analyze my options, which are few. In reality, there is nothing I can control about this situation or the outcome. I can only control my reaction. I choose to react calmly.

I will let go and let God. I will stay in faith that everything will be okay.

Another city rolls by. This time, I don't even attempt to pound the windows. It is useless effort and only increases my anxiety.

Then another city passes by.

"Well, your plan was to work your way down to the tip of Italy over the course of a month. Maybe you do it in a day instead," I attempt to joke and see the positive of the situation, exactly like Chris would choose to do. "What's the worst case here? Worst case is you live in a boxcar for the rest of your life. Hey, look at the bright side. You are homeless so now you will actually have a place to live!

"Okay, so now that worst case isn't so bad, why don't you take another deep breath and drop back into the knowing that everything will turn out fine," I instruct myself.

I open my eyes and actually laugh a little as I think about my new home solution. I watch as another city comes and goes but no longer feel panic gripping my heart.

Maybe reaching the tip of Italy in a single day is part of some master plan. I sure don't have the answer to that one, but I do know that this time faith is winning.

My heart is full of gratitude for this outcome, whatever the end result of this train situation. As I acknowledge that I have just won a battle against fear, I whisper "Thank you, God" and "Thank you, team."

It might have taken a team of trusted voices to keep my mind from heading into fear, but I conquered! I am victorious!

I see a flashlight beam start to dance down the aisle a car away. Soon the conductor arrives, unlocks the door, and frees me from my temporary prison. Rain-drenched and grease-smeared, but with a smile on my face, I hug him. I am sure he thinks I'm insane but I don't care. I hug him again, euphoric that I survived this test of faith.

All because I surrendered quickly in faith instead of allowing my head to become paralyzed by destructive thoughts.

The conductor leads me off the train at the next stop and points out the train I need to take back, all without communicating a word in English. I understand completely.

As I sit there at the station of some distant town and wait for another train for my hour trip back, a kind woman—who is also unable to speak to me with words—leans over, pats me on the hand, and offers me her last donut.

People of the world are so good.

# # # #

A handful of people I meet advise me to skip Naples. "It is dirty and there are pickpockets everywhere" is the general consensus. After Rome, I plan to head down to Pompeii and travel the Amalfi Coast before taking a train east to catch my ferry to Greece. Naples is on the way, so I decide to stop and check out this city for a few days despite warnings and objections.

On the train ride to Naples, there are three different stops for the heart of this large city. An elderly Italian woman advises me for my particular stop, then a young man helps lift my luggage off the train. Another Neapolitan man comes along at the station and directs me to tourist office, where an information clerk gives me a city map and provides the bus numbers for my correct bus. A local boy walks outside with me, and points out where the buses park off in the distance. A man in a suit helps me as I struggle to get my big bag up over the curb and down the cobble road. Already six people have helped me in this supposedly hostile city before I even reach my hotel.

At the bus station, I am led to my bus by a friendly woman. Once on the bus, two older gentleman and the bus driver watch over me and inform me when it is time for me to disembark. On the bus, a young girl recommends two places I should visit and a place where I must eat. I am at eleven examples of helpfulness within a thirty minute period.

After I get off the bus, an elderly woman helps me locate where I am on the map and which direction I need to walk to get to my hotel. After a short wrong detour, a shop owner takes pity on me as I struggle to pull my suitcase on the cobblestone and leads me directly to the door of my hotel so that I can't get lost again.

I open the front door of the building at the exact same time as a middle-aged tenant who proceeds to carry my bag up the three flights of stairs to the entrance of the Bed & Breakfast.

I am then warmly greeted by the B&B owner and I quickly inform him that I will only be staying a few days before I move onward to Sorrento. By the time I wheel my bag to my rented room, he has contacted his friend in Sorrento and arranged for me to stay in a large apartment with a balcony that overlooks the ocean, all priced at a budget rate.

I have gathered vast quantities of proof on my trip already

about the helpfulness of people, but this episode supplies me with enough proof for the rest of my life. In the single hour it took to land in Naples and arrive at my hotel FIFTEEN people helped me!

I sit on the bed of the B&B and my only thought is, "What if I would have listened to all those people's negative comments about Naples? I would have missed hitting an all-time high Help Record!"

It is a valuable lesson to me that while it is good to listen to the experience of others, it is okay to trust my own intuition and have faith that my experience might be completely different from theirs. This sure proved true with Naples!

# # # #

I complete my run of Southern Italy by spending an afternoon in Pompeii and a few short days in the cities of Sorrento, Ravello, Amalfi, and Positano on the Amalfi Coast.

In Sorrento, the beautiful room my Naples B&B set me up with has a balcony overlooking the ocean with an incredible view of the sunset. It's the idyllic place to reflect on my diligence over the last thirty days with <u>Project Love</u>. The rewards are remarkable! My vibration is so genuinely positive, people can probably feel it when they walk past me.

When I arrive in Sorrento at the hotel, I find that the call from my Naples B&B causes a man on vacation to be bumped from this room. I apologize and offer to switch rooms but he declines. Instead of the situation creating tension between us, Peter and I become instant friends.

Peter is an American who has lived in Paris for the last twenty-five years. We go grocery shopping together and exchange numbers and he parts with, "If you need a place to stay in Paris, let me know!"

I venture off on my own to check out the town. It's Halloween and I want to see how this holiday is celebrated in Italy. I love that there appear to be only three costumes choices: a witch, a ghost and Dracula. They keep the costume choices simple and focus on fun.

After my short Amalfi Coast tour, it's time to take my last Italian train to the Eastern Coast before I head off to Greece. Happy memories parade through my head about the places I have already visited. I've grown really attached to this country of *love* and feel sad to leave it behind.

I am leaving Italy with a full heart…a heart I never really knew was inside me.

As I head through the train station, I am a little behind schedule and distracted, so when I rush by an elderly woman in her mid-seventies I think, "She reminds me of my grandma," and continue to dash on by.

I take three more steps and stop. Whether I miss my train or not, I instinctively know I have sped past someone in need of help. I turn and look back at this white haired, fragile woman and am met by an expression frozen in terror.

"You look like you could use some help," I say with a big smile. "What can I do to help you?"

The look of relief that washes over her face is so intense, it gives me chills. "Oh, thank you!" she cries, "I'm so happy you speak English! I need to find the right train and I don't know which one to take. None of the cities listed on the board are my city! I'm so confused!"

"Let me find out for you," I offer and write down her destination city. I track down a conductor and locate her train.

"Good news! We're both on the same train and it's only one track over. Let me help you with your luggage so we don't miss it! By the way, my name's Michelle," I say as I grab her suitcase.

"My name is Helen," she replies as she hurries behind me. I am absolutely determined that we are both going to make this train. As we step up to our compartment, I start to lift our luggage up the stairs. Helen protests the entire time.

"Honey, you don't need to do that, I can get it myself. It's heavy. I don't want you to hurt yourself," she says in a worried voice.

I smile a big smile and assure her I am young and strong and that she doesn't need to worry about me hurting myself. She continues her protest but I ignore it and keep loading the bags because I recognize only too well exactly what I have on my hands. I'm dealing with someone who can't ask for or receive help. I'm dealing with the old ME!

We sit down in seats facing each other and after we get comfortable, Helen proceeds to tell me a little about herself and her situation. She's from the East Coast of the United States, seventy-five years old and traveling with a group, but this last part of the trip she has to complete alone. It's her first time traveling alone and she confesses she's completely terrified but this last city is so important, she is willing to take a risk. Helen is a devout Catholic going north to a sacred church to meet a priest she knows so that he can perform special prayers for her daughter who is having difficulties.

The priest will be waiting to meet Helen at the station but thoughts about all the terrible things that could happen have kept her awake many nights filled with dread.

"I even bought a safety whistle!" she informs me and shows me the shiny silver whistle that hangs on a lanyard around her neck.

I look at this woman, who could easily be me in forty years, and with a heart full of compassion I say, "Let me tell you a little story, Helen. Like you, I am also on a journey. My goal is to no longer let fears and old beliefs control my life but to have faith instead. Before, I did not trust that God had things under control. That was *my* job.

"My job now is to let go and let God handle things and to trust that He can. I want to trust that there is something much bigger than myself which always surrounds, guides and protects us all when we connect to It. I want to believe that no matter what I go through in life, no matter where I am, that God is watching over me and will point me down the right path and that whatever the outcome, I will always be okay."

Without getting into details about what a trapped head-case I was; I explain to Helen that whenever I now face a choice, I choose faith and have not been disappointed. "It's like God is always there, two steps ahead of me, wiping out obstacles or sending people my way to help," I tell her.

Then I relay a few of the stories about the wonderful people who arrived to help me when I was in need, who went out of their way to assist a random stranger while expecting nothing in return. I talk about the Help Record and the events that took place only days before in Naples.

"Helen, if fifteen people helping me in a single hour doesn't prove that someone is watching over me, I don't know what will!" She sits there beaming at me and soaks up all the positive energy I exude as I excitedly pass along my stories. I declare that the giving nature of people has been one of the best parts of my trip. How my heart feels full all of the time, because of the goodness.

She reaches across from her train seat and hugs me, close to tears. "Michelle, I prayed all last night and all this morning for God to help me get through this because I'm so scared and he did help me! He sent me an angel. He sent me you!"

I start to get choked up myself. It's my first experience as an *angel* and I am not quite sure if I'm qualified but then I remember Task #5 on my Project Love list: Accept and receive compliments and believe what someone says about me. I reply with sincerity, "Why thank you! I'm glad I could be here to serve as your angel today!" and laugh.

"Helen, a very wise friend of mine gave me great advice about receiving help. She told me that people WANT to help because it feels good to help others. If I don't let them, I actually do them a disservice. I need to accept help and ask for it when needed, and to give it as well."

I continue, "I have taken this advice to heart and my faith in people has grown to an unbelievable level! Be willing to ask for and receive help. Don't shortchange people. If you keep doing everything on your own, you'll never experience the gift where you realize how truly wonderful people are."

Helen hugs me and pulls out her little prayer book so she can write down my name to pray for my safe journey. I give her my name, but I ask her to add:

1. FAITH NOT FEAR
2. PEOPLE ARE GOOD
3. ACCEPT HELP
4. GOD IS TWO STEPS AHEAD

She is so excited and promises she will read these ideas every day. It feels so good to help someone by simply passing along what I have learned from my experiences.

Well, it might have taken a diligent thirty day self-love program for me to finally get to a place where I appreciate who I am enough to accept being called an angel, but what a rewarding experience to be grateful for! It feels like I received a "Good job" cheer from Chris, or a little pat on the back from God.

With these warm feelings in my heart, I leave the wonderful country of Italy and love and set off for another adventure . . . Greece!

Chapter 6:
Saviors in Disguise—Greece

The soreness creeps up my spine and slowly seeps into every muscle in my back. I bend over and grab the handle of my bag and moan as a sharp stab of pain shoots from my neck to my legs. Slowly, I attempt to turn my head to see how close we are to shore, but the muscles in my shoulders are like tight knots of fiber that are not about to stretch even a millimeter.

"I need to get to a hotel so I can unload my bag and take a hot shower," I groan. I start to fantasize about how good the warm water will feel as it beats against my aching back. "A soft bed tonight will make the rock hard ferry cot a distant memory," I convince myself as the ferry pulls into the port after a night of sea travel.

The port resembles a parking lot, with rows of gigantic ferries ready to head out to sea. As I reach the deck, the smell of seaweed and fish fills the outside air. The sun is shining and I soak up the rays, grateful after hours of lower-level darkness. It might have only been an eleven hour ferry ride, but I am ready for my feet to be planted on land again. I've decided that ferries are *not* my favorite form of transportation.

After struggling down the ramp, I finally reach land and begin the long walk to the harbor exit. "Excuse me, where is the tourist office?" I ask the first person I encounter, but he ignores me and continues to walk. One, two, three people I ask before someone finally points in the direction of the train station with an annoyed gesture.

"Please, I need to find a hotel. Can you help me?" I ask the man behind the counter at the station. He scribbles the name of a hotel and draws a circle on the map, then waves me away so he can help the next person in line.

I walk outside, sit on the curb and rub my throbbing temples, in hopes of stopping my headache before it spreads any further through my skull. I look down at the counter attendant's writing and then take a good look at the map. I do not recognize a single character or a single word.

"Toto, I've got a feeling we're not in Kansas anymore," is the only thought that runs through my mind as my head begins to pound.

"Baby, this is all part of the adventure, so go with the flow. People of the world are still good; you just haven't run into many of them yet in Greece. Think 'People are good—but different—in Greece.' You'll be fine," I say to myself in my Karen voice, as I attempt to give myself a pep talk while I trudge up the hill toward the hotel.

My throbbing head does not seem to agree. The aches and pains from the ferry ride leave me feeling physically beaten, and there is a dark cloud all around, even though the sun shines above.

"As for the language frustration," Karen's voice in my head continues, "You've been through this before, only this time there's a different alphabet thrown into the mix. You are a capable woman and you can do this. You just need a new system and a new attitude."

I can do this. There is an easy solution. When possible, I will have people write the names of certain things in English and in Greek so that way my bases are covered. That was a simple one to solve.

"As for the attitude adjustment, go back to your hotel and call it a day. Greece is one of the oldest countries in Europe. It will still be here tomorrow and it will be an even *better* Greece when you aren't sore, tired and dealing with a painful headache. Michelle Bain—Professional Tourist/World Traveler, you have complete approval to clock out early; sites unseen," the Karen voice says.

I am too exhausted and achy to combat negativity alone today. Good thing my team is only a voice away to help save the day!

JOURNEY TO THE IDEAL

# # # #

"What a difference a good night's sleep can make!" I sing the next morning with a fresh new attitude. I stroll through Patras for a few hours and absorb the change in food, language, architecture and culture from Italy to Greece. People I pass smile back today as I window shop and wander in and out of the small stores.

I venture off to find Pantokratoras church which is my primary destination for the entire city. This lady is calling to me and I have to meet her because I have never been to a true Byzantine church, especially one built on the ruins of an ancient temple of Zeus. I schedule my day around the church's hours of operation because it sounds so beautiful in the city guide I picked up from the tourist office.

After I climb all one-hundred-ninety of the famous Agiou Nikolaou steps and wander many blocks in search of the church, I finally arrive—only to meet with immediate disappointment because the gate is locked.

"Great, here we go again! Why is it so difficult for European countries to post simple hours of operation accurately or coordinate sites with their brochures?" I complain. I shake the gate frantically, as if my frustration will miraculously open the lock. Even as I say this, I realize I have probably been to over one-hundred sites in the last few months and this type of thing has only happened a few times.

Time for an attitude adjustment again.

"Focus on the positive. You are not the center of the universe. Things do not revolve around your existence, exclusively for your purposes, Michelle. The church is closed. Accept it and move on. You climbed almost two hundred stairs to get up here so you might as well check out this area. There will be other churches," I say as I attempt to redirect my thinking.

With that, I turn toward a street to the left and hike off. I wander up and down some winding roads for a half-mile or so before

I become a bit lost, which is unusual for me. In the distance, there is a cross mounted on top of a large dome so I head toward it. "I might as well visit this church since I'm close."

I laugh as I approach the church. Yes, it is my must-see church again, only I'm at a different entrance on the opposite side and this gate is wide open.

I walk through the gate and up the stairs to the main door but as I take a step in, I am blasted back outside by the force of the church's interior. I stand frozen in the doorway, almost intimidated to enter.

At this point in my trip I have already visited almost fifty cathedrals across Spain, Portugal and Italy—some of which are recognized as the most magnificent in the world. Pantokratoras church blows them all away in terms of pure visual overload.

If I continue to compare churches to women, then the woman I see when I enter this church is a flamboyant drag queen in a $10,000 show outfit with sequins, beads and feathers covered in loads of sparkling jewels with layers of colorful makeup. She is simply dazzling.

Every inch of every wall, ceiling, pillar, floor and piece of furniture is covered in bright murals, geometrical designs, scriptural paintings, and ornate carvings all saturated in color. Everything from floor to ceiling is accented in gold leaf so the entire place looks like it glows.

The intriguing trick of the church is that nothing is real. The murals, frames, sculptures, pedestals and borders are painted in three dimensional design so that they look like real marble statues, wood frames, and stone pedestals but they are really all paintings.

Small checker board patterns of orange and yellow decorate the bottom portion of the walls, while wide green and purple stripes cut between the panels. Vividly-colored murals of ancient religious scenes flank the upper portion of the walls, outlined by ornate tromp l'oeil gold-painted frames.

Perched between the murals are faux statues which glisten in gold and shiny marble and appear as real as solid marble statues. Hexagons in blue, flower patterns in red, and zigzags in yellow cover every open space from floor to ceiling—all entwined with gold leaf.

Pillars of dark blue, capped with intricate green and gold detail lead the eye up to the ceiling where faux domes depict elaborate murals of angels and the heavens.

Large maroon and mustard tiles cross the entire floor, broken by bands of smaller orange tiles which weave their way side-to-side and front-to-back. Only the wooden chairs are real and some of the items at the altar. The seats of the chairs are covered with deep purple fabric.

There is so much visual stimulation in this small space, my eyes cannot figure out where to focus. They dart over here, then head over there—distracted by all the strong, vibrant tones that leap at me from every direction. It actually makes me feel a little dizzy, especially with all of the optical illusions created by the faux painting. There is not a solitary blank inch in the entire church. Not one inch. I am completely mesmerized and struck with awe.

Immediately, my memory flashes back to the last time I felt overwhelmed by a surprising view. It was the hidden miniature nativity scene in Portugal. I remember the old man and the unsaid message:

"Behind every door lies a beautiful unknown and it will be shown to you...*if you just have faith.*"

Here I am, once again, in a similar situation. I turned away in disappointment when I met a locked door, only to be guided around the corner to where an open door awaited to expose beauty of breathtaking proportions.

Absorb this wonderful message that God keeps sending you in gorgeously wrapped packages, Michelle.

# # # #

I haven't quite decided if there is something about the air in Greece that makes my stomach constantly growl or if it's because I have passed by about thirty restaurants and have been too embarrassed to go in.

Why am I starving when food is all around? One word . . . ego.

Somewhere on the span of ocean between Italy and Greece, ego decided to hop on board and I am starving to death because I feel too stupid to ask someone a simple question like, "What is this?"

I ate Doritos for dinner my first night in Athens. Is my plan to live on Doritos for the next three weeks?

Pride in hand, I walk over to the small sandwich shop down the street from my Athens hotel. "You can do this! It is only silly insecurity causing you to starve," I say to myself, a quick second before I open the door.

I walk up to the counter with my customary "just looking" expression firmly in place, and eye the door to make sure I am still close enough to run out if someone asks me what I want.

"It amazes me how my mind can take one little fear and quickly grow it into something I need an escape plan to cope with. My stomach growls at the smell of real food, but this ego of mine is still perched on my shoulder, ready to yell 'run!'" I think in disbelief.

Take contrary action. Don't cave into ego thoughts!

"Let me guess, this is 'All Greek to you', correct? We can fix that!"

I look up at the blonde girl behind the counter who spoke these wonderful words, see her reassuring smile and blurt out, "I love you so much right now!"

Either I still have love on the brain from Italy or I am demented from lack of food!

We both start to laugh and instantly, my distress is gone. No emergency exit required. I need help and Olga appears to rescue me from starvation. She gives me a crash course on some of the basics of Greek food, explains every item and has me taste many things so I know what I like and dislike.

I have been saved! I will eat more than Doritos in Greece.

It turns out, Olga's father owns the restaurant and she works there almost every day. We quickly become friends and I stop in at least once a day for the next few weeks.

While we enjoy coffee together in a booth at the back of the restaurant, Olga, her cousin and I chat daily about Greek culture and history. Their involvement in government and their knowledge about world economics seems extensive compared to my limited understanding. Here, thousands of years of history push forward into modern day discussions about politics and religion.

For Olga, and many in her culture, the commitment to family also runs deep. Brothers and sisters live around the corner from each other so that cousins grow up together like one big family. Uncles take nephews under their wing and teach them the family trade. Fathers support daughters as long as necessary. Olga is my age and still lives at home. She explains that she would never move more than a few houses away from her parents even if given the choice.

As a transient without a home, far away from everyone I love, all of this touches a place in my heart where the word 'commitment' lies dormant. These restaurant discussions open up some serious personal questions for me such as, "What kind of commitment to my parents and sisters do I neglect when I chose to live on the other side of the States, thousands of miles away from them? Why is this so easy for me to do? Do I lack a sensitivity chip somewhere in my DNA which makes detachment effortless for me?"

I did not expect an analysis of my choices and my commitment to family to stem from casual coffee conversation, yet I can't ignore the questions that are now exposed.

Is the world showing me, through Olga and her family, another way I have missed out on important opportunities to love? Maybe if I choose a different path, I might find that there is a caring, dedicated family woman buried underneath my fear of commitment.

This idea is hard to digest after years of being a lone wolf who has kept life commitment-free in her quest to remain independent. I am just not sure that relationships, family and children are built into my DNA.

But then how would I know if I've never given the whole family thing a try? I always focused on work instead of family, because I was a proven success at that. I also sacrificed time with family for self-serving gratification, like making money. Is there another path I am supposed to explore?

I recognize that I have grown as a person on this trip, even in a short period of time. My developed self-love and practice of giving and receiving have set me on a new higher path toward the ideal me. But here in Greece, I am challenged with another area to face and review.

Olga shares with me some of her disappointments about lack of opportunities in Greece. Even with several degrees, she has found it difficult to secure a job financially lucrative enough for her to survive on. I tell her about my experience working jobs that paid well but that did not fulfill me.

"It might not be a bad thing to be in the family business surrounded by people you love," I suggest. "That's only my perspective based on my own experience," I add. "My intention is to live my true calling now that I have discovered it. I am going to write!"

Olga is one of the few people I have confided in about my new desire to be a writer. She immediately supports my announcement and says, "Michelle, you travel the world alone. Look at you! You are crazy but you are strong! If you say you are going to write a book, I know you will write a book. You must make sure and send me your first book in case I can't find it in Greece! Look at this. I sit with a famous author!"

It is so fun to share this dream with someone who is right here next to me, not by email. I feel the excitement grow within me as we laugh and joke about it over coffee. As I speak openly about this dream, I begin to connect with the reality of it. Feelings of joy flow through me when I daydream about writing on the beach, or when I visualize myself seated at a table, signing autographed copies of my first book.

All of this joy about my new dream triggers an unexpected attraction process. Suddenly, it appears I can't go anywhere without someone saying, "You should write a book."

Parthenon: "Wow, you travel alone? Will you write a book about it?"

Sounion: "Boy, a trip around the world. You should write a book about that!"

Delphi: "You are visiting how many countries? I would love to read a book about that trip!"

Mycenae: "What an adventure! You have to write a book someday!"

These are a few I distinctly remember, but it feels like the universe shot out an email blast to every English speaking person in Greece which reads, "If you see this chick traveling alone from California, tell her she needs to write a book!" It's almost ridiculous, it happens so frequently, especially because writing a book about my trip isn't part of my plan.

I don't even know what I would write about when it comes to my trip. I'm so absorbed in the many great lessons about myself, people, events, faith, and attraction. There's no room in my mind for ideas that concern a <u>travel</u> book. Who needs another Fodor's or Lonely Planet book anyway?

# # # #

As I stare in awe at the monasteries perched high atop their isolated rock mountains amid an ocean of golden leaves, I have only one thought: "Meteora is God's land."

Like a light fog, the spiritual aura of the monasteries drifts down from the mountains to the green valleys below and mists me with positive particles which vibrate with spiritual energy generated from centuries of prayer and dedication. Those little vibrating particles constantly surround me, like I float around in a bubble filled with all the good feelings I have ever experienced in life. Meditating in the morning has become a new, almost trance like experience here as I reach deeper levels.

The serenity and silence are so powerful here. I never want to leave.

I spend an entire day at a single monastery absorbing every ounce of its history, every spec of its prayer energy, before I retire back to town. The next day, I am back up in the mountains to discover what wonders the next monastery holds.

These are the last remaining six of the hundreds that originally existed, before they were destroyed by invaders. Life was not easy then. Building supplies, food, even people, all had to be hoisted up by pulleys to these isolated peaks, before modern conveniences made them more attainable.

Today, buses still do not travel through the mountains so I take a cab each day to visit them. Wandering herds of animals seem to control traffic on the winding roads. Often, the cab driver has to slam on the brakes to avoid a goat as it bounds across our path.

Other times, if horn honks achieve no results, the taxi driver and I get out and wave our arms in an attempt to motivate the lazy herd of sheep and goats to move along so that they quit blocking the road. There are no fences, only open land where herds wander in search of areas to graze.

What a different world from back home where trained domestic dogs aren't even allowed off their leashes!

Up in the mountains, the roads wind through beautiful acres of trees dressed in fall colors. The golden leaves spread like a protective canopy for miles, while thicket bushes and vegetation of all sorts sprout below. In certain places, the road follows along the steep cliff edge. Large rock plateaus jut out and serve as observation areas so that visitors can capture spectacular photos of the monasteries with rolling prairies as distant backdrops. These views are stunning.

On my third day, I spend some time at Varlamm Monastery where I visit the church and tour the museum. Afterwards, I ramble across the bridge back to the road. It's a sunny day and I don't want to leave the beauty of the mountain quite yet. I look off in the distance and see the town below and feel a rush of inspiration.

What a gorgeous day to be outside walking!

Based on the drive down the day before, I estimate it will take about four or five hours to walk back to the hotel. This gives me plenty of time to contemplate the alternative path the monks chose for their lives as I stroll along, soaking up the immense beauty of my surroundings.

I have nothing else planned. This walk will be a wonderful way to spend the rest of the day, but I need to get started if I intend to make it to town before dark!

Down the road I trek, full of inspiration and excitement. Each step squashes post-decision fears about the scarcity of people and cars up this way, or about my lack of map or phone. I am filled with the faith that I can make it back safely and this is enough for me. I walk for miles as I enjoy the fresh air and beautiful trees and stop to take photos of the views, only passing a few cars along the way.

My connection to God is so solid here; I feel almost like a physical presence is walking beside me, especially now. It's just me, God and this beautiful winding terrain.

Soon I reach an odd fork in the road where one road heads up and the other down. "According to my memory, the road that heads up eventually winds around and travels back down again toward the road that leads into town," I think as I take the road upward.

"Gosh, if someone got lost up here, it would be forever before anyone found them. There is no civilization—only these winding roads that wrap through these gorgeous trees and mountains," I realize as I walk.

After about another half-mile of walking, I notice the distant sound of jingling bells. As I continue to walk, the bells get louder so I start to look for a stick. Not a great defense mechanism, but I assume I will be able to wave it at the goats and they will run away. "Flailing arms worked before when they blocked the road so a stick will probably be even more effective," I decide.

I'm unable to see what's ahead because my view is blocked by a wall of stone where the road bends. Stick in hand, I round the corner prepared to swat at the goats. What I run into instead is about four times the size I expected. It is a large herd of gigantic, horned cattle.

I let out a yelp of surprise and fly back around the corner where I pin myself to the wall, still clenching my little stick.

"Is that my heart pounding or is it the thud of hooves as they stampede toward me? I can't tell. I think I just had a heart attack! What am I going to do? Those things are massively huge and they have horns longer than my arms!" I think in total panic.

I look down at my little stick, "This sure is useless, but what am I going to do? I have to get past them! That road they are blocking is the only way up," I cry as my panic grows. "Maybe I can hide here for a few minutes until they start to move on and then sneak by after they are gone. Yes, that's a good plan!" I decide.

I walk down the road another twenty feet and wait for what seems like eternity. Finally, I hear bells so I work my way back up the hill to the stone wall and slowly inch my way to the edge of it. Quietly, I move sideways, clutching my stick and peek my head around the corner.

I come face-to-face with the most enormous black beast I have ever encountered. It is less than ten inches away, has pure black eyes and horns that are at least three feet long. I am so close to it that I can feel its hot breath as it blows back my hair.

We lock eyes; my small blue ones stare in terror into its large black orbs. The beast lowers its head a fraction of an inch and lifts one hoof. I spin around and I start to *run*.

I run like my life depends on it because, to me, it does. My legs move as fast as an Olympic champion as I fly down the hill. My lungs feel like they are going to burst, yet I don't stop. I sprint at full speed for at least a half-mile, never pausing to glance back, certain that a big black bull from Spain has found its way to Greece and is breathing down my neck, ready to gouge me to pieces. I have never run so far so fast! My little stick whips through the air as I run and run. I have no clue where I am running. I only know I am running AWAY!

I run all the way back to the fork in the road, where I finally slow down enough to glance back to see if I am about to meet my end. To my utter relief, the big black beast is not behind me. I collapse on a rock, where I huff and puff, on the verge of tears.

"What am I going to do now?" I ask myself between ragged breaths. "There's no way I'm taking one step back up that road. I haven't passed a car in hours. Do I have to walk two hours all the way back to Varlamm Monastery and ask them to call me a taxi? Dusk is already setting in, will I even make it back to the monastery before dark?"

I stand there for a few minutes and stare at the ground as tears fill my eyes and I fight the urge to panic.

What should I do? I am out of answers on this one.

I hear the rumble of a vehicle engine and look up. "This can't be possible! There is a bus headed in my direction. Buses don't come up here! Am I hallucinating?" I say in total disbelief.

No, a real bus is coming toward me. I start to wave frantically and jump in front of it. The bus grinds to a halt. I rush around to the passenger door.

"No bus. No bus here, only taxi. I cut across today only, no bus," he tries to tell me but I refuse to listen. I blubber instead, "Bull, save me from the bull," then switch to making horn gestures on my head with my hands and *moo* noises when I realize he doesn't understand my words. He doesn't get the picture I am frantically trying to create for him through my sounds and gestures but he does recognize that I'm not about to accept no as an answer, since I have already worked my way up the bus steps. He finally surrenders and shuts the door.

Since buses do not travel this route, there are no other passengers on the bus except me. There's only one reason to explain why he cut across the mountain today—because I needed him to.

As we pull away from the fork in the road, I crumple into my seat behind the driver, vaguely noting that we are heading down. I bolt upright.

I had been walking the wrong way!

If that herd of cattle had not blocked my path and sent me back down the road, I would have been lost in those desolate mountains in the dark.

My big, black beastly horned nemesis had actually been my savior!

I can't hold the tears back any longer, this realization is too much after the miraculous appearance of the bus. Tears of happiness and relief pour out of me during the entire trip down the mountain.

I can see the driver's bewildered look in his big overhead mirror as he glances at this strange passenger who sits crying on his empty bus. He must have been worried about my sanity because he pulls the bus right up to the front door of my hotel, like he doesn't trust that I will make it unless he does.

In a country where everything starts out as "Greek to me", one thing becomes clear: *all the elements* of God's Universe want to help me.

I am being sent messages like crazy: Olga opening up my thoughts about family, random strangers telling me I should write a book, buses coming out of nowhere. And an animal I feared revealing itself as my saving grace—one that teaches me to look past external appearances and to recognize the God in everything.

With a growing arsenal of experiences like this, how can I ever doubt faith again?

Chapter 7:
The Golden Rule—Scotland

As the airplane tires bounce on the runway in Edinburgh, I am giddy with excitement. For the first time in three months, I will be in English speaking territory!

"I'll be able to read a sign and understand it!" I think with glee. "Better still, I will get to use my vocal chords again on a regular basis. If people talk on a bus, I can actually join in on the conversation. If someone asks me a question, I can answer instead of only offering a smile as I shrug my shoulders and shake my head.

"No more phrasebooks needed to find the grocery store. No more key expressions like 'please help me' or 'excuse me' written on my hand," I acknowledge. "No more pulling out my translation dictionary to figure out what the sign says above the mystery meat I am about to buy. No more. I will finally understand and be understood!"

I rush to baggage claim and then race outside to the taxi stand and hop into a taxi, stoked with enthusiasm about Scotland.

"Sae ye jist arrived in Scootlund? Whaur ur ye headed tae?" the taxi driver says across the seat.

"Um, excuse me, would you mind repeating what you just said please?" I ask, completely bewildered.

"Whaur ur ye headed tae?" he repeats.

"Gosh, I am sorry, but would you mind saying that one more time?" I ask him again.

What is going on? Has my plane landed in the wrong country? Have I landed in the Twilight Zone instead? They do speak English here in Scotland . . . right?

# # # #

After my initial bewildered shock about the strong dialect wears off, I am flooded with relief to recognize that they actually do speak English in Scotland.

It becomes comical to me. I joke via email with people back home that I must have DDD (Dialect Deciphering Deficiency) since it is harder for me to understand the Scottish than people from the four non-English speaking countries I have visited.

While at the Edinburgh Castle, I chuckle as I hear a Scottish man ask, "Whit? Dornt yeu understand English?" to another tourist. DDD must be a popular disorder.

It's probably because I start to feel rude when I ask someone to repeat something three times, but I find myself listening much more closely to every word that is said around me, hoping it will help me decipher my next conversation better.

I have never been a particularly good listener so this is a new practice for me. I focus intently on conversations that surround me, and even flat-out eavesdrop in a few cases, as I suck up every word and pay detailed attention.

With all this focus on conversation, I have the most beautiful realization: Scottish people are some of the most polite people in the world. My newfound listening skills allow me to catch fabulous examples of this everywhere I go.

"Cheerio!" rings out up and down every road as neighbors greet neighbors. "Och, sorry thaur!" someone apologizes, even though he hasn't actually bumped another, but because he has come within a foot's length of possibly doing so. "Please, yeu go first," is offered in the busy line at the market.

Doors are constantly opened by men for women, and then by

women for men. Everywhere I look, I see and hear more examples of impeccable manners and acts of politeness.

The highlight for me is that not a single person ever steps on or off a bus without saying, "Thenk yeu," to the driver; even if a person only rides for the length of a single bus stop, it is a courtesy that is never neglected.

To me, Scotland is a prime example of a country built on people who treat others how they want to be treated. They understand and live by The Golden Rule.

Maybe this is just the experience I'm attracting, but as I witness this day after day, I believe this country sets a standard for the world to follow when it comes to good manners and politeness toward our fellows.

Up to this point, the truth that "People of the world are good" has been proven to me on many, many occasions but to see this extend into common everyday politeness across an entire country has an even stronger impact. I think about how I am always in a rush back in the States. Even when I have time to spare, I still rush. I am in such a rush, I finish people's sentences instead of listening, so that I can say what *I* want to say.

Do I live by The Golden Rule and treat others how I want to be treated? No . . . but I could! I could be a person who is polite and listens because I know what it's like to want to be heard. I could be a person who puts other's needs, wants and desires first, instead of always thinking of myself as top priority. I could slow down and appreciate people in the present moment.

Look at how harmoniously the Scottish exist because they treat others how they would like to be treated. I could do these things, instead of choosing to live behind excuses, like "Life is too busy."

"It's okay . . . the world isn't going to leave you behind, Michelle," I reassure myself. "From now on, take an extra breath and treat others how you would like to be treated. Little acts of courtesy go a long way. It only takes a second to do something simple like glance at someone's nametag and thank them by name or to let someone go ahead of you in line.

"Small courtesies will spread into larger courtesies and before you know it, you have deeper, more meaningful relationships with people because you treat them how you want them to treat you."

I want to slow myself down. I want to really appreciate the many people that cross my path every day and extend a new level of courtesy, as I have witnessed here in Scotland.

In support, Scotland gifts me with a simple little reminder before I leave. As I sit and stare out the bus window on my way to the ferry to Ireland, I catch a glimpse of a statement in big gold block letters on the brick wall in the roundabout.

"Whit's yer hurry?" is the question imbedded on the wall.

Chapter 8:
Go with the Flow—Ireland

The ferry across the Irish Sea is short and sweet compared to the ferry from Italy to Greece. It's more of a luxury boat and it docks where the *Titanic* was built, which is exciting and eerie at the same time. A luminescent glow seems to cover Ireland, even from a distance, because of the bright shade of the green grass.

I head to Belfast in Northern Ireland first, before I travel even further north where the grass truly does glow and where the fables stand tall amongst the solid cylindrical rocks of natural wonder.

THE LEGEND OF GIANT'S CAUSEWAY:

"Once upon a time, Ireland had a giant called Finn MacCool. He was rather small for a giant, but he was very clever. Across the sea, in Scotland, there was another giant called Benandonner. He was an enormously tall giant, but not very clever.

Benandonner was a real showoff and boasted about being the strongest giant on earth. So Finn invited Benandonner over to Ireland for a contest and even built a causeway across the sea for the Scottish giant.

The day of the contest finally arrived. When Finn saw Benandonner approaching, however, he realized that he really didn't stand a chance against that large and fearsome giant. Finn decided to play a trick on Benandonner.

Finn put on a nightgown and a bonnet and went to bed. When the Scottish giant arrived, Finn's wife Oonagh told him that Finn wasn't at home. Benandonner didn't believe her. "Where is the coward hiding?" he shouted and started searching the house. When he heard a noise in the bedroom, he rushed toward it and flung the door open. But Oonagh warned him, 'Be quiet or you'll wake the baby.'

'That's your baby?' Benandonner muttered when he saw the person in the bed. He didn't realize that the 'baby' was Finn. Instead he was shocked by the size of the child – 'If the baby is that big, how much bigger and stronger might Finn be?' Benandonner panicked. Hastily he ran back to Scotland destroying the causeway behind him."

This is the Irish legend of how the Giant's Causeway came to be. The 40,000 vertically aligned hexagon cylinders are really created by volcanic eruptions over 60 million years ago, when highly fluid molten rock was forced up through fissures in the chalk bed. Then, rapidly cooling lava contracted and variations in the cooling rate resulted in the world famous columnar structure that many refer to as the 8th Natural Wonder of the World.

But as I stand amidst the thousands of massive columns and stare in awe and wonder as the ocean crashes around me, I swear the writer in me catches a glimpse of the giant, Finn MacCool, as he looms in the distant fog.

I love this country and its creative legends. Northern Ireland is breathtaking. It's so sad to me that the tour guide on the bus has to end his pitch with, "You have seen some of the most amazing castles and the 8th Natural Wonder of the World. You have also seen rolling hills and valleys of the greenest grass on earth. What you did not see is a single gun or any uproars. Please tell everyone!"

Except for the old man who gives me a tour of the glorious Celtic church in Belfast affectionately calling me a "Yank," I encounter only beauty in this country. He's a cute old man, so I give him a break since I know he's flirting with me.

The Belfast Castle is gorgeously decorated for Christmas and there are only holiday festivities in the air. All the people I meet are lovely and very supportive of tourists.

Many people back home suggested that I skip Northern Ireland and I am reminded of all the people who suggested I skip Naples. I am grateful that I trusted intuition again. Northern Ireland is another place I will return to someday.

# # # #

By the time I cross the border into the Republic of Ireland, I have either shipped home, or left at some hotel, all my material possessions except for one small suitcase.

As each country goes by, I love myself more and as a result, I seem to need a lot less, especially clothing, so I unload pounds of ego baggage along the way. I am down to about a fifteen pound bag by the time I arrive in Ireland. That is about fifty pounds of ego shed without a single regret!

I soon decide what I can use in Ireland though is an extra suitcase filled with good ol' everyday *patience.*

I start my tour in the grand city of Dublin. It's a fun town, full of energy and life, where pubs are the predominant business. I think I read somewhere that there are over 750 pubs in the city alone!

Despite it being winter, the weather is sunny so I walk almost everywhere. Every road I walk down, a shop owner waves and stops me to chat. Soon, I am caught up in conversations about the lovely weather with each person I pass. An hour after I enter a gift shop, I finally leave empty handed, but with an abundance of knowledge on the history of the town.

I thought I liked to talk, but these people <u>really</u> like to talk!

Every site I visit, the line wraps around the outside, as we wait for the late ticket salesperson to return back from break. They seem to schedule a lot of breaks for staff at tourist attractions here. There I stand when the ticket person arrives, tapping my foot with an impatient look on my face.

When I finally make it to Dublin Castle, I am four hours later than I planned due to delays in transportation, conversation, and general operational flow at that castle. My patience is non-existent at this point.

"What is wrong with this country? Don't they have consideration for other people's time? I only have a few days here to see everything. Are they trying to mess up my plans on purpose?" I fume in an accusatory tone to no one in particular, since I'm alone.

The first sentence out of the guide's mouth is, "If you haven't realized it yet, we are very relaxed here in Ireland. Our philosophy is 'When God made Time, He made a lot of it' so don't ever expect an Irishman to be on time or ever expect him to be in a hurry to get anywhere!"

Here's a chance to work on some massive reprogramming, Ms. Type 'A', Always-on-a-Schedule, Compulsive Planner who thinks late people, or entire countries even, are out to sabotage her agenda.

I can choose to fully embrace this new philosophy of slowing down or else I can lose my sanity in this land that knows no time. It's up to me: gain patience, slow down and go with the flow, or feel never ending frustration and go crazy. Ireland or old ways, Michelle?

I remember Karen's words the day before I left, "Michelle, a few things will take place whether you like it or not. The first is that, no matter how well you planned this trip, things will never go exactly as you planned. The sooner you accept this and become flexible, the less pain you will experience. As much as your ego likes to think so, the universe does not revolve around you and your meticulous plans. You have fought this fact for too long already. Use this trip as an opportunity to learn to go with the flow of life."

Where is the fun in "things must always go how I want them to or how I plan them?" Life is always changing. Many times, the best experiences meant for my true direction come from paths I can't predict because they haven't even entered my reality yet. Paths I miss because I am so laser focused on following my plans. If I change my ways and slow down and go with the flow, I leave enough space between my way and God's way to see the true path I am supposed to take. Plus, it cements me in the NOW!

I decide to pull out my new slogan from Scotland, "Whit's yer hurry?" and put it to work daily, because what is life if it's not about enjoying the journey? I want to experience relaxed joy, like these happy-go-lucky people who always have time to stop and gab or tell a good story.

I understand what Karen recognized long ago: if I go with the flow, then I won't always feel exhausted from constantly swimming upstream. Flexibility is essential to a happy life. Each time I pause in my day to chit-chat with a stranger, I acknowledge, "This is a much more joyful way to be."

My newly adopted philosophies are soon put to the test though. On my third day in Dublin, it starts to rain.

As I hide in my room from my arch enemy, I scour the newspaper for good news that the rain will end. I have experienced un-seasonally good weather in every country up to this point. It has been at least ten degrees hotter and sunnier than normal. I joke that I bring "California sunshine" with me wherever I go and I'm determined to keep the streak alive in Ireland.

The news reports that a storm is on its way to Dublin which will last almost two weeks before it migrates south. I immediately say, "Forget go with the flow," and devise a new plan: I will travel west tomorrow to Galway and the Western Coast and then take a train further south before the rain arrives. My new motto becomes, "I am smarter than nature and I *will* outrun this rain!"

As I head off to Galway the next day, it appears my plan has worked. After crossing the borders of Dublin, the skies clear and I enjoy hours of spectacular rolling hills of fluorescent green grass on the four hour train ride west. I arrive in Galway, excited that my plan has succeeded. The sun shines brightly in the sky.

One hour later, the rain starts. It's more like a monsoon sweeps in. The downpour is steady—hour after hour. The rain is so heavy, the streets flood, the stores close down and transportation stops.

In my plan to outrun the rain, I have trapped myself in a city on the other side of the country where it does nothing but continuously rain non-stop for three days straight. The news informs me that the storm diverted and headed west instead. Dublin is sunny and dry.

Confined to my hotel room, I stew over how badly my plan has backfired and how going with the flow would have been a much better choice. This fresh pain proves my attempts to control every outcome are not always the best way. I missed out on the opportunity to explore more of Dublin in my quest to create an 'ideal' experience.

Maybe this is the ideal experience, Michelle. Maybe a harsh example is exactly what you needed to cement in this lesson about not always planning, since this is a long-standing issue which runs pretty deep.

There are hours of introspection and inner struggle that go on in my room as the storm rages outside. Learning to be spontaneous and to take things as they come may not be an easy feat for me to accomplish, but for the sake of my future sanity, I have to make it a priority. If I need proof that planning is not always the best action, I have been delivered gallons and gallons of wet proof. I get it.

As soon as the weather breaks and transportation starts to run again, I bolt south. In the South, I choose differently—everything I do is unplanned and spontaneous. I divert to Blarney Castle and kiss the Blarney Stone. I know I already have the "gift of gab" but it sounds like a fun thing to do, so I do it.

I visit Cork and then go to Waterford and tour the Waterford Crystal factory where I am brought to tears by a memorial piece one Irish glass carver created. It is a beautiful sculpture of three fireman in dedication to September 11th which he made during his off-time. Waterford was not on my original agenda and I would have missed this amazing commemorative had I stuck only to my plan.

It rains the rest of the time I am in Ireland and instead of attempting to outrun it, I enjoy the vivid neon green grass it produces instead.

Stop and smell the roses along the way, Michelle. This might not be on your agenda, but roses are beautiful after the rain.

# # # #

Throughout my last days in Ireland, something pressing has been on my mind. I attempt to shake it off but it persists and finds its way back into my thoughts time and time again. It has to do with India, where I will travel in a few short months. The thought that keeps repeating is "DON'T GO ALONE."

The thing is, I can't figure out if it is anxiety or intuition speaking the message. It's easy for me to see how it could be fear. This country will be dramatically different from my current travels in Western Europe, so my dread about the unknown might be kicking up a notch. Yet, I have so much proof that God is with me on this trip so I want to believe it is intuition.

I set aside the rest of the day to do some research on different group related travel options for India because the message is so consistent and so loud. I am learning to go with the flow in Ireland but something inside me says, "It's okay to have a plan for India."

I decide to walk down the road in Cork and visit an empty church I passed earlier while exploring the town, in hopes that some silence will help clarify if this message is coming from intuition or fear.

The church is small, with old stone walls and dark, worn wood pews. There are no murals or statues and the only light comes from a round, clear glass window above the entrance. "A milk maid—plain but solid" is my first thought as I walk inside and sit in one of the wood pews.

I close my eyes and say, "What do you think God?" and then

wait to see if anything comes to me. I don't hear a whisper, but the expression "Thunder of Silence" enters my head. The silence is so loud, my eardrums vibrate. I can only handle this intense silence for about ten minutes; it is so loud my eardrums feel like they are going to burst! With a nervous laugh, I decide, "It's probably time to get to my India research," and quickly leave.

Back in town, I find an internet café so I can start investigating tour groups. There's still some lingering anxiety from the church experience and I am suddenly clear that, regardless if it is intuition or fear directing me, I do not want to travel alone across India. "There has to be a group I can hook up with," I say to console myself and to keep stressful thoughts from growing.

Before I jump into research, I take a quick look at my email since I have been bouncing around and haven't checked it in a week. "Yay, there's one from Sunny! An email from home will be a good thing to help stop bad thoughts right now!" I think with joy.

Sunny is my middle sister. I have a great relationship with both my sisters, Sunny and Lesa, despite the fact that they both live in Baltimore and I don't see them very often. When I am in the States, we talk on the phone all the time and we have been emailing regularly during my travel.

Sunny has the only child in our family, my young niece, so I always love getting emails from her because she has fun stories to tell and photos to share. I open her email first . . . and tears of joy instantly spring to my eyes.

"We decided that you should not travel to India alone—so Lesa and I are both coming with you!" she says in her very first sentence. I sit there and stare at the sentence in total shock.

This isn't an idea that has ever been discussed. Neither of my sisters mentioned wanting to travel to India in any of our conversations! I reread the sentence to make sure it is really there. My heart starts to sing, "Thank you, thank you, thank you!" as I read the rest of the email.

"Maybe this is how I see family more—through family travel," I think as I remember all my questions about family love and bonding back in Greece. "I wonder if I could ever get my parents to leave the country."

That is a thought for another day. At least right now I can bask in the excitement of traveling with my sisters in a few months. And float in the comfort of knowing that I will not be going alone.

Just like God told me, in a silent voice that was so loud, it was deafening.

Chapter 9:
Generosity—France

"Up . . . then down. Up . . . then down. Constant, never ending gigantic waves of motion. That is what my world consists of right now. It seems impossible that a ferry this large and heavy would still have the ability to get tossed up and down by something like water. Always the same motion: *Up . . . then down. Up . . . then down.*

"I can't believe that stupid storm I tried to outrun in Ireland found me again, only this time it got me good. I'm completely trapped, unable to even sit up because of nausea, in a small cabin surrounded by miles of sea. There is no escape. There is no way I can outrun a storm when I am stuck on a ferry in the middle of the English Channel. The ferry in Greece might have had hard cots but at least the weather was smooth. This storm is my worst nightmare!

"Endless, endless motion. *Up . . . then down. Up . . . then down.* I wish I could physically be up without having to be back down two seconds later. I did not plan for seasickness. I sail all the time and have never been seasick a day in my life!

"*Up . . . then down. Up . . . then down.* If I could at least sit up long enough to grab a book. I have to try again. I cannot lay here for twenty more hours with nothing to do! Okay, quick—I can do it!

"Okay, okay, okay—so I can't do it. That was close! I almost had the smell of vomit added into this retched equation. So, I guess I *will* lay here for twenty hours since I can't seem to sit up long enough to even breathe without almost hurling."

I almost cried when an hour into the trip they announced that it would take us twenty-two hours instead of sixteen to get from Ireland to France due to the storm. I could have taken a flight and been to France in a few hours, but nooooo, I decided it would be more *economical* to go by ferry! I convinced myself that it would be fun to watch movies and gamble as an adventurous tradeoff, worth the added time. It was a third of the cost, after all, way worth it!

"Right now, I'd pay a thousand dollars to be on solid ground! I wonder if anyone has ever died of seasickness. What do they do? Send a helicopter over to pick up the body? I wonder how much it would cost to have a helicopter come and save me right now. It would be worth it. If I could sit up long enough, I'd go find out.

"*Up . . . then down. Up . . . then down.* Here I lay—still—flat on my back. So this is what it would be like as an invalid? I never really thought about what it would be like to be stuck in a bed all the time. All those people in hospitals or in wheelchairs, I never put myself in their shoes before. I have been so selfish and taken a lot for granted! Imagine being trapped like this longer than a day . . . for weeks, years, even a lifetime!

"I need to have more compassion for others. It is that selfish part of me that gets so caught up in my own little world—I forget to see how fortunate I am. I'm on a roll with gratitude lists and helping others since Italy and <u>Project Love</u> but when I get back, I need to start doing more for those less fortunate. Branch out into new areas so that I make a difference to others in gratitude for my health!

"Whoa boy, that was a big one. It felt like the boat was about to tip over from that wave. Okay, enough about the waves. Let's think some positive thoughts. Must stay out of negativity.

"Hey, now that I think about it, I'm exactly halfway through my trip—wow! I might as well do a little trip recap since I have nothing better to do.

"I went to the Guggenheim Museum in Bilboa! How amazing is it that the exterior is completely metal? I went to The Alhambra in Granada. That Moorish architecture captures my designer's soul. Then there was the Botticelli art in Madrid, and the Gaudi architecture in Barcelona. What about all the fabulous cathedrals? Those were some pretty amazing gals, I tell you.

"Remember the initial panic when no one spoke English? That seems like a lifetime ago already. Universal communication—who knew?

"Ah, then there was my precious beach in Valencia where I finally discovered my true calling!

"What about Portugal? I felt so instantly at home there. Yep, I will be back there someday, maybe to write my first book! Then when I saw that hidden nativity scene, so beautiful.

"Oh, Italy . . . I love Italy! The Cathedral in Milan with its 3,400 statues, the leaning tower of Pisa, the Colosseum in Rome, the ruins of Pompeii—such history! Mmmm, scrumptious gelato—what a delightful food that is. Delicious pistachio, or banana and chocolate—no wonder I ate ice cream three times a day!

"Most of all, I love that I started my journey of self-love there. Man, self-love is so awesome! It will take a lot of nurturing and practice, but I started the process . . . at long last! My entrapment on the train, a true test of faith not fear, which I passed! Oh, and Helen—how incredible it was to be able to pass on advice about the goodness of people, how to receive help, and ideas about faith to that remarkable woman? She called me her angel!

"Onto the Parthenon of Athens, Delphi, the islands and the thousands of years of history that are imbedded in every inch of Greece. I need to put some additional thought into ways to see my family more after experiencing the unity of Olga and her family. I'll think about that later. Today, I'm on a trip around the world!

"Remember how excited I was to get to Scotland so I could finally speak English, and then couldn't understand what they were saying? How funny was that? Then there were the castles, Oban and the Highlands—which have such an aura of mystery to me—before heading to Glasgow. I will keep my new expression 'Whit's yer hurry' while I learn to slow down.

"Lovely, green, rainy, gabby Ireland. I will always admire the

Irish with their rolling green hills and their stories of Giants. What wonderful concepts: abundance of time and go with the flow. I learned my lesson when I tried to outrun the rain!

"Then there was that last miracle. The word that describes it best is *profound*. I mean, that whole silent church experience and then my sisters telling me they will meet me in India. I think about that whole situation and it still gives me goose bumps. It will be such an experience to travel with them, all the Bain girls off on an adventure together. I am so grateful that although they are younger than me, we all have such a good relationship with each other.

"It will be interesting to see how our personalities all come together since we haven't traveled with each other before. I'm sure it will be fine, but I have to remember not to pull 'big sister rank' like I used to. My mom is so stressed about us being together. Not because of personalities, but because something could happen to all three of us. I used a little advice from *The Secret* video and told her not to put that out there or else that is what she will attract. I am glad she agreed to try to stop thinking those thoughts.

"This has already been a truly remarkable trip on so many levels. I love living in faith not fear and to feel bliss and freedom from structure, control, relentless drive and false happiness. The joy of living a dream has given me so much!

"Next, I head off to France. I wonder what this new country has in store for me. They say the people are rude to Americans who don't try to speak French. I think I will stick with my own philosophy and assume that 'People of France are good' and they like me and want to help me too.

"This is fun, reviewing my trip. How exciting I still have half left to go! The big question is—now that my summary is pretty much complete—what am I going to think about for the next . . . nineteen hours?

"Only an hour has gone by? Man, I am toast! *Up . . . then down. Up . . . then down. Up . . . then down.*"

I manage to lie flat on my back without vomiting for another nineteen hours until the ferry docks in Cherbourg, France. I'm sure that my face is about as green as the grass in Ireland from the seasickness. Lovely sight. I don't care. My only thought is "Get me on land!"

My legs feel like Jell-O after not using them for so many hours and from the constant large swaying motion of the ferry. As I stand at the exit ramp and wait for the ferry door to open so I can make my escape, I strike up a conversation with a friendly, middle-aged man from Ireland, named Larry. He says he travels to France all the time for work. I mention to Larry that the ferry delay caused me to miss the last train out of Cherbourg and asked if he had any recommendations on how I might get to Tours, since he is familiar with the area.

"Why don't you ride with me?" Larry offers. "I have my car here ready to be unloaded from the ferry and am heading in that direction anyway. It would be no bother."

In spite of only meeting him a few minutes ago, I agree because my alternative is to find a hotel in Cherbourg, which would cut a day off my visits to the magnificent French Chateaux of Loire Valley. Plus, my instinct says Larry is a nice, normal guy—no red-flags wave.

It turns out that Larry, the salesman, is exactly what I need after the twenty-two hour ferry ride alone with my thoughts because he talks the entire way. He has visited France often for years and informs me of charming little facts about the history of many towns.

In the passenger seat, I listen, nod and ask questions when appropriate, exhausted after the ferry trip but grateful for his company. He offers to divert a few miles off-path to show me a war memorial that is popular in France. I object and tell him that I don't want to be a bother, since he is already going out of his way to help me with a ride.

"Nonsense!" is his reply and off we head on our detour.

As we approach our destination, I see a figure dressed as a war soldier and his parachute chords are tangled in the tall spire of the town's church so he is suspended like he is about to fall. Larry has a long story that goes with this scene and proceeds to tell it to me, but I almost instantly forget the facts because I am so tired. He doesn't seem to notice my lack of retention since he has already moved on to the next story. Only later do I realize the importance of what I saw. It is a memorial representation of D-Day and the Battle of Normandy in World War II.

Larry drops me off at my hotel in Tours with a quick wave good-bye and a couple short beeps on the horn. Despite being extremely tired, I rush to my room and start to pour over the many pamphlets I picked up at the front desk that show photos and tell the history about each of the chateau. These are magnificent estates that seem straight out of a storybook with their manicured grounds, castles and moats.

During the many hours on the ferry, I had a good time rehashing one of my young fantasies involving a handsome prince who arrives on a beautiful horse to whisk me off to a wonderful life in some enormous castle on the hill. As a young girl, I spent *hours* staring out my bedroom window in hazy daydreams involving princes, horses and castles on hills. I would twist a long towel on my head so that it hung down my back and pretend it was the long blonde hair of a princess that would blow in the wind when the prince whisked her away on his horse.

Remembering those days of my youth makes me so excited to see real chateaux! I want to see them all, but since there is not enough time, I pick six to explore.

Over the next week, I wander through the elaborate interiors and beautiful grounds of the chateaux in Loire Valley in the hazy state of fantasy I experienced as a young girl. These enormous structures are magnificent and romantic with moats, gardens, beautiful décor and captivating histories.

Although a prince does not ride up on his trusted steed and

whisk me away, the young girl inside me smiles, happy to have her dream partially come true.

# # # #

"Hi Michelle,

Peter emailing . . . remember we stayed at the same hotel in Amalfi Coast and went on the hunt for a grocery store together? You know . . . the American living in Paris for the last twenty-five years? Well, I checked out your website—great photos! Your schedule says you should be in Paris soon. Call me when you arrive. I have a fully furnished apartment that is vacant— you can use it for free. I know you are on a tight budget. It is in a great district, right where you want to be for site-seeing. I will explain when you call.

Travel safe,

Peter"

"He was a nice guy for the short time we spent wandering through the grocery store and such, but no one can be <u>that</u> nice!" my suspicious mind immediately responds after I read his email. "There has to be a string attached somewhere. I would rather pay for a hotel here, in the bad part of town, than feel like I owe someone something."

"Stop for a second, Michelle, before you go down that path," I tell myself sharply in my make-believe Chris voice. "Remember Sam in Spain—no strings. Larry from the Ferry—no strings. Why must Peter in Paris have strings? Give this situation the benefit of the doubt. Place a call before you shut off opportunity. You are low on cash, this hotel is disgusting and your instinct before said Peter was a solid guy. Make the call!"

Some people really are that nice with that good of a soul. Peter lends me a wonderful apartment within a short walk to the Eiffel Tower, complete with a washing machine. I have it all to myself for my entire week in Paris at no charge. Not a single string.

"It's open as long as you want it, we won't be using it for at least another few months. If anything happens and you head back this way, know it's available to you," he adds on the phone as we decide a place to meet so I can return the keys.

A week in Paris by the Eiffel Tower at no cost and my instant response had been to say no based on an old idea about owing people for kindness.

From now on, Michelle...we say "oui"!

Chapter 10:
Selflessness—Switzerland

I am about to land in Switzerland and every minute I remain seated on the plane feels like an eternity. For the first time in months (well, besides the ferry from hell) I wish I could hit a fast forward button. Chris is arriving in Switzerland from the States today also. It is hard for me to contain the joy and excitement I feel about seeing my best friend.

"By tomorrow, Chris and I will be gliding down the snow-filled mountains of the Swiss Alps, carving up powder on our snowboards. *Swish, swoosh, whoosh*—a little air action and miles and miles of snow!" I think as I anxiously count down the minutes.

"Then at night, we'll warm our toes in front of a toasty fire as we sip hot chocolate and reminisce about a rewarding day on the slopes. It's going to be a fantastic, memorable experience. I know it!

"What a dream to spend Christmas week with my best friend snowboarding in Zermatt, Switzerland and then to spend New Year's week boarding with her in Corcheveaux, France. Two weeks of international slopes and two weeks with *Chris*; life cannot get any better than this! We have a lot to catch up on since we haven't seen each other for almost four months.

"The dynamic-duo takes on The Matterhorn!" I cheer. One of our favorite things to do is snowboard, which is why this trip is a dream come true for both of us. Before this, we had snow trips in different states but this is our first international encounter.

A majority of the time, these trips are sensational and fun. On a trip the year before though, we had a not-so-pleasant situation when Chris broke her pelvis at Mammoth Mountain on the last day of a weekend trip.

It was truly horrible. She cracked it landing tailbone-first on an ice patch as she exited a lift. I will never forget the pain she suffered for five hours in the back seat on the ride home to Los Angeles. This episode is not one of our fondest memories.

A recent visit to the doctor confirms she is repaired and ready for action so with doctor approval in hand, we decide this is our year to hit the slopes of Europe since I am already there.

At our hotel in Geneva we meet up at last. "Chris!!!" I squeal like a little girl, as I run up and give her a big hug. "Michelle, my BFF!!!" she squeals right back. After parroting her voice of advice in my head for months, it's like music to hear her live. Although it has only been four months, so much has happened to me on my trip, I feel like I haven't seen her in four years.

We don't dive into a trip review yet though. There will be plenty of time for those conversations over the next few weeks. Instead, we tour the town, find a fondue restaurant, gorge on cheese fondue, and then go back to the hotel. We both agree a good night's sleep is essential, yet hours fly by as we jabber away, like two little kids on Christmas Eve who are all excited about what Santa is going to bring.

The next morning, we jump out of bed with gusto—despite our lack of sleep from a late night gabbing—gather our things and catch the earliest train from Geneva to Zermatt. Chris brought over two roller bags filled with our gear (one which I packed before I left the States) so we have everything we need for this adventure.

"I can't believe we are both here and that we will be snowboarding near The Matterhorn within hours!" is our common statement as we anxiously watch the miles of white, snow-filled mountains pass by our train window.

As the train pulls into the town of Zermatt, we both stare in wonder at the picturesque winter setting. The entire scene looks like a postcard. Snow-capped mountains loom in the background while the quaint town, with its cabins and lodges, sits nestled below.

The chilly air is refreshing after the train ride and a warm sun welcomes us to town. With all the bright snow gleaming on the rooftops and along the roads, Zermatt seems to glow, especially with the pure-white mountain backdrop.

Luggage is tossed onto the bed of our cute studio apartment, and we fly out the door to go find a map of the runs. My jaw hits the ground as I stare at the enormous map posted at the bottom of the gondola. I feel like I am viewing a picture of the human circulatory system: a main spine with what looks like a hundred little red and blue veins stemming out of it in every direction.

"There are so many runs, Chris, and they flow in different directions and extend for miles. We can snowboard in Switzerland and in Italy all in the same day. This is incredible!" I exclaim.

Day one and two, we decide to stay on the Switzerland side, so we can get comfortable and develop a lay of the land. The rides in the large gondolas are long because the mountains are so high. Chris and I have a great opportunity to mingle with others and snap photos of the breathtaking views below. Then we *swish* and *swoop* down the runs; some take as long as forty-five minutes to complete.

I am having the time of my life!

Exhausted by evening, we cruise through town and search for quick food so that we can return to the apartment and unwind. Chris and I sit in our PJs on the sofa and catch up on events of the last four months as we relax, in preparation for another full day on the slopes the next morning. Our place doesn't have the fireplace to warm our toes but the hot chocolate tastes as good as I hoped.

"It would be so nice to read for a few minutes before bed. I wish I had a good book," I say and start to tell Chris about a book that Peter from Paris recommended I read, called *The Alchemist*.

"No way! You are not going to believe what I bought you for Christmas!" Chris exclaims as she digs my present out of her bag. I tear it open and sure enough, it's a copy of *The Alchemist*.

"I have to read it right now!" I am a slight speed reader so within a few hours I read the entire thing. The book is completely enjoyable and has interesting messages that coincide with my current life journey. The portion that really resonates with me is the idea of detaching from separatism and becoming one with the elements, which I find fascinating.

We get a little bit of a late start on day three, but Chris and I mutually decide that we are ready to explore Italy, so we travel to the other side. It takes over an hour and two gondolas rides to reach these higher peaks.

After a few short warm-up runs, we head back to the top so that we can board down the longest run. Both of us look at each other in excitement; this run will take us all the way over to a town in Italy — the farthest point from Zermatt.

By now, it is already one o'clock. We want to have a few hours boarding over there before we need to head back toward the Switzerland side. Darkness starts to set in about four o'clock on the Italian side of the mountain, but we determine that we still have plenty of time.

About three-quarters of the way down the long run, it happens. I am some yards ahead of Chris, but I heard the "Owww, ow, ow, ow" coming from behind me and immediately skid to a stop. I spin around and see Chris rolled up in a ball on the snow.

"Oh no, not here . . . not now Chris!" I think to myself as I pull off my board and hike back up toward her.

"Keep going. I'll be fine. I don't know what's up but something hurt with that fall. Give me a few minutes to let the pain pass and I'll be okay. I'll meet you at the bottom at the gondola," Chris yells, waving me away.

For a second, I actually think about following her instructions. Shame rushes through me and I snap back to my senses.

This is my best friend!

I continue to climb up to where Chris is now standing. The

pain on her face is obvious. "What happened?" I ask.

"I don't know," Chris responds, her face still etched with pain. "It feels like it's by my pelvis but it can't be because the doctor said it was healed. I just can't spread my legs apart at all or else I feel like I'm going to die."

"Can you walk?" I question, wondering what we are going to do if she answers that she can't.

"I think so," she replies.

In silence, we start to walk down the mountain. The amount of unspoken mental chatter feels like a deep snowdrift surrounding us. As we realize how long of a walk there still is to the bottom, Chris attempts to put on her board. I hold onto her as we try one way, and pull her up as we try another way, but she isn't able to move any distance without crumpling onto the snow in pain.

We take our boards off again and continue to walk a few feet in silence. My stomach cringes in sympathy as I watch Chris take each slow step, but some part of me feels this ugly anger at the same time.

"How could she do this to our dream holiday?" I think resentfully. "How could she do this to me?"

"You have to be joking that you are really having this thought!" I say to myself in a rare voice Karen uses when she is in baffled disbelief that I am spinning so fast that I completely miss something obvious that is slapping me in the face. "As if Chris would chose horrible pain on purpose to mess up your plans, Michelle. Quit playing the victim. This is your best friend! There is no room for anger here, only love and compassion. Have you learned nothing? Your best friend is in agony here, this is NOT about YOU."

I stop walking instantly and turn to my best friend. "I am so sorry Chris!" I say in apology. "What can I do to help you?" I ask with true sincerity and a great degree of shame and remorse.

"I don't know. I only know I did not mean for this to happen," Chris states.

"She read my mind. Of course Chris read my mind, I am sure

the anger and disappointment is clearly readable in my expression. Did I expect my best friend to be naïve and not notice that my silence is really negative emotion?" I take a breath and absorb for a second how horrible it feels to know the additional pain my selfishness causes others, especially someone I love.

I never want to be a woman this ashamed of her reactions again.

"I'm sorry Chris. I am such a selfish idiot. I'm so sorry," I tell her with that same level of compassion I felt when I said similar words to the woman in the mirror. Chris deserves more than my selfishness and I want her to know it.

"It's okay," She replies. "If I were in your shoes I would probably feel the same way. Trust me, I am disappointed right now too. Let's figure out a way to get back down the mountain."

Still supportive, even in her pain. What a remarkable woman.

We make it to the bottom of the run to the town in Italy after a long, slow walk that eats up much of our daylight. Upon arrival, we discover the last bus has already left and that there is no other form of transportation to Zermatt. Our only option is to ride the gondola back up as far as it goes, and then see what help we can find from there.

I apologize to Chris again while we are in the gondola. Thankfully, she recognizes my sincerity and forgives me for my lapse into old selfish ways. We let go of our recent past and become a team again in our common mission—to get back to Switzerland with as minimal impact as possible for Chris.

At the end of the upward gondola trail, we face an even larger obstacle for the next part of our quest. The next lift we arrive at is similar to a pulley system with a round disk seat that hangs from a rope, which rests between the rider's legs. A snowboarder has to attempt to keep the board pointed up the mountain, while balancing on the seat. It is difficult for a healthy boarder to manage, let alone one who possibly has a broken pelvis.

I make Chris go first so that I can keep an eye on her. The disk hits exactly the wrong spot on her inner thighs and she immediately falls off. This time there are tears with the "Owww, ow, ow."

"It's obvious she's not going to make it to the top on this lift," I decide. "I need to find help."

I ride the lift to the top and am grateful to see the ski patrol. I explain that we need help below. They hop on a snowmobile and rush down to load Chris on. She sits somewhat sideways and is able to make it to the top of the run.

Here, we strategize on the best way for all of us to get off the mountain. It is already starting to get dark and we are dealing with a rush against time. We only have forty minutes to make it to the main gondola which goes to Zermatt before it shuts down for the night, and that is approximately how long it takes for this run. There are no other ways to reach the bottom at this point, except possibly by helicopter.

All the stories about mountain deaths that we read earlier as we waited to get our photo taken with the St. Bernard dogs suddenly seem very believable. "We have to get out of here!" we all agree.

The ski patrol asks Chris to try to snowboard again. She makes it a few feet and collapses in pain. Their next idea is to lay her in a sled, strap her in and have ski patrol pull her down the mountain while on skis. The look of sheer panic on Chris's face is one I will never forget. "Do NOT let them strap me into that thing," is her frantic plea to me as they pick her up off the ground.

"No, not possible to sled. What is another option?" I demand. There are at least three languages involved in the conversation now; the Italian and Swiss ski patrols and myself. Our voices get louder as the stress level rises. We all know precious minutes are ticking away.

A helicopter is another option but it will take too long for it to arrive and is expensive. It's now dusk and temperatures are starting to drop quickly as the sun disappears behind the mountain.

The final option is the most painful, but it is the only real choice left because we are out of alternatives *and* out of time. The last gondola to Zermatt will shut down in minutes. We all have to get there fast. Chris will have to sit side-saddle on the seat of the snowmobile and endure the bouncing pain.

"Michelle," the Italian patrolman says to me in broken English as he attempts to deliver the final plan, "you will have to snowboard down and we will take Chris on the snowmobile. You must go fast though, faster than you have ever snowboarded, with no falling—only speed—or else we will all miss the last gondola," the ski patrol informs me. Now it is my turn to look at Chris in panic.

I nod my head at the patrolman, strap on my board, adjust my goggles and take a deep breath.

Here I go. No screw-ups allowed.

I start down the forty minute run, completely aware that I have to make it in a fraction of that time. There can be no errors, only speed. The entire scene becomes surreal; like I am out-of-body, watching myself on a movie screen.

As I descend, I glance around for a brief second and realize I am completely alone. I am the only person left on the mountain now that the snowmobile has started down, surrounded by the remaining ski patrol. One pulls the sled and the other skis by Chris in case she falls off the snowmobile.

It's just me and endless miles of white.

I take another quick second and admire how the night sky is starting to reflect off the snow, which adds a beautiful purplish hue to it. All around me there is silence; no noise, except for the quiet *swoosh* of my board and the distant sound of the snowmobile far ahead.

How peaceful. To be alone in this beautiful silence.

"Remember *The Alchemist*, Michelle," I whisper to myself. "Be one with the elements. Be one with the snow. Become the snow. You are part of the snow. Now you are part of the wind. Race like the wind! Look ahead, don't look down."

My heart begins to race as I catch a little edge, but then the silence takes over again and I relax and let go. Every time I start to waver a little, I think about Chris far ahead and how I have to make it without falling because there is no time for mistakes. Chris needs me to make it, even if my legs are shaking because they are so tired, or else she will have to sit on that bouncy snowmobile for a very long time.

As my legs start to ache more, my thoughts switch to an invigorating new mental scene where I become a female James Bond, in hot pursuit of the snowmobile racing far ahead. James Bond would never wipe out and neither will I.

I snowboard faster than I ever thought possible. The gap closes. Shaky legs and all, I am determined to catch them as I fly across the white terrain. The thought of falling is no longer in my head. My focus is only on catching the snowmobile. The gap continues to close. Faster. Closer. "Catch them," my mind cries . . . and I do!

We make it to the gondola with only minutes to spare. They quickly strap Chris onto a gurney and load the two of us into a gondola. Because of the length of the gurney, the fit is too tight and the doors will not shut all the way.

"What? They don't have straps to tie to the gurney or to bind across the door gap?" I ask in total disbelief. They don't. Instead, I have to push against the open door with my legs while I pull back on the side rail of the gurney; a human bracket that keeps Chris and the gurney from rolling out the open door into the snow miles below.

"Don't worry, Chris, I won't let you go. If you go, I go. I promise," I commit to her.

She doesn't look at me with panic this time (like she did over the sled idea) even though the results of this situation could be much more catastrophic. She looks at me with total trust instead. I might have had a selfishness relapse earlier but I pulled it together to be the friend she again trusts and loves.

Being the amazing woman that she is, in spite of the pain and terrifying circumstances, the next words to come out of Chris's mouth are, "Michelle, watching you chase that snowmobile was seriously unbelievable. I wish I would have had my video camera with me. It was just . . . epic!"

I so want to be like Chris when I grow up . . .

We make it to the bottom where an ambulance takes us to the medical clinic. Here, we receive confirmation from the doctor that Chris does have a broken pelvis. The break is in a different spot from the previous one.

The doctor informs her that she can walk with crutches as much as the pain allows, but there will be no more snowboarding for Chris this trip. Crushed, we limp back to the apartment, sad and disappointed.

"I refuse to leave. I'm all the way here, it's my first time in Europe, I have time off work and I can't fly home yet anyway. We can stay here and then we'll go to Corcheveaux, France as planned. You'll be fine on the mountain by yourself. I can relax, hang out, read and do a little shopping if I get bored. Everything will be great," Chris announces in a determined voice. I cannot think of a better plan, given the situation. I never anticipated this roadblock and had not come prepared with a Plan B.

The next day, I hit the slopes alone. I snowboard the longest, most amazing runs I have ever boarded. One long, winding run takes me almost fifty minutes from top to bottom. It is shear heaven . . . except that Chris is not there to share it with me.

This is not going to work. There has to be a new plan, a better plan that involves both Chris and I.

"What are options where Chris can walk?" I think while on the next gondola. "What if we go to Paris instead? Chris has never been to Europe. Think how excited she would be to experience Paris. Peter's apartment is still available with an open offer and would be easy to get in and out of with crutches because it has an elevator. Plus, the Paris metro stops directly at every major tourist attraction so there is limited walking and cabs are always an option."

What a plan! What a beautiful, selfless, put-someone-else-first-for-a-change plan! Get back and make it happen, Michelle!

When Chris comes back that day from her follow-up doctor visit, I am already there to meet her at the door. "Chris, pack your stuff. We are going to Paris. The arrangements are already made and we are going to have a marvelous time!"

We *do* have a marvelous time! Chris does extremely well hobbling around on crutches. It is easier on her pelvis to remain standing, rather than climbing in and out of taxis, so the metro proves to be the best mode of transportation.

We eat quiche and pastries at quaint little restaurants and visit the Eiffel Tower, Notre Dame and Arch de Triumph. One night, we take Peter to *Moulin Rouge* as a thank you for loaning us the apartment. The show is wonderful and something I never would have seen during my solo travels.

Although I had been to all of the tourist sites in Paris the week before we met up, this time it is even better because I am able to experience it with Chris, who sees it all with new eyes. Someone in Ireland once mentioned having a case of the "ABCs" (Another Bloody Castle/Another Bloody Cathedral) and I realize I had developed a case myself without being aware of it. I visited so many castles, museums and monuments over four months—I too have started to take their magnificence for granted.

As I watch the look of awe and appreciation on Chris's face, it brings freshness to my own view. These sites are wondrous, and I look at each with new eyes too.

My favorite experience is the Louvre Museum. We mutually agree that for me to push Chris in a wheelchair is our best option to tackle this enormous structure. As we roll along, Chris and I gain a new perspective on how people react to disabled individuals. Some people rush by, afraid to make eye contact. Others go out of their way to walk around and avoid us. Others smile and say a friendly hello, almost stooping as they do so.

It makes for interesting conversation between the two of us as we discuss this while we wander through the museum. I admit that I don't really know how I respond when I see someone in a wheelchair but I plan to pay attention to my response from now on.

Chris notes another unique observation as a person in a chair. She comments on how exhibits are very biased toward the non-disabled. Exhibits are situated high and she often has to hold the camera above an object and take a picture downward so that she can see what it looks like.

This is something I never would have noticed either, an unfairness that gives me new compassion and understanding toward people that push for equality.

Chris hugs me. "I am so glad you are my best friend. Thank you for taking me here!"

"I am so glad you are my best friend too," I reply as I hug her back. "Thanks for putting up with me sometimes. I'll get there, I promise."

"You're on your way, Michelle," is her supportive response.

Chapter 11:
Appreciation—Czech Republic

Her name was Josephine and she came over from Moravia to the United States on a boat when she was a young girl. She struggled cleaning houses, determined to make a life in this new foreign land of America. At a young age, Josephine wed an immigrant man from her home country, Czechoslovakia, and they had four beautiful children. My grandfather was one of those children. Josephine was my great-grandmother.

My grandpa looked so much like her. He had the same shaped face with its slightly rounded characteristics and the same bright eyes. Most important to me, the two shared the same big smile which was so embracing. Their smiles seemed to light up their entire faces. This is what I remember about both of them.

My mother looks like them too, the resemblance is amazing. It can never be mistaken whose daughter my mother is. Same shape face, same eyes, same engaging smile. Then I am born generations later, and I am blessed with these same Josephine characteristics as well.

As I travel to foreign countries this trip and meet many people from many cultures; I admire the vast array of physical characteristics. There is such a diversity! People with dark skin and square faces. People with dark hair, tight lips and big dark eyes. Pale skinned people with flaming red hair and stocky bodies. I meet people with many different nationalities, always noting how different they are from me.

Then I arrive in the Czech Republic, the land of my ancestors, and see my own characteristics, the shape of my face, my eyes, and my smile reflected in hundreds of similar faces. A place where faces look like my great-grandmother, my grandfather, my mother and me.

Prague itself is a magical city, one of the most magnificent on Earth. The beautiful castle, churches and buildings all have a picturesque element and there is a feel to the place that many recognize as exceptional.

As I wander, I listen as people talk and I'm transported back in time to conversations between my great-grandmother and my grandpa in her living room. I was only a child and never understood what they were saying to each other, but I do remember the intense feeling of pride that washed over me. It was this pride of knowing "She is from somewhere far away and I am like her." As a child, I even took on Josephine as my Catholic confirmation name because I wanted Josephine to be tied to me forever. She symbolized the "world unknown" and having her in my life planted a seed in my young mind.

Thirty years later, that small seed finally blossomed into this glorious journey. As I walk down each cobble stone street and stare into the many familiar faces, I think, "These are my people. This is where I come from," and a deep sense of gratitude washes over me. I eat goulash and dumplings the same way I did as a child and smile as I remember days from my younger years.

Over my week stay in Prague, I tour the Old Jewish cemetery. A chill runs up my spine and I get goose bumps as I walk along the central path. Twelve thousand tombstones are crammed together in tightly packed rows, many stacked on top of one another so that the small area almost appears to be a solid mass of cement and marble. Here and there, a small tribute is built out of tiny rocks on top of a tombstone, with a little slip of paper folded up inside. A note left as a token of love.

Inside the main building, drawings made by children in the concentration camps hang on the walls. My eyes fill with tears as I read the descriptions below each drawing and learn how the child died. The drawings capture tiny glimpses of their souls. So many lives lost over reasons I will never understand.

At the Church of our Lady of Victories the next day, I pray to the Holy Infant who is said to work miracles. I ask for eternal guidance that I may stay on this new path of awareness when I return back home and not lose site of the many lessons I have been blessed with over the last four and a half months. I pray for Chris to be well so that we can continue new adventures together and for true miracles like a peaceful world and abundance for all.

Prague arouses a substantial amount of emotion in me. After years of emotional suppression, I suddenly find myself overwhelmed by them. I feel both raw and alive and I want to cry over everything: the sadness of needless deaths, the abundance of beauty, the happiness of the connection to my past. Yet, I do not cry. Some habits are hard to let go of, even when it doesn't really serve much of a purpose except to give me another element I control.

Although I am not able to visit the little village where Josephine was raised, I travel onward from Prague to Brno, which is my great-grandfather's hometown. I sit in a church and wonder, "Did he sit here as a child? Did he run down the cobblestone road outside, in a rush to get home after a busy day at school? Was he happy here?"

What strength and courage it must have taken them both to leave all they knew in search of a different life in America. What a gift they have given me, this seed of adventure. Here I am, as an adult, walking in their past.

What I inherited from them is far beyond physical aspects such as eyes and a smile. What they gave to me is their strength and courage so that, like them, I could leave behind all I know in search of a different life and a better self in lands far away.

Thank you, Josephine. Thank you.

Chapter 12:
Surrender—Central India

With each experience, I discover more rewards when I let go of my ingrained need to control all outcomes and instead accept the guidance of faith. What I fear will go wrong usually doesn't and situations continue to work out better than I could have imagined.

I wish I could snap my fingers and immediately let go of my natural instinct to control, but I will have to work on this issue the old fashioned way—one experience at a time.

I almost mess up this entire India trip with my sisters before it even starts. Old big-sister thoughts immediately take over which say, "I have the most travel experience and I am the oldest so I should run the show." In keeping with this old role, I research and select all the places we will see over our three weeks of travel together.

I email my list to them only to find out that Lesa, Sunny, and Greg (Sunny's boyfriend) have a completely different agenda. Our plans do not match. I attempt to convince them to follow my plan by emphasizing that since I am oldest and wisest, my plan is the best. The response is "Big deal!" My defenses start to build and I prepare for a battle to make things go my way. Then, I remember the profound silence in the church in Ireland.

Is it a battle I want, or is it the joy of traveling with my sisters?

I quickly send an apology email that promises I will not use the "oldest and wisest" card anymore and emphasize that I want this trip to be about my journey with them, not about destinations, and that there is nothing more I could ask from this trip in India than for us to be together and for it to revolve around what they want. I surrender control and let go of the outcome.

After this email, we are able to come to one quick agreement: it doesn't matter what amazing fort or temple or mountain we see, we all want to experience one thing . . . spirituality, in whatever form that best presents itself to each of us.

With our new common goal, we all make the decision that we should fly into Mumbai to meet and then immediately catch a flight to Varanasi; the holiest city in all of India. "If spirituality is our main objective, what could offer this better than the holiest pilgrimage site of the entire Hindu religion?" is our reasoning.

As I fly to Mumbai, I am brimming with excitement. India is the place on my list that I felt the most intense draw toward and now that the time has arrived, my excitement is beyond maximum capacity. Back in Europe, many other travelers warned me to be ready for sensory overload—their advice only seems to grow my enthusiasm.

It's a good thing I feel so positively fueled right now or else overload might actually have caused me to high-tail it back to the safety of my airplane seat. There are no spoken words that could ever have prepared me for what it is like to step off the airplane into a country of one billion people who appear to be in constant motion. There are people everywhere and the energy of all this motion is enormous! At least a million people seem to be at the Mumbai airport, like a sea of bodies ready to swallow me up as soon as I leave the protection of the airplane.

My eyes scan around quickly, bombarded by all of the movement and by the vibrant colors of the women's saris. I search face after endless face for my sisters. Noise comes at me from so many directions: thousands of voices, loud engines of electric rickshaws, and mysterious music that blares out from who-knows-where. My sinuses protest immediately against the thick pollution and I start to sneeze, but then my nose detects the aroma of spicy food and my mouth begins to water at the thought of how delicious food will be here. All my senses are alive and alert to these dramatic new forces.

The hot, dry air seems to hang on my skin. Despite this, I quickly put on my long sleeve shirt in defense against the mosquitoes biting at my arms and neck. As they swarm around me, ready to attack, I think, "I'm glad I went for the malaria shot after all!"

"Yay, you're here! What do you think? Crazy isn't it?" my sister Lesa says as she surfaces from the crowd and grabs me into a huge hug.

"Crazy doesn't even come close to describing this!" I reply in stunned amazement as we gather bags before heading out of the airport.

The assault on my senses soon doubles, if not triples, as we venture out into Mumbai, en route to the domestic airport. Our electric rickshaws swerve within centimeters of collisions as we weave between the piles of honking cars and the mounds of people.

I cannot tear my eyes away from all the people! Many squat in the street, or lie by the side of the road as if completely oblivious to the chaos that surrounds them. Dogs and cows walk over these street people like they are sticks in the road.

This is life to them, just a part of life.

My brain feels like it is in some state of shock. All of this is like nothing I have ever experienced and I never imagined a world like this exists. I actually laugh as I think back to Los Angeles traffic. Traffic here makes L.A. traffic jams seem like a walk in the park.

The visible poverty everywhere is also astonishing: shack houses built out of rusted metal serve as homes, cars are held together by rope. Shoeless men muck through the muddy waste that serves as a sidewalk. Children who look like only skin and bones run beside our rickshaws with outstretched hands, begging for food or money.

"Am I ready for this?" I think with alarm, and remember back fondly to what I now perceive as plush travels through Western Europe. "I guess I will find out!"

One thing is certain—I am so grateful that I am not alone.

\# \# \# \#

"There it is, you guys, the holiest city in all of India—Varanasi," Greg says to us as we reach the place in the sky where the city comes into view. We all crane our necks to look out the small airplane windows. Below stand hundreds of temples and ancient structures which have survived for thousands of years. We can even see the famous Ganges River as it flows along the edge of the city.

Murlie is the first person we meet after we step off the plane. There he stands, in his striped knit sweater and tan pants, his dark, short hair brushed off to the side. He looks relaxed and expectant—like he has been waiting for us to arrive. Not a drop of perspiration dots his face, despite the extreme heat. I like him instantly, especially as I look around at the other drivers who rush toward us with their sweaty shirts and tense energy.

With a warm, welcoming smile Murlie offers to drive us to a hotel. We all immediately feel a unique level of comfort with him and so we quickly inform the barrage of other taxi drivers that we are "taken".

Murlie remains our personal taxi driver for the rest of our stay in Varanasi. He is a godsend. I don't know what we would do without him. Not only because he knows his way around the city but because anytime we need anything, Murlie's instant response is, "No problem!" Then he finds us what we need.

After we leave the airport in his new, shiny white car, he taxis us from hotel to hotel until we find a vacancy and then he makes sure we eat. From here, he drives us to the heart of the city where he introduces us to Sambu. Sambu becomes our tour guide for our stay in Varanasi.

Sambu has a genuine smile, is vivacious and fun and has great knowledge of the city. These two are a wonderful team and a tremendous resource for us to have. We feel so much gratitude that Murlie crossed our path out of the gate.

At this time, we aren't aware that drivers and tour guides work in teams and that there is an entire business system in India that revolves around it. We catch on a few days later and laugh at how special we thought we were initially to receive such undivided attention. "Who cares? The system works for us," is our general consensus.

Our visit to Varanasi is filled with memories we might not have experienced if it were not for these two amazingly patient men. They fit our personalities easily—like they are meant to be the ones to guide us through this experience. I have no clue if the price they charge us is fair, but to me, they are priceless because what they provide is ease and peace of mind in an otherwise hectic environment. I would pay triple the amount for the depth of experience and the accommodating nature they bring to our visit.

No matter where we start each day, we know Murlie will be right where he left us when Sambu brings us back. It's like a dad who is there to collect the kids after school—we know he will be there to make sure we arrive safely at our next destination. This is such a relief because the traffic here is usually six lanes of cars, cows, pedestrians and bikes all going in every different direction, with constant honking as all attempt to avoid each other. A complete mess of a system, and every place we need to be seems to be on the opposite end of where we are.

We leave the navigational skills up to Murlie and Sambu so that we can enjoy all of the activity along the way instead of having to worry about which way to turn or which narrow path to take once we are immersed in the city center.

"Do you visit friends during the day or runs errands at least while we are gone, Murlie?" I ask him the second day, after he collects us from Sambu. He responds with a surprised look, like I asked a very silly question. "No, Madam—I wait right here. What if you decide to come back early and I am not here for you?"

I have a difficult time with this part of our arrangement. As Miss Independent, I am definitely not used to being chauffeured around and catered to. It makes me uncomfortable and the thought, "Why do I deserve to be treated like this when it causes another person to serve me?" pops frequently into my head. The four of us will be off exploring with Sambu and suddenly I think about Murlie standing there in the hot sun, until we return. "What if he sweats to death as he sits there in his car waiting for us for so many hours?" I think, which is followed by "Is this genuine concern I feel for him, or is this some weird guilt about accepting so much help?"

Regardless, I go with it. Murlie is downstairs every morning, waiting for us outside the hotel at the precise time we arrange the night before, ready to transport us to our daily adventures with Sambu.

"Where do you live Murlie?" I ask him on our fourth day.

"Far away, by the airport, with my wife and young son," he replies.

"Isn't it difficult to drive all the way out here to meet us every morning?" I continue to probe.

"I actually sleep in my car in the lot next door to your hotel because it is so far away," he informs me. He has been doing this for three nights already. Mortified, I tell him that he has to leave and go see his family tonight. Of course, his standard reply is, "Madam, really—it is not a problem!"

"What a sacrifice to make!" I think, but then I look at all the times I—like many others—have had to travel away from family for work. Sometimes I would be gone for weeks at a time for work events.

Isn't it kind of similar? Granted, I didn't have to sleep in my car at night, but if it cuts his costs and gives him more money to take home to his family then I'm sure it's worth it to him.

We all get paid to be of service to people in some way, shape or form I guess. I'm just on the receiving end this time, with a service being provided that I'm not quite accustomed to.

Murlie has a great level of humility that I do not possess. He never would have mentioned his sacrifice if I had not brought it up whereas I complain about my sacrifices all the time.

What a great example of being grateful for work with quiet humbleness. How admirable! I need to be more like Murlie—filled with gratitude and humbleness about my work when I return.

In a similar fashion, Sambu collects us from Murlie with a huge smile each morning. Sambu takes his job as a tour guide seriously, which is to our benefit. Under his guidance, we discover temples, rituals and shops we never would have come across on our own. His historic information and explanations are priceless. Those two may be grateful for work, but we are also equally grateful for their services.

My India sensory overload transitions as time passes. Instead of feeling assaulted by all these sights, sounds and smells, I grow more attached and appreciative of them each day.

At the silk shops, we sit and sip tea for hours as roll after roll of brightly colored silk is strewn before us. Wrapped in yards of luscious fabric, custom saris and Punjabis are measured and fitted to our taste and size. The vivid colors and soft textures of the hand woven cloth are mesmerizing. It's impossible to pick only a few out of the many beautiful bolts of fabric. We want them all—and of course they would like us to buy them all!

It is quite a networking business they have here with the guides and shop owners. It doesn't dampen our experience since the four of us are having fun together in all the shops. Sunny plays fabric model at one point and I snap photos of her wrapped in about twenty different silks. We have a great time.

The sensual experiences flow beyond the visual. A cow plods by and brushes up against me, and I smell its strong scent and feel the energy of this sacred animal as it wanders past. How animals and humans intermix here in India fascinates me. Cows walk into shops and nestle down; they trust that the shop owner's respect for their sacredness will be honored.

What surprises me is that the shop owners actually do honor them as sacred, even if inconvenient. It's shocking to enter a stall and see a big cow lying in the middle of the floor. "You sure wouldn't find that in Beverly Hills," I joke. "I just can't see some woman all dressed in Prada stepping over a cow to get a closer look at a Gucci bag!"

I laugh as I watch monkeys leap from building to building, snatching up fruit from the vendor carts along the way. Goats and dogs wander between people, as if they are two legged creatures as well. "*All are One* seems to be the general tone of this city," I realize as I view the harmony that exists between man and animal.

While tantalizing tastes of Indian food burn my tongue with their spices and textures, it's the aroma of an Indian buffet that brings me running. I don't have to run very far though since buffets are abundant.

"I'm very lucky," I say to the crew, "I seem to be able to eat anything here without a problem." Soon, I am eating everything from fine cuisine, to food wrapped in banana leaves bought from a street vendor without issue. I joke that it's because I'm so used to eating junk food instead of healthy food—my body has built up a weird immunity or something. My sisters and Greg all run into digestive issues but not me. I gorge on a large variety of delicious meals made of potatoes, vegetables and rice with no problems. It is heavenly!

What I really notice about my senses is how distinctive my sense of smell is here. I don't remember detecting this sense as much back home. Besides the aroma of food, which is sharp but pleasant, there are many other prominent smells. Some sting the nose, like car exhaust and fires, while other scents from incense and oils float through the air like perfume. Soon, even bad smells seem good.

At one point, we all become so attached to one unique smell that we ask around to see if anyone sells incense like it. What is the smell that we so fondly associate with India? Not the temple incense or the vials of scents from the medicine man. The smell we come to love is none other than cow dung bricks!

All of these sensual stimulants, combined with the activity of thousands of busy people, are invigorating but it is the power of sound that steals my heart in the end. I will never forget waking before daybreak to a gentle noise outside, which grows louder and gains momentum the farther it progresses up the road.

"What is that?" Lesa asks me, since we are sharing a room and she hears the same sound. We both rush to the window and peer out to see a group of people walking in a procession through town. The melody grows louder as more people join and the energy of the sound channels along the road up to our hotel window.

"Lesa, they are chanting 'Om Namah Shivaya' as they journey to the Ganges River to pay homage to her at dawn," I whisper.

In Hindu faith, the Ganges River is revered as a goddess whose purity cleanses the sins of the faithful and aids the dead on their path toward heaven. Hindus travel great distances to scatter the ashes of loved ones in the Ganges. It is even said that a single drop of Ganges water, carried by the wind over a great distance, can cleanse a lifetime of sins.

As Lesa and I realize the scene we are witnessing, chills break out on our arms. The sound strikes an emotional chord inside my heart, it is so magical. To hear these chants of dedication seems almost surreal on some level. It is one of the most spiritual sounds I have ever experienced.

Every morning, we rise to this glorious sound of chanting before dawn. As we look out into the darkness from our window, we see the silhouettes of many monkeys perched on the rooftops all across town. They honor the first glimpse of sunlight in the distance and salute the procession of people below.

It is an important ritual among the truly faithful to submerge themselves in this sacred water each day. One morning, we join this holy act and pay homage to the Ganges ourselves. Before dawn, we slip silently into a small row boat. Our guide paddles us out to a distant riverbank and then docks the boat on shore.

As the sun slowly rises over the city edge, my sisters, Greg and I all join hands and wade into the water. The cold water dances on my skin and I feel the tiny energy particles of this great river invigorate each cell of my body. With words of prayer, we all dip below the surface.

"Please forgive me my selfish ways and always stand by me as I grow to be a more loving, giving person who lives in gratitude every day," I say in prayer.

As I stare into the eyes of each of my sisters, we bond on an entirely different level, absorbing the significance of this event. We are not sisters at this moment. We are particles amongst particles accepting the energy of millions. Our submersion in the Ganges River is one of the most memorable experiences the four of us encounter during our stay in Varanasi.

Varanasi has been the ultimate pilgrimage spot for Hindus for ages and is the oldest surviving city in the world. Hindus believe that one who is graced to die in Varanasi will attain salvation and freedom from the cycle of birth and re-birth. Because of the spiritual significance of this city's location on the Ganges River, ceremonies take place almost every evening.

At night, we watch the Ganga Seva Nidhi ceremonies performed by Brahman priests near the river's edge. Next to the ceremony site, the fires of the crematorium burn brightly as bodies are reduced to ash so that they can be delivered to their resting place in the sacred Ganges River.

As I sit and watch the ceremony, temple bells ring and chanting voices sing in the two thousand temples scattered throughout the city. There is so much devotion present. Few words are used amongst the four of us during these times. There is no need for words. No need to express the thoughts that flow through our minds, because there is a *feel* and this feel communicates it all.

\# \# \# \#

"There is no way I can ask a person here to accept less for a trinket than what they state is the price," I admit. "I know this is what they expect me to do. I read about it in the guidebooks. I know negotiation is factored into the initial price already. I know I am on a tight budget."

I also know this country is filled with a level of poverty I will never personally live and I can't bring myself to ask for less. Even jobless and homeless, the wealth I have in the eyes of the average person here would be considered a small fortune. I can't bring myself to barter about price! Call me a sucker but I would rather not eat at all than ask someone, who could possibly be starving, to go down on a price for any type of food or ware that they are selling.

Right now, I am so appreciative for the abundance of money and opportunity available to us in the States. I never fully comprehended how good we have it in North America. I have led such a sheltered life in comparison. Even when our family faced financial hardship or struggle, it was not even remotely comparable to what a majority of this population suffers through on a daily basis.

How could I have lived in such ignorance and lack of gratitude? Because I never experienced this much contrast to realize how good I have it — that is how. Contrast brings awareness. Holding onto the awareness will be the bigger challenge.

My new belief is that every American child should be required to visit a third world country early on so they have a chance to gain new perspective, and maybe a new level of gratitude, to use as their life foundation as they grow and age.

Lesa must feel the same about the poverty and bartering. When she actually does attempt to negotiate, the man says "$5" and Lesa belts back at him, "I'll give you $6!" I start laughing so hard I almost wet my pants. Lesa looks at me like, "What?" but I can't stop laughing long enough to tell her. Plus, I don't want to embarrass the man in any way or have him jack the price up to $7 since he knows he obviously has us like putty in his hands. We laugh about it later when I tell her, but she still doesn't believe she said it. She says it must have been a Freudian slip.

What the people of India lack in financial prosperity, I feel they make up for in family unity and in the idea of Karma. As sisters traveling together, we are welcomed into many homes. We learn a great deal about family bonds in India and how tight family units remain for generations.

In some cases, three generations of a family will continue to maintain the same residency. Sometimes up to twenty-four people all live in the same home. This family unity is remarkable. Each generation helps the one before, because they know that the next generation will help them in return.

One of the shopkeepers explains the depth of this belief to me when he says, "If I do not take care and honor my mother in this life, Shiva will not bless me in the next life. It is the law of Karma." I felt similar pangs to those I experienced in Greece—about my choice to live away from my family. Only in India, these pangs are sharp jabs, since I realize more each day how much I enjoy my sisters.

What has a lasting impact on me is how genuinely happy many of the people of India seem, in spite of owning so little. They seem content to be filled with gratitude regardless.

It inspires me to see such a dramatically different, non-materialistic component to happiness, especially compared to what filled my own empty Box. People chant and sing as they stroll to a temple, offering smiles and prayers to us as they pass by. Neighbors join in to help one another wash clothes and carry bundles of fresh laundry. Happiness shines everywhere, yet these people have so little in terms of material possessions.

If I ever needed proof that money, titles, jobs and possessions do not lead to my happiness, the people of India provide a beautiful example of this.

Watch and observe, Michelle. These people have so little, but they glow with acceptance and contentment. True happiness comes from within, with God and spiritual connection as the key. Life is not about seeking "more." It's about a heart filled with love and about finding joy and gratitude for who you are, not what you have.

# # # #

To top off our Varanasi experience, we find out that we happen to be in India during the largest festival of the Hindu religion, the Kumbh Mela. This festival is held every three years and rotates between four cities. As our luck would have it, this time it is an Ardh Mela—a larger festival that takes place every six years—and it is in Allahabad; the single point in India where the three holy rivers (Ganges, Yamuna and Saraswati) converge.

This festival is an extremely big deal. Even as a non-Hindu, I see the value of our timing and location. There are an estimated twenty million people that make the pilgrimage to the festival and it is only three hours away from Varanasi.

Murlie agrees to drive us to Allahabad and we leave early in the morning so we will have plenty of time to walk around the grounds before dark. We set off, me in the front seat with Murlie and Sunny, Greg and Lesa all in the back.

A few hours in, traffic starts to slow on the highway.

"What's happening? Can anyone see?" Sunny asks from the back seat.

"It looks like they have some kind of checkpoint set up or something. The police are standing there waving cars in so they can inspect them but it's weird because they've let every car go by so far. I don't really get why they have the checkpoint set up," Lesa replies from the back seat on the driver's side where she has been peering around Murlie to see up ahead.

It is true, the policeman waved every car through, except for when it is our turn. He motions for us to pull over but instead, Murlie stays focused straight ahead and keeps driving. Everyone in the back seat yells to stop but I quietly say, "I get it, keep going!" Murlie and I know exactly what's going on.

The policeman raises the five foot metal staff he is using to direct traffic and swings it down as hard as he can onto the roof of our car as we drive by. Everyone ducks, afraid the windows are next. Murlie hits the gas. I peek up from my crouched position in the front to glance into the side-view mirror. I can see the policeman behind us swinging at the tail end of the car. My heart is beating so fast, I can hear it in my ears.

Thank you for protecting us!

After putting miles of distance between us and the checkpoint, Murlie pulls over at a gas station to inspect the damage. We all climb out and stare at the deep dent the metal rod has caused in the roof of Murlie's new car.

"He was going to extort money from us, or something worse, wasn't he?" I ask as we stare.

"You are correct, Madam, which is why I could not stop," Murlie confirms back to me.

"I'm so sorry about your car," I say as tears well up in my eyes in gratitude for our quiet protector.

"Do not worry about the car. It is ... not a problem," is Murlie's reply, as always.

There is a second police encounter when we arrive at the festival. After leaving the car in a lot, we all cram into a rickshaw to take us to the entrance, since there are no vehicles allowed near the festival. As we head toward the main bridge, we see the enormous tents of the gurus off in the distance. Murlie asks the rickshaw driver to pull over so we can take a few quick photographs of the spectacular view. We jump out, ready to take our shots.

Out of nowhere, a policeman rushes over, raises his stick, and is about to cane our rickshaw driver. Murlie quickly jumps in the way. Heated words are flung at Murlie by the policeman, which he calmly addresses and replies to. The poor rickshaw driver doesn't even look up. He stands with his hands behind his back, an innocent victim waiting for his fate to be delivered to him. After some discussions, the policeman puts his cane away and waves the rickshaw driver off. The driver immediately hops into his rickshaw and races away.

It turns out, this spot on the bridge is a high security zone because of the important gurus attending the festival and no one is allowed to stop. This is completely understandable, but the brutality of how the situation is handled still has us reeling in a state of shock.

What is interesting to me are the visible status dynamics that appeared. Murlie, as a cab driver, outranked the rickshaw driver and was able to plead his case and eventually save him from punishment. The four of us, as tourists, represented a higher rank, which allowed Murlie to take action without repercussion. The poor rickshaw driver, who wasn't even allowed to raise his eyes, definitely had the "bad end of the stick."

I don't know if the policeman wants to keep an eye on us to ensure we do not cause any more commotion, or if he wants to guarantee some type of tourist protection, but he becomes our personal escort for the remainder of the walk to the festival. I glance sideways at him a bit suspiciously, not knowing what to expect after these few police experiences. Whatever his intent, there aren't any issues as we trek to the entrance, surrounded by thousands of others on the same mission.

As we enter, I again feel that same stirring of overwhelm that I experienced when I first stepped off the plane. In the procession to the entrance, there are thousands of people. Inside, there are literally millions.

"There are more people here than I have ever seen in my entire life. I am one amongst millions. One small person wandering in a sea of people," I think as I realize suddenly how small I feel. "I bet I wouldn't even be a blip on a radar if a satellite were focused down on me right now. Small and insignificant—like I'm a blade of grass in a field of green."

"But this isn't entirely true," I quickly realize as I look around at all these millions of faces. "This isn't true at all. My sisters and I do stand out. Out of twenty million people, we are the only white faces I see at this festival!"

With this awareness, I notice something else: we have a following! We are surrounded by a group of about twenty people that seem to follow our every step and listen to our every word. We walk two feet, the crowd moves two feet. I say something and twenty sets of eyes study my face the entire time.

"What an odd site! Three blonde-haired, blue-eyed women and their crowd of spectators wandering through the Kumbh Mela," I say, finding this completely hysterical. So funny in fact, that I laugh aloud. All twenty followers start to laugh, for no other reason than because I am laughing.

My sisters do not find any of this amusing, especially Sunny. She has social anxiety issues and looks like she is about to panic. Greg steps in and takes her hand to calm her down before she flips out. It seems to work. With his dark dreadlocks and beard, and olive Filipino skin, Greg stands out as well, but mostly because people mistake him for a shaman. There are many of these holy men here though. We, as blonde-haired, blue-eyed women, are definitely more unique.

I break free from our posse for a few minutes and head off alone in the direction of a jewelry booth. I collect inexpensive pieces of jewelry as souvenirs when I travel so I automatically gravitate toward jewelry whenever it is around. As I stand at a booth admiring all of the beautiful pieces, I'm not really paying much attention to the people beside me.

"It okay—look," I hear a man's voice say next to me. I assume it is the owner of the stand so I turn to talk to him with a smile. But it isn't the owner, it is a man dressed in traditional Indian garb.

"It okay—look!" he repeats and this time I notice a small Indian boy about seven hiding behind him. The boy peeks out at me with enormous brown eyes and a little smile that he hides behind his hand. He quickly lowers his eyes and squeezes back behind his father's arm when I glance at him.

Oh my gosh, I might be the first Caucasian woman this boy has ever seen!

I lean toward him and squat down so I am on his level and with a big smile reassure him, "It *is* okay, you *can* look." As he peers back at me, he smiles a gigantic smile and giggles. I smile and giggle back, amazed by this new role life offers me to play.

Yes, in any given minute, I am exactly where I am supposed to be.

# # # #

After Varanasi, we travel northeast to Agra to see the Taj Mahal. I wish I could say the train ride there is an enjoyable one filled with beautiful scenery and glorious sites. Instead, it is close to the most miserable experience of my life, only second to the Irish/France ferry.

We book our tickets for the twelve hour trip in Varanasi not far in advance of our departure and get hustled by the ticket agency. The agent keeps telling us, "There is no availability," but he suddenly finds seats in the expensive section when we turn to walk away. We fork over the cash with resentment but look forward to nice accommodations for the cost.

When we walk across the street to the station, there are about another million people also waiting for trains. Bodies sprawl everywhere.

Finally, after mass amounts of confusion over which train and what car, we load into our car—only to realize how badly we were truly hustled. For the next twelve hours, we will ride in a car class that is only one level better than riding with the chickens and livestock.

There are bars on the windows instead of glass, and frigid air blasts in from outside the entire time. Hard vinyl-covered benches serve as beds. All is exposed in the open; there are no compartments with food, toilets, blankets or pillows.

"This uncovers the mystery of why everyone has so many bags with them," Sunny says as we watch all the people around us unpack blankets, pillows and food. The four naïve American tourists have nothing but the small packs on their backs for this long overnight ride.

"This is insane. I am freezing to death. I have never been so cold. How could we—no wait, not we—how could *I*, the Professional Traveler, have been so stupid not to have investigated all the train options before we bought the tickets?" I say to myself in judgment and anger. "I have to wise up. This is a different country and they play by different rules and I have to start adapting to those rules or else we all might die.

"Okay, so that might be a little extreme, but it sure doesn't feel like it right now as I lay here getting frostbite!" is the begrudging conversation in my head.

At one point, I pull almost every piece of clothing I have with me out of my bag and layer it on. All my socks, all my shirts, all my pants. Layer after layer. Then I wrap a tee-shirt around my head to block the wind from blowing in my ears and lie there in a shivering ball. I look around at Sunny, Lesa and Greg and see they have done the same. "This is a nightmare!" I continue to think.

On top of this, trains in India are notoriously late and so the trip actually takes sixteen hours instead of twelve. We all wake up the next day horribly sick with head and chest colds.

I am beyond grateful that I am with my sisters right now, versus being alone or with anyone else. Our family has a strong level of resilience and we need that edge more than ever as we face these new challenges. Instead of having a pity party over how crappy we all feel, we say, "Roll with the punches, all part of the adventure!" to encourage ourselves between coughs and sneezes. I am saved by the group from my own negativity.

As the train rolls over the last bridge before it enters the city of Agra, I look out the window in admiration at the early morning scene below. Beyond the light haze, acres of brightly colored laundry are spread across the dried, empty river bed like a huge patchwork quilt. A large camel saunters slowly along the laundry edge, as if hoping one of the pieces of blue fabric might actually be a cool drink of water. Off in the distance on the left bank, the sun rises over the magnificent Taj Mahal while ahead, on the right bank, looms the miles of brick of the great Agra Fort. It is a beautiful, picturesque scene.

"This single moment has made the entire miserable train ride worth it," I think with appreciation. "This postcard image is one others only dream about and I am here seeing it live. Sick or not, I am so grateful!" With this thought, the whistle blows and we pull into Agra.

Babu and his crew of rickshaw drivers are the first locals we meet as we depart from the train. Like Murlie, they offer to take care of us and get us to a "great hotel." Babu is a likeable guy about my age, who presents himself as the leader/negotiator for this bunch. While the four of them seem to share no physical similarities, they still have a common trustworthy *feel* to them.

"Should we test our luck again and go with the first person to come up to us?" I ask Greg and the girls.

"Might as well since it worked last time," they consent. We agree to let Babu and his crew take us to the hotel. Like Murlie and Sambu, we end up spending our days in Agra with these four as our rickshaw tour guides.

"Maybe if we stay busy, we will wear out our sickness!" I suggest. We decide to give this a try and so after some hot tea, our crew of rickshaw drivers escort us to the beautiful marble palace of the Baby Taj. After this, we go to the massive Agra Fort before traveling to the gardens of the Black Palace, across the river from the Taj Mahal. It is an action packed day despite many sneezes and coughs.

As we stand in a field and snap distant pictures of the Taj Mahal, we are approached by a group of young children. They look at us with their big brown eyes and stretch their empty hands toward us through the fence begging for money. It is such a heart wrenching site, I want to give them all the money I have, but before I reach into my bag, Babu stops me. Instead, he hands them some candy and tells them to get back to school.

"Please do not ever give begging kids money, only candy or something. When you give them money, they think this is the better way to live and so they skip school to beg. It never pays off in the long run," he wisely tells us. He is right. The pity I feel for them makes it difficult to resist—especially when they stare at me with those big brown eyes—but I appreciate Babu's logic and respect his advice.

While we wander from the field back to the trail, we come across a group of teens who have quite a few loud comments to share about us. Out of some mysterious "nowhere" again, a policeman suddenly materializes next to us and sharply slaps one of the teens across the face. The boys take off in a hurry. The policeman tips his hat and continues in another direction.

I am again shocked by the open physical violence of the police. Babu explains that the Indian government is strongly promoting tourism and that it is a prime initiative of the country. Key locations basically have a no-tolerance rule when it comes to tourist harassment. "Ironic, since we were about to be extorted by the other police!" I think.

As we travel from site to site, we pass donkeys and camels hitched to carts. Men peddle bikes with huge piles of lumber slung between racks mounted by the seat and handle bars. An entire family of four zoom by us, all squeezed onto a single motor scooter. "Well, they definitely don't give out tickets for not wearing seatbelts here!" Lesa jokes.

I mentally compare the scene to our U.S. highways packed

with single passenger cars. Even though Agra is a fairly modern city, time feels like it has turned back a full century.

The next day, we are up and out the door before dawn after another cold shower, since I didn't realize there was a hot water switch that needs to be flipped in advance. We leave early because we want to catch the sun as it rises over the magnificent Taj Mahal.

The image of the Taj reflects mystically in the beautiful fountain pool at the base of the palace. As I stare at the reflection, I have another moment where I think, "Life can't get any better than this moment right here and now."

After spending hours admiring the Taj Mahal, Babu asks if we are interested in experiencing a real, non-tourist Shiva temple. If so, he will take us to a little Brahman village about an hour away to show us the temple where he personally prays.

We excitedly agree, especially me. I have a deep personal interest in the Hindu religion after my experience a year or so ago. Chris and I went regularly to an ashram by Malibu for about six months to experience Shaktipat, which is a form of meditation. It was led by a guru who studied in India for decades.

I loved the experience, with the chanting and meditation and there was a great sense of spirituality about the place. The guru was extremely wise, and his lectures were both profound and simple.

All of the messages were about letting go of materialism and bad habits that distract us from focusing on God within. Unfortunately, I was too stubborn and too deeply branded and I refused to give up my vices. I was a captive to my ego inside my Box and unwilling to let go.

Here, in India though, I want to let it *all* go. A temple sounds like the idyllic place to deepen my growing connection to God and the faith-filled belief in something greater than myself. We head off to the temple.

On the way, Lesa and I have the most wonderful conversation about family and Karma with our rickshaw driver, Deepak. Deepak is the grandfather of our rickshaw bunch. He is tall, very thin and I would guess him to be in his early sixties. When he smiles, he only has a few teeth left on top, which for some reason makes his smile even more pleasant. He always wears a thick jacket and a winter cap, like he has been stuck on our hell-train before and now plans for the coldest weather wherever he goes.

Deepak tells us how it is his duty to care for his mother and how he would never make a serious decision without her approval, even though he is obviously old enough to make his own decisions. He explains the role Karma plays in his life and that only good acts should be performed every day and good thoughts should always fill the mind.

"If a person accomplishes this, good things will come back to the person," he tells us. This is how Deepak lives each day of his life.

How many dozens of books have I read about this same idea? It is quite different to see people who actually live this belief. Book knowledge is one thing, but reality and action are everything. I admire this man, a content rickshaw driver, who bases his life on always doing the best he can for others.

The temple is in a small, remote village on the banks of the Yamuna which is one of the three holy rivers. Babu won't enter the temple because he didn't shower today so he waits out front with one of the other drivers. We enter with Deepak and Nuli—a short, quick little man in his early thirties who seems to pair up with Deepak in the rickshaws.

Inside, the air particle vibrations are so strong, I physically feel them from the temple door. Similar to the cathedrals and churches, here at the temple I detect the presence of a collective positive energy. I enter with my bread offering and after I perform the simple ritual Deepak explained beforehand, I sit on the floor and soak up the waves of electricity that seem to float in the air.

My ears begin to ring loudly and that thunder of silence is again with me to the point that my head feels like it is about to explode. Then a silent calmness settles in and washes through my body like a soft purple wave. I don't ever want to leave; the aura of peace and tranquility mixed with this pool of positive energy are so sensational. I sit in a trancelike state for what feels like an eternity and a single second at the same time.

Finally, after quite a while, my consciousness returns back to the temple. I am the only person from our group who is still inside. Outside, all of the others have climbed up into the tower, except for Deepak, who stands down by the water's edge. I decide to join him and walk up to him with a smile, still glowing from my experience in the temple.

We stand next to each other and stare into the river for a few minutes in peaceful silence. Deepak turns and faces me, then extends his cupped hands out to me. In them, he holds a small piece of the offering bread.

"Please allow me this gift. It would be an honor to share bread with you," he says as he stares into my eyes and smiles his happy toothless grin. My heart floods with warmth and love. I smile and with tears of pure gratitude respond, "Deepak, it would be my honor too."

Then we each pinch off a piece of the offering bread, place it into the other's hand and eat the bread at the same time. There we stand, Deepak and I, in front of the Shiva temple on the banks of the holy Yamuna River, blessing each other with prayers of happiness.

People of the world are so good!

With that, we gather the others and make our way back through the temple courtyard toward the entrance. On our way to the exit, we pass a snake charmer with a huge cobra coiled in a basket in front of his folded legs.

Snakes are by far one of my greatest animal fears in life. If given the choice of being trapped in a cage with a man-eating tiger or a one-foot long garden snake, I would take the tiger every time. The way snakes strike is unpredictable and since I don't do well with the unknown, they spark a feeling of terror in me.

This is probably why God chooses the exact minute I am experiencing my highest spiritual connection to suddenly bring me face-to-face with my worst nightmare. It happens so fast it is all a blur. I see the snake for a fraction of a second before I blink. Just that quick, Nuli, the fast little rickshaw driver, picks up the snake and drapes it across my shoulders and says, "You need to hold the snake."

He didn't ask the questions, "Does anyone want to hold the snake?" or, "Do you want to hold the snake?" or, "Are you afraid of snakes?" He instead states, "You need to hold the snake," and then in the next blink, I have a hissing cobra wrapped around me.

We are all stunned into a total state of shock, especially me. I have a moment where I'm not quite sure this is really even happening but then Sunny starts to panic and orders Nuli to get the snake off me, and I snap back to reality.

The cobra senses the tension and rears itself, flares its wide hood and hisses. Now I am completely past initial shock. Suddenly, my mind is sharp again and it is in full action as it flies through the limited options I have at this moment.

I can throw it and hope I don't get bitten in the process or I can take my chances and try to calm it down.

I have a split second to make a choice. Since there is nowhere to throw it, I choose to attempt to calm the cobra down. "I read *The Alchemist*. I can do it! I will become one with the snake," I decide.

"Snake, I'm not here to hurt you. I know this isn't where you choose to be and I'm sorry," I attempt to say to the snake through osmosis as I try to send positive vibes out from my body into this angry reptile wrapped around me.

I am supporting the upper half of the snake with my left hand. The snake curves around, turns and faces me. It looks directly at me and I can feel it judging my integrity.

"Are you really my friend, Michelle? I know for a fact you hate snakes," is the message it slithers at me.

Is this really happening or have I lost my mind? I am staring into the eyes of a cobra . . . and attempting to communicate through energy!

This is the most out-of-body experience of my life- way beyond the snowboard episode or any meditation experience. Still, I continue my efforts to be one with the cobra.

"I am not here to hurt you snake," I send out as he curves his body so that his head is back behind my line of vision. Suddenly, a chill goes down my spine. The type of chill I get when someone breathes close to my neck. I feel the flicker of the cobra's tongue against the hair by my ear.

In that instant, I have total clarity that I have zero control of this situation or the outcome. I pass from thinking that I can calm the snake into complete surrender in less than a second. I do not scream. I do not panic. I do not pass out. I do not throw the snake. I simply surrender that whatever happens next is beyond my control and I accept that I am about to be bitten by a cobra . . . and I am calm.

I fully surrender to faith not fear. Whatever happens is meant to be.

"I understand, this is your nature, this is not your fault," I think as the wave of acceptance washes through my entire being.

Sunny screams right then and almost faints. We all know what is going to happen next. The cobra whips around, hissing and I feel my neck muscles tense. It shoots out in full strike mode—but not at me.

Instead, it strikes out unexpectedly at the group, coming within inches of Greg's face. Greg springs back in reflexive alarm and suddenly the group looks like a pile of dominoes as everyone knocks into the person next to them.

I feel every ounce of energy in the entire snake zap into my body as it strikes. It's like I stuck my finger in an electric socket. The energy transfer is so intense, for a few seconds, I feel like I really *am* the snake!

Maybe some part of The Alchemist philosophy worked!

The snake charmer jumps into action and pulls the cobra off of me before more chaos takes place. I say nothing because I can't even speak. It's like the snake did strike me, paralyzing my vocal chords.

I walk back to the rickshaw and climb in, completely silent. I am not there yet, I am somewhere in another zone still where the thunder of silence rings so loudly in my ears, I am temporarily deaf as well as unable to speak.

Slowly, my hearing returns and I listen to the chatter of the group; they are filled with adrenaline about what just happened. As they recall each detail, I realize something—their story does not match mine.

To them, this was an exciting story about a striking cobra. To me, this was an experience about acceptance and surrender.

I faced one of my worst terrors in life, actually stared it in the eyes, surrendered completely . . . and survived unharmed. Future events will seem incomparably small from this day forward. My cobra, in the temple of the snake god, Shiva, taught me to accept and surrender and set me free from fear.

Chapter 13:
Acceptance—Rajasthan India

We seem to develop a trend in India, where we attract frigid transportation. Our path westward from Agra to Pushkar puts us on an overnight bus that is as cold as a refrigerator. All of us think we covered our bases this time when we upgrade to the bus's upper sleeper section, but broken window seals prove us wrong. Even after we stuff the cracks with tee-shirts, the huge gaps force constant cold jets of air to shoot directly at us for eight hours.

Lesa and I are in one cubby, and Greg and Sunny are in another. The two of us huddle together trying to keep warm while the wind whistles into our ears and faces. Our Agra chest colds feed on the freezing air and grow with a vengeance. Pneumonia feels like it is on the way.

In addition to the cold air, there are no restrooms on the bus and the bus never stops. My bladder has been about to explode for the past two hours. I cross my legs so tight they go numb. I can't move because I am afraid it is going to burst out of me. It is excruciating.

At 2:00 a.m., the freezing bus finally pulls into a dark, empty lot in the middle of a shut-down town. "This cannot be a bus station!" I think. "It's just a dirt parking lot with a bunch of people standing around."

We are ushered off the bus, into the lot. There are no other buses. I see no movement except for forty or so people who are milling around. Beyond the lot, there is not a person, car or bus in sight. It looks like we have entered a ghost town.

"Where are we? What are we supposed to do next? Do we wait here all night for another bus?" are the questions we pass between the four of us.

"We have to find someone that can tell us what's going on," I say. "More important, I have to find a bathroom in the next ten seconds or else I'm going to spend the rest of the night in pee soaked pants!"

I rush up to the first person I see and ask where the restrooms are.

"Over there, outside toilet," the tall elderly man says and nods his head toward a cement wall under some lights over by the road.

"No, I'm looking for a bathroom," I repeat, thinking maybe he misunderstood me.

The younger man he is with points at the same cement area about fifty feet away. "Toilet — over there," he confirms.

"Over there" is a cement stall with three walls, no toilet — not even a hole in the ground — and no door, so it is open for all to see.

"Screw it! I don't care who watches me pee. Going in front of an audience is better than grossing everyone out on the next bus ride because I smell like pee," I say as I walk over to the cube, pull down my pants, squat and let 'er rip. For a second, my concern about people watching me is replaced by my concern about the splash factor but even this fades quickly as absolute relief floods my body.

When I find my way back to the others, they tell me that while I was away on my potty-break they found a bus driver who explained next steps.

"We are supposed to get on another bus in a few minutes and that bus will take us three hours to our next drop-off point," Greg says. The next bus arrives and every seat is already filled. It is standing room only and the standing room is already taken as well.

The driver directs us to sit scrunched in a space behind his seat that is used for luggage. The four of us sit with our legs crossed for three long hours. Initially consumed by pain, my legs gratefully go completely numb after about an hour.

"Well, at least there is no freezing air blowing on us," Sunny feebly jokes. We all laugh in agreement, but I think each of us really wants to cry. I know I do. I try to tune-out in meditation but my head can't seem to escape the distraction of the clucking chicken three rows back.

Three hours later, we arrive at the next dark, empty lot. It is still pitch black out at 5:00 a.m., but it is clear that we are in the desert because of all the sand. My stomach starts to clench up as I realize that we are about to be dropped off in a remote desert area in the black of night surrounded by nothing but sand. There is no town or civilization around.

"Should we just stay on the bus?" I ask the others.

Greg replies, "I am sure they know what they're doing."

Lesa makes the decision for us when she says, "I don't care if we get stranded, I *have* to stand up!"

We all stagger off the bus like we are drunk, knocking into each other since we have no feeling in our legs. I stamp my feet around the empty dirt lot and attempt to get my circulation flowing again. As the nerves come alive, it feels like I am standing barefoot on a bed of pointy needles, which is still better than folded leg cramps.

The bus pulls away and leaves us, along with ten others, standing in the empty lot. The four of us huddle in a tight group, shivering, sneezing, and praying for sunlight and for the next bus to come soon.

My mind starts to reach into the darkness, "What will we do if it doesn't come? We are in the middle of nowhere and have no phone. Even if we did have a phone, who would we call?"

I haven't had a panic attack during this trip and I refuse to have one now. If I can survive the cobra situation without having one, I'm sure not going to have one over "dark and stranded."

I pull my mind away from the dark, "I'm so grateful I am here with family instead of facing this situation alone. At least there is a little safety in numbers."

I look around; there are no chairs, no benches, no concession stands. Just dirt and open desert . . . and no bus. "It will come," a man standing nearby assures us. I look at him with apprehension. "It will come," he says again.

We wait another hour in our huddle. As I stand there, I think about the freezing trains and buses, open urine stalls, barren lots of dirt and buses that might or might not come.

"I will never take my car or a toilet for granted again," I joke aloud. "Give me L.A. traffic any day!"

# # # #

The man was right—the bus does finally come. The four of us arrive at the entry to the city of Pushkar feeling ragged, tired, sick and irritated. All of us cough constantly and my bones feel like they are about to shatter apart from sheer exhaustion.

There is a cloud of negativity building all around us. It seems that none of us have the mental energy to muster up any type of positive attitude. We all agree that we have to get to a hotel fast before we collapse right there, in the road.

"Do you need a hotel?" a young boy asks as we start to trudge forward. "I can take you to a nice hotel."

"I'm sure you can," I snap in irritation, "but I'm also sure that there is probably a 'nice hotel' about twenty-feet away from where we stand. We will head down the road here on our own and find out." My patience with this entire experience is gone and the last thing we need is some child sending us on a long, wild goose chase only to probably end up at a crap hotel.

"No problem," he replies with a smile and lowers his eyes. He is a young kid, about twelve, dressed in blue jeans and a plaid short-sleeved button-up shirt. He has enormous eyes, which he constantly averts. There is nothing harmful or menacing about him, he actually looks like a sweet kid, but I am not in the mood to be potentially swindled at this moment.

We proceed to walk up Main Street, stop at a hotel, balk at the outrageous price and then leave. When we come out, the boy is there, a few feet ahead. He looks down at his feet, attempting to be inconspicuous.

The next place is no good because there is no hot water. We move onto the next place—no availability. Each time we come back out of a potential hotel, the boy is there, still pretending like he is not following us.

"I know there are a lot of hotels in this area, but since we are only staying in Pushkar for three days, should we stick with our pattern and go with the first person who approaches us?" I ask Greg and the girls. "Should we suck it up, follow him and see what this kid's place is like since he's not going to leave us anyway?" We all decide to give it a chance.

There are no cars or rickshaws in this city, only hand carts and mopeds and the occasional camel-drawn cart, so we slowly follow the boy by foot. He proceeds to lead us all the way to the other side of town.

We finally arrive at the hotel after a trek that feels like miles of winding alleys and roads. By now, we are so tired, we don't care about cost or room conditions. Whatever this place holds, we will take it because there is no energy left to search for anything else.

"Mama Luna's—well this should be interesting," Sunny mumbles as we drag ourselves past the gate, up a flight of stairs, to the two rooms the boy leads us to. The rooms are simple; only a double bed, a small side table and a wicker chair, but they are clean and colorful with bright green paint on the walls and striped blankets that hold every color of the rainbow.

I open the bathroom door and smile. "They have Western-style toilets here instead of squat holes. We can stay." (Hot water and Western-style toilets are my two criteria after a little incident I had in

Varanasi where I lost my balance over a squat toilet, head-butted the door open, and exposed myself to an entire yoga class.)

Lesa and I throw our bags on the floor of our shared room, ready for an immediate nap, while Greg and Sunny go to their room and do the same. The boy stands in our doorway though and says, "Come . . . follow" and gestures toward another narrow set of stairs near our room which look like they lead to the rooftop.

Reluctantly, Lesa and I pull our weary bodies up off the bed and follow the boy up the stairs. Greg and Sunny follow. "What an odd place to put the reception desk," I grumble, assuming that he needs us to sign some rate agreement or registration or something.

Chinu, the hotel manager, greets us at the top of the stairs. "Welcome to Mama Luna's," he says and extends his arm in a sweeping gesture.

The boy wasn't leading us to reception. He was leading us up to heaven!

On one side of rooftop terrace, thick cushions line the floor topped by piles of soft pillows. A canopy of sheer, wispy fabric covers the entire area, which allows the sun to beam down upon us with all its splendid warmth while also blocking out some of the desert heat. Soft music plays in the background and the tantalizing aroma of sandalwood incense fills the air.

We sink into the pillows; they are like soft, inviting clouds to our tired bodies. Then, the boy arrives again, this time with hot tea and honey, deliciously warm and soothing for our hacking lungs and sore throats.

As we lay there in nirvana, absorbed in bliss, Chinu begins to chant and I feel like I really am floating in heaven.

"I am never moving," I whisper.

"Neither am I," Lesa murmurs from the cushions next to me.

"Seriously, I don't think I could move if I tried," Greg adds from the cushions across from us.

"I don't know if I have ever been as happy as I am this second,"

Sunny sighs from her space in the cushions.

"I am serious you guys. I'm never moving," I repeat. "I think we should skip the rest of our plan to work our way down to Southern India and stay right here instead."

"Wonderful," Lesa consents before she rolls over to take a nap.

"I'm good with that," Greg says as he sips another drink of warm tea.

"Like I said, I'm so happy right now, you couldn't tear me away," Sunny adds as she lays back and looks up at the sky.

Without even visiting the city itself, we make the unanimous decision to take a three day visit and turn it into a two week stay.

See how easy life can be when you go with the flow and do what feels right, Michelle? Ahhh . . .

# # # #

Pushkar is a desert city so it is vastly different from the previous cities we visited. Instead of smog and pollution, there is fresh air and open desert. From the rooftop, I can see temples housed by tall hills off in the distance.

Small hut villages surround the city. Women from the villages walk by below, balancing tall vases filled with water on their heads. Chinu tells us that some of these women walk up to six miles each day to retrieve fresh water because there are no wells in their villages.

Camels plod past pulling carts loaded with produce, while men with hand carts maneuver around them to deliver other wares. There are no vehicles allowed in the city. Chinu informs us that electricity is a luxury in Pushkar and that it is only offered at certain hours each day.

The colorful rooms are comfortable at Mama Luna's, although the bathroom shower takes some getting used to. It is really a yellow bucket that sits on the tiled floor below a raw tap that sticks out of the wall at shin level. The choices to rinse are; scoop out the water with a cup or dump the bucket directly on your head. It makes things kind of convenient because every time someone showers, the bathroom floor gets washed too. A small, electricity driven water heater is stuck to the wall.

After a few cold showers, I finally leave myself a note by the bed so I remember to click the water heater on when the city has electricity so we have hot water the next day. It amazes me how quickly I adapt to the lack of showers and electricity. I guess because there is no choice. I would trade hot water for cold in an instant if it insures that I have a Western-style toilet.

What an interesting thing to be grateful for—a toilet I can sit on! It's all about perspective and finding the good in whatever the current situation offers. I feel like I am getting there!

As another of India's holy cities, there are rules listed on large signs throughout Pushkar: "No alcohol." "No profanity." "No public displays of affection." These are some of the many rules posted on the wall by the sacred Brahma Temple. I like a city with rules. It seems like almost everyone who lives here believes the rules exist for their best interest also. There is an air of harmony wherever you go.

Pushkar is a city of temples. There are over four hundred scattered both in the city and in the surrounding hills. The holy Pushkar Lake acts as the nucleus at the center of the city. Surrounding the lake are layers of white buildings and temples so that the lake is illuminated from the reflective white glow. The visual to me is one of purity and cleansing; no one is allowed in the lake.

On the outskirts, scattered buildings of pale blue, light yellow and grey are interspersed to add contrast to all the whiteness. From the temples, the harmonious sound of chanting voices float throughout the city, offset by the occasional chime of a temple bell.

Our decision to set roots in Pushkar is one of the best supporting decisions we make toward our quest to have a spiritual experience in India. The rush to "see and do" in the previous cities dampened the spiritual vibe since we were constantly busy and on-the-go to the next destination.

Here, we are able to relax and absorb our surroundings without the rush of time. Before, we maintained a group mentality, but now we are able to go our separate ways to explore so that we have individual experiences as well.

One of my personal favorite practices becomes yoga at a beautiful white temple. The first time we go, I think that we are at the wrong place. There is no one present, only an empty white temple that opens up toward the sacred lake.

Soon, an elderly yogi dressed in white appears and leads us to an open area with rugs. He hardly uses any words, but proceeds to take us through a variety of light yoga postures and breathing techniques.

At the end, as we meditate in silence, another man dressed in white arrives, rings the temple bell, sits in front of a statue of a Hindu god and sings his morning prayers. My entire body breaks out in chills as the hum of his voice pulses through my cells. Tears well up in my eyes as I feel the emotions of gratitude take over my heart. I have never experienced yoga so pure.

Unlike the yoga I practiced in the States, the focus with our yogi is not on movement but on connection. I feel so relaxed and free, I am afraid I might float out the door and end up in the lake.

We return for yoga here most mornings our first week. Many times, it is only my sisters, Greg and I in the temple with the yogi. It's like our own little secret spot that only we know about. To me, it is a very spiritual experience and I feel God's presence all around.

Our other secret spot is the highest part of the rooftop of Mama Luna's where we can watch the nightly wedding celebrations that take place in the open courtyard hall next door. There are large wedding ceremonies in halls scattered all across Pushkar each night. As we roam the city during the day, we pass grooms dressed in traditional wedding garb with ornate headdresses as they parade throughout town on white horses. Processions of people and musicians follow in their wakes. These processions continue for hours until the grooms finally arrive at their respective halls, where the ceremonies take place in the evening.

If there is a ceremony at the hall next door, we run to our secret spot and watch from our rooftop seats. I feel like we are eavesdropping and that we shouldn't watch something so personal, but I can't seem to help myself. In this world of arranged marriages, I am too drawn by the fact that we are about to witness the bride and groom as they see each other in person for the first time.

The ceremony is exciting but very formal. Closest family surround both bride and groom as they are presented to each other. Then the celebration begins as the married couple goes to the main hall where there is a festive dinner as well as lively music, song and dance. We fall asleep to the sound of the music as it plays late into the night, a celebration of a love we all pray fulfills both the new bride and groom.

One special evening, it is a different kind of night. The astrological signs indicate that this particular date is one of the most blessed days of the year for people to wed and there are over ten weddings. Grooms on white horses seem to parade down every road and in the late evening, fireworks light up the sky all over the town as music fills the air. I feel so fortunate to experience this special day as the fireworks and happy sounds of celebration etch themselves in my memory.

This concept of arranged marriages both fascinates and frightens me at the same time. It triggers my independence and fear of the unknown in a huge way. The thought of committing to marry someone without knowing them is more unknown than my psyche can handle.

Lesa and I are able to get an in-depth explanation of how it all works one day, when we go to one of the local's homes to have henna painted on Lesa's feet. We are there for hours as the young bride-to-be draws the intricate henna designs and it gives us plenty of time to ask questions. The future bride looks like she is about twelve years old, but in fact she is twenty-one. She is beautiful: petite with long dark hair, an engaging smile and she is extremely skilled at henna. She is also very open to our questions, which we are excited about.

"So you won't see him until the wedding day, not even once?" Lesa questions her.

"No, only a photo, but his mother says he is a very nice man," she responds.

"Of course his mother is going to say he is a nice guy. It's his mother!" my mind thinks.

Do not judge, Michelle, this is not for you to judge.

"How do you pick someone?" I ask, totally clueless as to how this whole arranged marriage ball would even get rolling.

"Actually, his family picks you. This is based on your family's standing, the amount of dowry you offer and what you look like," she explains.

"So it is all about money and looks—just as I expected. No love or anything like that," my judgmental mind silently concludes to itself while my physical voice says, "So then what?"

"After the families agree, then the astrological signs are read to see if you are a good match. If the signs show you would be a good match, then a marriage date is selected based on the signs," the girl continues.

"So it is about looks, money and astrological hocus pocus. This is too much!" my mind continues to itself.

Too much for you, Michelle, but maybe instead of judging, you should stop and accept that this is their way of life and that it is not for you to judge.

"Who pays for the wedding?" I ask as I hope for some positive news that the groom has to at least put some skin in the game.

"Always the bride, the entire celebration," she replies,

squashing my hopes. "Our family will sacrifice everything for this wedding. That is the way it is here," she informs me. I feel anger start to simmer inside me over the injustice of this entire arranged marriage process.

"That does not seem fair at all!" Lesa cries, voicing my thoughts. Not wanting to offend, we drop this whole financial discussion. Both Lesa and I obviously hope for some positive outcome for this young girl as a bride-to-be. "Okay, so what happens after you get married?"

"I leave the next day after the wedding and move away to his city. I am very lucky, he is only a few hours away from Pushkar so I will be able to visit my family every once in a while. Some women never see their own families again once they are married," she explains with a look of gratitude on her young face.

"Torn away from her family for the rest of her life too? This is too much to comprehend. Please tell me some advantage this girl gets from all this!" my mind begs.

"But what if you don't like him?" I probe aloud, "Can you leave and come home?" I can't accept the idea of her being ripped away from family to then be stuck with a man she did not choose and might not love.

"No, that is unthinkable. I will grow to like him, hopefully love him. It is all arranged so I have no choice. His family says he is a good man though and I have seen his picture, so at least I don't have to worry about if he is mean or ugly," she confidently replies.

We both stare at this young girl. She is an example of total acceptance. I might have had a moment of true surrender and acceptance when the cobra was about to bite me, but this girl has acceptance on an entirely different level.

To her, this lack of choice is a natural part of life. To me, this lack of choice feels like a death sentence delivered by the hand of the unknown. I admire her courage and the grace with which she accepts all this. While in the temples, I shoot out little prayers of hope that she does end up with a man she loves.

Speaking of love, the four of us feel love ourselves in Pushkar, and it comes in the form of an eleven-year old boy named Shammah. Of course, this is not romantic love. The love he seems to bring out in us—especially in me—is a maternal "this boy has my heart and I want to protect him and save him and give him a better life" kind of love.

This sweet little stealer-of-hearts is the young boy who led us to Mama Luna's when we stepped off the bus. Shammah is about five feet tall, super thin, has one grey front tooth, short black hair with sweeping bangs and the biggest smile of any boy I have ever met.

This smile never leaves his face for a minute; not while he cooks food for every person in the hotel, not while he cleans every room in the hotel, not while he gathers all the supplies for the hotel, not while he hand washes laundry at the hotel. Shammah does all of this with dignity and with a smile, at age eleven. He truly melts my heart.

We give Shammah a pretty large tip based on the first half of our stay. We hand it to him directly when he is alone, instead of passing it through Chinu. After about three days at Mama Luna's, I decide that something about Chinu rubs me the wrong way. This pot-bellied manager, who looks like he is stoned all the time, never seems to lift a finger to help with the workings of the place. We never see him leave the lounge area of the roof and we all unanimously decide that no tips ever make it past his pockets to the kids who are doing all of the work. Right or wrong, we go direct to Shammah this time.

Shammah rushes up to us the next day, excited to show us the cassette player he bought with the money. The pride and joy he expresses over this cheap, outdated technology uplifts me and breaks my heart at the same time. I am reminded again about how much I take for granted back home. I buy him a stack of batteries to go with it and contemplate giving him my iPod because he works so hard and receives so little.

I ask Chinu many questions about Shammah, which he

reluctantly answers. I probe him with questions like, "Does he get paid?" (Yes, I buy him new jeans sometimes and give him a little money if he needs something) "How old is he?" (Don't know, sometimes he say eleven, sometime he say thirteen) "Where is his family?" (Not in Pushkar) "Does he go to school?" (Sometimes).

Very vague, untrustworthy answers for someone supposedly responsible for the young boy's life. I dislike Chinu even more.

What I learn through observation is that Shammah sleeps outside on the rooftop and only attends school a few days a month. This infuriates me. I want to go ring Chinu's neck for sitting there on his butt all day while this poor child is deprived of an education. I know Shammah is involved in some type of slave labor.

"I am taking him home with me," I inform my sisters. "Shammah deserves a better life. He deserves to be a kid!" I mean it. This little boy is too special to lead this kind of life. I know it might be a common practice to use orphans or give-away kids as slave labor in India, but I am determined that Shammah will not continue to be one of these unfortunates.

Sunny has to act as my voice of reason with this situation. "Michelle," she says, "do you really think he would have a better life in California? Look at him. He is full of more joy and gratitude than many kids I know in the States. He is happy to do his daily duties with pride and to have a place to sleep at night. His life is simple but the kid seems to have a lot of joy in his heart. Do you really think subjecting him to the materialistic, complex world of California would make his life better?"

I digest this over the next few days. Each time I see Shammah's smile, I ask myself, "Is it because his life is simple? Is that why he is so happy? Is he grateful because he knows his situation could be worse?"

Wandering through a field on my way back from the Blue Temple at the base of the mountains, it hits me. Like the bride-to-be, Shammah is in full acceptance. This is a different world here that plays by an entirely different set of rules. Rules which mean sometimes young kids work hard instead of going to school. Shammah accepts what-is and has a joyful heart because of his acceptance.

What a huge example of acceptance wrapped in such a small package. Shammah, my heart-stealer . . . and teacher.

# # # #

To stay in one city for longer than a few days is a new experience for me after the last many months. It is so relaxing to start the day off with yoga at the temple, and then to spend the rest of the day engulfed in books, hikes and city exploration.

If I need a laugh, I head to town to peruse the local shops so I can hear my favorite expression, "Same, same—only different!" It's silly, but every time I hear it, I can't help but giggle.

Here in India, when you walk into a booth, they display an item—be it a shirt, skirt, bag, pants—and then stack piles of the same design in a variety of colors and sizes behind it. When a shopper shows interest in the display item, the shopkeeper immediately starts pulling variations from the stack repeating, "Same, same—only different!" so that you clearly know that these extras in the back are all the same as the display, only different. As they pressure you to buy, they pull more and more out of the stacks and repeat the phrase many times hoping that they come across the golden nugget in the piles.

At the same time all this is going on, usually the shopkeeper next door is standing in the front saying, "Same, same—only different," but the phrase takes on a new meaning because he is using it to try and convince you that while his wares may look the same as this booth's wares, they are different.

"I love this expression!" I think every time.

Probably because this statement takes my "serious" I.T. sales job and summarizes it into four simple words. I basically do what the shop owners do. I attempt to find what triggers an account's interest in my stacks of computers and laptops and then try to convince them that while my commodity product may look the same as the competition's, somehow it is different. India is just really obvious about the process.

The marketplace provides simple entertainment in other ways also. Like when I watch a woman swat at one of the sacred cows as it nabs a mouthful of fruit off her cart or when I halt to let a family of monkeys run in front of me, as they cross the street.

I love that I am able to appreciate and be a part of these small moments. Life is so dramatically different here!

One day, I decide to summarize how polar opposite Pushkar truly is from L.A. by describing my path from a temple back to town:

"Take the 1,000 stairs from the temple down to the bottom of the mountain, pass the family of angry monkeys that throw rocks and the tree full of green parrots all the way down to the fork in the road.

"Head right until you come to five camels tied to a tree. That is where you turn right. Don't go left or else you end up in another village!

"Keep right until you finally get to the white ashram. Ask permission to cut through because it will save you a good ten minutes. The yogis and guru there are very hospitable—even to travelers!

"You will end up by a big field. There isn't a trail, but keep heading through the field toward the grey temple and you will be moving in the right direction. Not the green, blue or white temple but the grey temple.

"Cut to the right until you get to the holy bridge by the lake. Don't forget to take your shoes off when you cross it! Follow along the water's edge until you get to the other side, over by the restaurant with the big bamboo awning.

"Oh, and watch out for the narrow alley that leads up to the bridge because you never know what is coming at you around the corner. I had to wedge myself into a doorway to miss getting trampled on by a herd of stampeding cattle one time.

"You have reached your destination."

Imagine my Garmin navigation system trying to show and say all that!

I maintain a slow pace of reading and relaxing for over a week and then get a bit antsy, so I enroll in a six day yoga course which lasts five hours a day. I have always wanted to learn more about authentic Indian yoga and this course offers the opportunity.

The jolly sprig of a yoga instructor is a man in his late twenties who studied in the Himalayas with true shaman and gurus. He is very focused on authentic, original yoga which is exactly what I want. We do yoga without mats, on braided rugs and even this small detail adds to the authentic feel.

There are six of us in the class, all from different countries and we have a great time. There are two sessions per day: two and a half hours in the morning, and then we convene again in the early evening for another two and a half hours.

I know it is that deep, ingrained branding from my Box driving me to do all this, but I immediately feel more at ease about staying another week in Pushkar, now that I have a daily agenda to follow and someplace I *need* to be. Michelle Bain: Professional Tourist/World Traveler is back to work.

First I go to class, then I have free time where I meet back up with Greg, Sunny and Lesa and go mountain hiking to see a temple or go to some event. Then, I leave them and head back for my second session of class. After that session, we all meet at the hotel and go somewhere to eat.

I walk the same route every day, back and forth to class. Within a few days, I am a regular on my route. Shopkeepers quit asking me if I want to look at their wares and exchange greetings and ask me about yoga class instead. I am into a life of routine, just like home in California and just like in Europe.

There is an elderly man with a long grey beard and white

clothes who always sits in front of a particular temple that I pass on my daily route. Each time I reach him, I stop, bow toward him with my hands together in prayer and say, "Namaste," which means "I bow to the God within you." He then does the same back to me. We do this every day without fail as part of my daily routine.

My agenda and timing flow smoothly until day number three. On this day, as I hike back from a temple between morning and afternoon sessions, I feel tension in my shoulders as I look at my watch. I am *late*. I speed up my walk and make it to the session right on time.

The fourth day, between sessions, we visit the hut of a guru. I check my watch in anticipation. "I didn't think this would take so long," I say to myself. I leave the others at the hut and start the long hike back at a quick pace, still following my normal path. I make it with a minute to spare. The tension of yesterday has spread from my shoulders to include my neck.

On day five, I find myself cutting through a farm to make it on time, alone again. The tension in my neck and shoulders grows as I hop over fences and run through the field. I make it, without being late.

Day six, graduation day from class, I am running so late from break time adventures that I actually have to jog my route to class. "Slowly" one shop owner calls as I cruise by. "Slowly" another man cries as I turn the corner at a fast clip. "Slowly" my jewelry friend yells to me as I rush by his shop in a blur. By the time I arrive at class, seven people have called out the exact same word to me. Seven!

During meditation this final session, there is only one word in my head—*slowly*. In a few short days, I have converted from a relaxed, slow paced person who is connected as a human being to her surroundings, into one who is stressed and rushed. It takes seven people yelling Gods message for me to finally realize that I have regressed into old behavior.

As I walk my daily route after class, contemplating my relapse, I come to the grey bearded yogi. "Namaste," I said to the old man, bowing with my hands in prayer as I always do. Instead of returning this usual blessing, he grabs my hands and holds them until I look up at his wrinkled brown face.

"Slowly, slowly . . . *always* slowly, slowly," are his words of prayer back to me this night instead.

Chapter 14:

No worries—Australia

"Forty television stations to choose from, all in English with American style commercials! Ten types of toothpaste to select from! Hot water by the gallons! Non-harassment window shopping! Fresh air in wide open parks of green grass! Electricity! I love you already Australia!" I exclaim in joy.

I skip along the sidewalk in Sydney, feeling fresh and alive. The warm air feels so good on my bare legs, now free from the conservative attire of India. I visit the famous Sidney Opera House and many other amazing sites, but find myself more fascinated by the abundance of product available in two aisles of the local drug store.

"I never noticed how many different types of shower gels are on the market before. I guess a little dose of deprivation does a person good," I think as I wander the store aisles and ogle over the endless options.

After a few days in Sydney, I catch my flight to Queensland. I only have three weeks in Australia and it's a large country so I decide to fly to my most important must-see destination. Even though my other fear is sharks, The Great Barrier Reef is the main reason I want to visit Australia. I am flying to Cairns, a "Reef Hub" where many tours launch, and then I'll work my way down the coast to Brisbane over the next few weeks. From there, I fly back to Sydney for my international flight to Fiji.

As I glance down at the Coral Sea from my small plane, I feel that old familiar urge to head to the beach so I can center myself before I tackle the sea. I need a day to relax on the beach with my toes in the sand so that I can psych myself up before I venture out into great unknown water adventures filled with scary things like sharks!

I am met with a disappointing blow. "What? There are no beaches in Cairns?" I reply in disbelief to the hotel help. Instead of sand leading into the water, there is marshy muck. They try to compensate by building a large man-made water lagoon, which is completely packed with every tourist in the city.

Move into acceptance, Michelle. Don't let a little thing like this get you down.

Instead of sulking, I let my disappointment get canceled out by the positive vibe that every person here seems to possess. From the hotel staff, to the locals I pass when in town—everyone I meet has a relaxed, positive energy about them.

I've heard the famous Australian expression, "No worries mate," in movies, but it is such a treat to hear people actually use it. It appears they also live by this philosophy. Their attitude is contagious, and soon any lingering disappointment is a distant thing in the past.

"Okay, so 'no worries' here, eh?" I say to myself. "How can I use this expression to help me face my shark paranoia and anxiety about the unknown in the ocean?"

I am part of the *Jaws* generation. Being the extremist that I am, I fed my fear of sharks until it grew into a massive phobia by the time I was ten years old. The crystal clear swimming pool in our own back yard was not even safe in my mind. A splash of my own foot had me out of the pool at lightning speed, as it still does today.

The big downfall of my phobia is that I love to waterski, especially in the fresh lakes of Michigan. As a teen, I would carve up the glass-surfaced water like a champ and then all of a sudden . . . the phobia would hit. My heart would start to race and my legs would shake as I glanced over my shoulder every few seconds ready to see a fin.

I think part of the reason I'm such a good water-skier today is because I'm too afraid to fall. Floating there, waiting for the boat to come around freaks me out. I am *sure* a fresh water shark is in the lake somewhere, ready to get me.

I will never forget the first time I ever went snorkeling. I was in Cancun on a jet-ski and I jumped off the jet-ski all set to snorkel . . . and landed right in a school of fish. I almost hyperventilated as the fish touched my legs, arms and body—sure that I was being attacked by a shark. I clambered back onto the jet-ski and was out of the water for the rest of the trip.

Gradually, the phobia did start to lessen a bit after some hypnotherapy, but not much. I am now able to get out on a surfboard in California but only when I see dolphins around. I figure if dolphins are near, then sharks probably aren't. That's my rule. If the dolphins leave, I am out of the water.

Needless to say, all of this has limited my ocean diving experiences so far in life. I am determined to conquer this fear by using the acclaimed underwater beauty of The Great Barrier Reef as my prize. From documentaries I have watched, it is the most beautiful diving area in the world and something worth overcoming old issues to see.

This is not fantasy land, I know my issues are not going to instantly disappear just because I want them to. They will be there, for sure. I need to have some serious ammunition ready to combat my thoughts so that I don't cave in to them and chicken out.

"Okay, back to this 'no worries' idea," I say as I lay in bed the night before my first scheduled dive. "I think I need to make up my own definition of what this expression represents. 'No worries' to me will mean that I have no reason to worry, whatsoever, because God has this situation under control and God won't let anything happen to me. God will meet me in the water and will not bring any friends with sharp teeth. There is nothing to worry about. God has it covered."

The next morning, I get on the boat, which is going to take me far from shore and dump me into the ocean. I repeat, "No worries. No reason to worry. Nothing to worry about. God's going to meet me there," over and over as the boat travels to the drop point and then repeat it again as I layer on scuba gear.

As I look down into the black sea from the exit platform, I say, "God's down there, just do it Michelle, let go. Go see God," then I step off.

As promised . . . God is there. Only God isn't simply there—God is suddenly *everywhere* as the world transforms into an underwater paradise. Tiny neon orange and purple fish jet back and forth while humongous silver fish slowly drift by. Seaweed and sea fans gracefully sway back and forth as the sea's current brushes against their flexible structures. Bright yellow coral juts out like cacti amid the vast stretch of lava-colored reef which expands as far as the eye can see across the sea floor.

A barren sand patch comes alive as a hidden fish materializes for a second before burying itself again under the soft sand. An eel peeks out of a reef crevice before slithering out fully and then disappearing into the dark waters. Pairs of barracuda hover in the distance as they decide if these human additions to their world are friend or foe.

Suddenly, like a freeway intersection in high traffic, dozens of fish appear in a frenzy of darting activity. The swirl of orange, yellow, blue, green, and silver is almost more than my eyes can keep up with. I look in every direction as quickly as I can as the brightly colored fish dart around and rush away.

All of this is God.

Our scuba group slowly moves toward a ledge. There is only darkness beyond and below as the sea bottom drops off into nothingness. I stare down from the edge into the endless abyss and then turn my gaze forward into the massive darkness ahead.

It feels like I am being absorbed by the immensity of this dark environment and the depth of the silence that surrounds me. I stare into the dark, almost mesmerized by its beauty. There is a calmness that invites me to join it.

This dark unknown is God too.

Then a quick thought breaks in about what could also be out there. I look around in alarm and am surprised to see the scuba guide floating next to me. I was so caught up in the darkness, I didn't even realize he was there. He gently grabs my hand and looks at me. Through his mask, I can see into his eyes. They say to me, "No worries."

As we head back to the group to enjoy and appreciate more of this colorful underwater nirvana, I feel like I have climbed with faith over yet another hurdle and it didn't require some big catalyst, like a striking snake, this time. It was more of a graceful glide over past beliefs and it left me knowing *I will never have to face the unknown alone. God is in all places, even the darkness.*

# # # #

Every place of interest in Queensland seems to involve either a boat, bus, all-terrain van, yacht or walking tour. Needless to say, I meet quite a few people in Australia, even some other serious travelers who have been all over the world. There are many hours of interactive conversation as I hike through rainforests, camp on Fraser Island, and snorkel in the beautiful reefs of Whitsunday Island.

I notice that I keep things very superficial when it's my turn to talk, telling much about my travels but little about my life. It's my way of stopping them from asking questions about my future which I have no answers for.

When conversations manage to break past the present into the future, I feel bombarded by the worry their questions spark. "So, you quit your job before you left? What are you going to do when you go home? Where are you going to live? What about money?" they ask. The gigantic knot in my stomach grows. I only have a few weeks before I return and then I will be face-to-face with my old reality again.

Seeds of financial insecurity become planted and start to frequent my thoughts. "I spent every ounce of the money I had delegated for this trip and so now I am going into debt," I acknowledge. "I only have the little cash I set aside for return start-up, which is not going to last more than a month or so."

"Keep the faith, Michelle!" I remind myself in a Chris voice. "You have been provided with everything you needed on this trip. Why does that have to stop when you get back to the States? Do you think that attracting what you need and staying in faith are only possible when you travel?"

Is that what this is all about? Do I fear that everything I learned while away will instantly disappear when I set foot back in the States? Am I afraid I will lose sight of all the new ideal qualities I have discovered?

With all the tours, I started to skip quite a few of my normal meditation sessions. As my concerns grow, I begin to meditate again and spend more quiet time alone, opting to focus on connection with God instead of gallivanting off on yet another tour.

It is important that I focus on visualizing a happy ending to all of this.

I also begin to write in my journal daily as I brainstorm future options. Career is causing me a dilemma because although I discovered my true calling in Spain, it has been many months since that revelation and a part of me is in doubt now. Plus, I need something that is going to pay the bills right away.

I decide to dust off what I know about the Law of Attraction and put it into good use as I write down a list of things I want to attract when I get home.

<u>What I want to manifest upon my return:</u>
1. A job making as much money as I used to, that does not involve a large learning curve, so I can focus on a plan to move into a writing career.
2. An apartment in Santa Monica, so I'm closer to freeways to

reduce driving and because it has creative and tourist energy.
3. Some major action toward my writing career.
4. To be by the beach so that the serenity of the ocean is near.
5. Enough money to pay off the trip debt within three months.
6. To continue to love myself and to win the ego battle. Not to get caught back up into materialism.
7. Serenity within this all, so I still live in Faith not Fear and stay outside of my Box.

This is my list of seven goals which I keep simple and focused on short-term. With my list, I return back to morning visualization habits and spend a good hour getting into the feeling place of each goal coming true, because I know this is an essential part.

"When I get a job, it is so effortless. I step off the plane and there it is! Not only that, I hop in and take off—easy as can be. I have so much time to write because I don't have to train!

"Ah, sitting at night behind the computer writing is so great! Creativity flows like water. Money flows like water too! It's no problem to afford a place by the beach in Santa Monica and to pay off my debt. And the energy of Santa Monica—I love it! I meet creative people every day and build an entire new network of friends who support the creative side of life. Actors, playwrights, other writers—it will be so different from my old life!

"I am so stress-free, how fantastic! What I really enjoy is continuing to grow as a loving, giving, helpful, creative woman who loves herself and others unconditionally. I shoot love out of my eyes like laser beams! Everyone I meet wants to help me as I strive to be the best me imaginable. Forget materialism and ego, I'm in love with life and me!"

Every day, I visualize this and say, "God, with Your universal laws, please help make it all happen!" Then I run through a list of all the wonderful things I have to be grateful about before I enjoy the day splashing in the water, hiking through the rainforests, or watching the surfers at the beach. At night, I read the list again and go to sleep with a smile.

Soon, the stress grows less and the knot of anxiety is smaller. I have faith that it will all take care of itself somehow.

No worries, Michelle, no worries . . .

Chapter 15:
Inspiration—Fiji

"Only four days left. Four days. Almost six months have gone by and it seems like it has been a day. So many countries, so many languages, so many cities, so many sites, so many people!" I think as I lay alone on the beach in Nadi.

"I have seen the world and I have achieved my dream. Wow. Thank You God. Thank You for being there with me. Thank You for showing me how good people are. Thank You for keeping me safe. Thank You for all the joy and happiness of each day. Thank You for teaching me so many lessons about life and about myself. Thank You for self-love," sings my heart with gratitude.

"I love the wonderful world of opportunity that You provide and I promise to always be grateful for the small things in life and not to take these gifts for granted. I will cherish life, slow down and enjoy it to the fullest. I will hold onto what really matters, not to what I used to value.

"Please give me the strength to stay on path so that I always feel the joy and happiness I feel today. Please help me to be the most loving, giving person I can be and to spread joy and faith to others. Please show me how I can give this beautiful gift I have received back to others, so that they, too, know that life is about faith not fear and that dreams can come true," are my silent prayers.

# # # #

I do nothing for my four days in Fiji but lie on a deserted beach, listen to the soft, warm waves as they gently roll onto the shore, and contemplate my journey and my future.

There is an email I received my last day in Australia that occupies my attention. Partially, because I am in awe that I could already have received a solution to List Item #1, but also because I am not sure I want to accept this as the solution. The email is from Chris telling me that my old job is open.

I asked for a same-pay, no-training-required job and here it is.

"Could I take this job I used to dread, approach it with a fresh service-based outlook and find joy and gratitude in it this time? I would be able to get an apartment without issue if I had a job. Plus, rumor has it that the big sale I walked away from is back on the table. I might knock out my debt and have time to write. With all of this in mind, do I give it another try?" I ask the waves.

"But I was miserable! What about writing? Sure, I won't have to train but I still worked eighty hours a week. How will I make this all happen? Will I even be good at writing? It's so dramatically different from my old professional sales and marketing world. Can I make the transition? Will I succeed?" I ask again.

I wish I had a sign!

A man and woman stroll up during my game of mental ping-pong. They are the only people who have passed by me in the last two days. After a pleasant conversation, they invite me to join them for lunch at their hotel, which I eagerly accept. My thought pattern is hauntingly familiar and I need a break from it before it continues to spiral. I can almost see the old mechanical arms reaching out for me.

Their distraction could not have come at a better time.

We all sit down and start friendly lunch conversation. Danial is energetic, talkative and full of positive vibes. The couple explain that their visit from Australia to Fiji is only for a few days and is more for a visa reason than a vacation. I tell them that I am in the last two days of a six month trip and what an adventure it has been.

The usual questions come up about "What are you going to do now?" I laugh and explain how my old job is available and that my manager wants to meet with me as soon as I return.

"How spot-on!" Danial exclaims.

I agree it fits my needs in many ways and then find myself explaining how "work equaled identity" to me before and how miserable I was at the job in the past.

"Besides the things it fills on my List, it might be good growth for me to have the opportunity to approach my old job with a new self to see what that produces," I add. "It's like a do-over."

"If I am really honest though, my heart is somewhere else already. I discovered on my trip that I am meant to be something else. I don't know when I am supposed to head down that new path," I explain without mentioning my new path is to be a writer. Verbalizing all of this information aloud has triggered my ego and suddenly I am hesitant to tell others about my writing dream in case I sound stupid.

Danial proceeds to tell me, "Michelle, I had a great career for many years in Hollywood as a stuntman. I met so many people and had a wonderful time and was very successful and made a great income. I gave it up a while back to pursue my dream and I am the happiest I have ever been. I write books and screen plays now and I love it. I have books on the market and am producing my first film. This life is incredible!"

I choke on my soup. The hairs on my arms stand on end.

What are the chances that I only meet two people on the entire island, and one is a man who gave up his old career to be a writer . . . my exact dream? This has to be God talking to me through someone again!

"That is what I am meant to do too!" I exclaim, suddenly rejuvenated by faith.

We spend the next hour talking about how he made the transition and brainstorming writing ideas we both have. I am so encouraged! Danial doesn't think my dream is silly because he shares my dream. He understands the fears that are now zinging at me about changing careers and provides proof through his example that I can also meet with success.

I feel his happiness and excitement about writing surge through my own veins. A talk with someone who has "Been there, done that" is so inspirational and helps me choose to stay on the path of faith.

It is my turn to receive an angel sent by God.

Right when I desperately need added strength to help me feed positive energy to my new idea, my angel arrives with direction, guidance and inspiration. My heart is vigorously renewed with faith that writing is my purpose. *When* is no longer important. I will start to build a strong foundation so that when the time is right for my new dream to come true, I will be ready to walk the path with confidence.

I rush into town to search for a book Danial recommends, which focuses on utilizing the power of positive thinking and the subconscious mind. I want to read it on the flight home but the selection of bookstores in Nadi proves slim. I surrender to the fact that I might have to wait to read it until I return.

The next day at the airport, I'm early so I stop and browse at the small magazine stand. As I peruse the covers, something catches my attention. On the shelf sits a single copy of the book Danial recommended . . . waiting there, just for me.

LAP II

CALIFORNIA SHOWS ME THE WAY

Chapter 16:
Depression and Isolation—Santa Monica

Astronaut Buzz Aldrin said in his autobiography, "After walking on the moon, everything else in life seemed insignificant." My trip around the world was not as monumental as a walk on the moon, but now that I am back, I definitely understand what he felt. Normal life seems completely insignificant in comparison to my months of adventure and discovery.

In commitment to my List, I find a great apartment in Santa Monica next to 3rd Street Promenade, so that I am close to freeways and tourist activity. The beach is across the road so I can resume my daily runs by the ocean.

This city is one of the few that still honors rent control, so it hosts a neat mix of residents. Some of my new neighbors are elderly and have lived here for ages, while others sublet as they struggle to get their foot in the door of the entertainment industry. The vibration here is exactly what I hoped it would be when I added it to my List.

What I really love about Santa Monica is that I am far away from my Box and the negative memories generated by those old behaviors and beliefs. I'm alone in this new place, just like I was when I traveled, which makes a tiny part of me feel like the adventure hasn't ended yet. I have an undisturbed, commitment-free start since my old life in Redondo Beach is a forty-minute freeway commute in stop-and-go traffic, which places me conveniently out of reach.

"Why are you moving so far away?" Karen asks when I tell her I found an apartment in Santa Monica.

"When my cravings for accents and foreign languages become too overwhelming, I can walk a few blocks to the Promenade and get a quick tourist fix," I explain. "I need that. I need less drive time if I go back to the old job. I need a fresh start. Santa Monica is ideal."

I don't tell her the truth: that I don't want to move back to Redondo Beach because I feel like my Box is there, ready and waiting to lure me back into a world of rigid structure, strict agendas, egotism, judgment, materialism and fear of failure. Nor do I tell her that, after being alone for so long, I simply can't stand the idea of being around people.

"If you move to Redondo, your old friends will ask you to go places and do things and expect you to call them back when they reach out. They are like vacuums ready to suck up the last of your freedom. Don't let your freedom get sucked away!" my mind selfishly cries. "You still want to do what you want, when you want, not make and keep commitments. You want to be alone—run away!"

Each time my cell phone rings, I cringe and let it go to voicemail. "They are trying to steal your freedom," my mind accuses, "Don't become a slave again; stay free—don't pick up!" Isolation and avoidance of anything related to my old world are my new paths in Santa Monica. I justify my absence to others with the handy excuse, "I live far away now. Plus, I need time to acclimate and space to adjust back into reality."

What I'm really saying is, "Leave me alone! I don't want to adjust. I don't want reality. I don't want to be around people. I only want to sulk and wallow undisturbed in a state of depression while I live in the memories of my trip."

Each morning, I drag myself out of bed and look out the window, with the hope that some gorgeous cathedral or castle has miraculously replaced the apartment complex next door during the night. "Same boring building still there," I moan before I climb back into bed, completely dejected. "There is nothing outside but another average day."

What if I can't do this? What if I never adjust to living a normal life again and I spend every day longing for the past in a total isolated depression?

What if the lack of excitement and adventure leaves such a void in my existence that I function in a complete state of discontent for the rest of my days?

I have been here before, in a place where I reek of discontent and non-acceptance of what is. A place where depression comes and shatters the lenses in my rose colored glasses, smashing them like a soccer ball to the face. A place where only grey lenses exist, which zero in on all that isn't right and see the world as mundane and boring. A place where gratitude is non-existent because my vision is too clouded by hazy darkness.

Santa Monica? Redondo Beach? They are just geography. I know *exactly* where I am . . . *I am back inside my Box.*

# # # #

"Same, same—only different." My favorite expression from India now sounds like a curse.

Same possessions. When I unload my things out of storage, I feel no gratitude, only repulsion. Each item reminds me of thousands of hours wasted working late and hours of joy sacrificed—all to buy a bunch of material stuff I can obviously live without since I did for so many months. I hold a massive garage sale. I have the same feeling about the sports car and sell it also.

"If I get rid of things that symbolize my old, materialistic, ego-driven self, then I won't become that person again," seems to be my strategy for escape this time.

"Baby, it's an inside job. It has nothing to do with stuff," Karen says over the phone, but I continue with determination to seek more ways to purge my old self.

Same job. After weeks, I decide I have to do something besides lay in bed all day hoping for a miracle outside my window, so I go back to my old job. Even though it is logical to return, in my state of depression, I still need convincing before I make the final decision.

"You said you wanted an opportunity at a do-over," Karen points out, "to see if you have a different experience by bringing a different attitude to the same environment. Not that I would tell you what to do, but this *is* a chance."

Yes, I did express exactly this idea to her before.

"Won't it be easy too? Isn't that what you want so you can focus on writing?" Chris reminds me.

Yes, I do want easy and no training like I wrote on my List in Australia.

"Haven't you used up almost all your return funds?" my mom asks when I call her. "Why wouldn't you take it?"

Yes, I am in debt, almost out of money and have constant stress about lack of finances.

So why is it so hard to make this decision when there are so many reasons to say 'yes'? One reason—fear of failure. Only this time, it isn't the fear of failing at the job that strikes at my ego, it is the fear of failing at being a different person.

What if I'm not able to succeed at a do-over and end up miserable again? Now that I'm no longer Michelle Bain: Professional Tourist/World Traveler, I'm petrified that I'll fail to change my attitude and that my past thoughts will run me down the unhappy path of destruction again.

In the end, the financial anxiety blaring at me triumphs, not some last-minute burst of faith in my ability to overcome old ways. With a heavy heart, I take the job and hope for the best. Yes, I am back in my Box with fear and negativity as my motivators once again. Karen is right—there is no amount of stuff I can sell and no amount of distance I can place between my old and new life that can stop my past ways from finding me.

Same possessions, same job—only a different me? It appears not, because wherever I go . . . there I am.

\# \# \# \#

"I *will* be different, no, I *must* be different!" I declare to myself with as much conviction as I can muster from my state of utter discontent. I am running along the beach, engaged in my new morning mental struggle between old and new. "I can't go through such an adventure and come back only to be the same woman both inside and out. I have to hold onto the lessons and change!"

It has been a few months since my return and I am already back to working over sixty-five hours a week at my old job. I sit in traffic now and reminisce about the shining memories of the past and complain about the miserable reality of today.

I daydream about writing and have no excitement about my old job. My "be grateful and treat work as an opportunity to be of service" idea has flown straight out the window. I am an in-debt paycheck worker—that's all.

Besides the stress of winning sales and hitting quotas, there is a new challenge this time around. There are rumors that the company might be sold and many employees are on edge because usually there are staff reductions with a sale. My ego is determined that I will not be cut and demands that I take more action to prove myself indispensable. My old machine-mentality returns to implement my ego's plan.

"I have to change my attitude before I hit some point of no return. I have to find a way to escape my Box here in California," I think as I jog. Since I gave up meditation in my depression, I search for all of the whispers of hope somewhere else and remember the statement "attitude of gratitude" from some of my past readings.

I have a flashback to Italy and my gratitude lists and how wonderful it felt to read the lists and to carry them with me. "This is action I can take here! Starting today, I will do gratitude lists while I run," I decide as my new plan.

"I'm grateful that I had safe travels and a safe return. I'm grateful I found a place to live quickly. I'm grateful to have my own transportation, versus buses, trains and metros. I'm really grateful that I don't have to wear the same tee-shirt every day for a week," I list. Gratitude cracks a window open and allows a little fresh air to drift in.

"Instead of reliving memories, why don't you make more effort to bring your experiences into your life here?" Chris recommends as an added action idea.

"I have been thinking about exactly that," I agree, "but I was too bogged down by depression to take action before. Now that gratitude is helping me see through the grey fog a bit, I might be able to move forward with that idea!"

I stay aware and look for opportunities. For instance, I find myself cursing traffic and remember how cold it was on that bus ride in India and switch to thoughts of gratitude instead. In a rush at the grocery store, I almost leave before I let "Whit's yer hurry?" pop into my mind and instead I slow down enough to notice the cashier's tag and thank her by name.

On my morning runs, as my mind starts to race through my daily agenda, I feel my pace automatically respond as it quickens in anticipation. I stop myself and remember, "Slowly, slowly . . . always slowly, slowly," so that I turn off my mental to-do list and enjoy the fresh air and the sound of the seagulls and ocean waves instead.

I especially nurture self-love, since I am back in the land of glitz and glamour. Perfectionism hasn't struck yet, but I know it's there somewhere, lurking in a corner. To cut it off in advance, I bring back Project Love and remember to recognize and appreciate my finer qualities: my energy, intelligence, talents, business skills, beauty and courage for going after my dream. I laugh about the pre-trip hair drama and how insignificant that all was.

I take small actions with writing as well. I complete the *Artist Way* program which helps open up new channels of creativity and provides tools for overcoming obstacles I will encounter as an artist. I buy books about writing and purchase a program for my computer. I start outlines for books I will write and talk about writing with people I know and trust, who help inspire my dream.

I dedicate time to understanding the subconscious mind and attend a live Esther and Jerry Hicks seminar on Law of Attraction. When I let it, The Law of Attraction continues to work wonderfully in my life: almost everything on my <u>List</u> has come to fruition. Only two things remain incomplete: #5—enough money to pay off the debt and #7—serenity within where I live in faith not fear and stay out of my Box.

My work hard mentality is back, ready to make #5 happen. "Don't forget, things can happen without psychotic amounts of effort!" I remind myself, but my old message still overpowers and the number of work hours continues to increase.

The monster battle to win #7 feels nearly impossible, especially since I have already been dragged back inside my old mental world. Gratitude lists and positive actions may crack more windows but the dark, stagnant air of depression still dominates and old negative thoughts still echo loudly inside.

"I am seriously going to lose my mind if I have to do this boring, stressful job one more day, Karen," I cry. "Then it sounds like you still have some work to do on attitude adjustment," Karen responds.

I know this is true—I am trapped in negativity again and feed it on a daily basis. The battle against my pessimistic thoughts just feels too overwhelming to conquer. My concern about being cut in a company downsize continues to grow, which fuels my relentless drive to win. There is no joy or happiness, only a driving goal to pay off debt and the fantasy of running away.

In desperation, I break out of isolation and reach out to one of my other friends. "You need to go to this seminar offered by a company called PSI. The introductory course, *The Basic*, is only a weekend long and it changed our lives," my friend recommends. "It dives into all areas of self and will help you see the messages your mind creates and why. You have to do it! Call this guy right away," she says and then rattles off a phone number.

I call, because I am desperate for anything that might pull me out of this harmful spin-cycle. Ironically, PSI has a *Basic* seminar which starts in two days and the director finds a scholarship for me so I can go for free. "Hope for escape is within my grasp," I tell Chris who decides to go with me. "I will get technical tools to use toward a mental change, since worldly experiences obviously aren't enough!"

There are a few hundred people which attend and the entire seminar is about personal issues, self-growth, unlimited potential and how to make every situation a win-win for all people involved. For three days, I am surrounded by people striving to make a difference in their lives. I meet some amazing men and women and the awareness of the importance of people is brought back into my consciousness.

The Basic doesn't get me out of my Box, but it definitely throws open all the shades so that light enters. I walk away knowing that my period of self-centered aloneness has to end. When I isolate, I become fixated on my issues because that is all there is inside to focus on. A life that revolves only around me keeps me trapped in a dark, depressed and lonely world.

It may <u>appear</u> to be easier without people and commitments, but life sure becomes a miserable place when I make the choice to isolate.

My emotions feel raw and overworked after all of the exercises and discussions, although on the outside I still look calm and cool. At the wrap-up, I sit like a zombie and stare at the stage as people go up and discuss what they've learned. "I might have a new awareness about my need of people, but I'm way too chicken to be that emotionally vulnerable in front of them," I joke with Chris.

There is one guy in particular that I take notice of onstage. Paul is a 6'4" tall, well-built man with wavy dark-blonde hair who has amazing dimples when he smiles. When he speaks, this wonderful accent flows from his lips (after my travels, I'm a sucker for an accent). My first thought as he walks on stage is, "What a good looking guy."

Paul starts to talk but quickly stops as he chokes back tears. Some searing pain in his soul seizes him. I can feel his hurt all the way from the middle of the room and my heart leaps up into my throat. There he stands, vulnerable and exposed. With each sob, I feel compassion surge through me.

There is a level of respect I instantly have for him, because he is able to risk pride and show emotions in front of strangers with a courage I do not possess. Light might shine into my darkness now, but I am still inside where the voice of my ego says, "No one can see my cracks, even in a self-help seminar where it is almost expected."

But my compassion does flow inside somewhere too. I feel it as I watch Paul and also sense this feeling of envy swirling around inside me.

He is so in-touch with his heart.

Paul's tears subside enough for him to finally tell his story. It involves a marriage that is ending, three young children, old childhood wounds and lost dreams. I look over at Chris and joke, "Someone needs to save that poor guy."

His life might be a mess but he has one thing I envy—a strong connection to his heart. I want that!

On the way home, Chris and I talk about why I allow the shades in my Box to be pulled down. "If I am uncharacteristically honest, Chris, I can hide in the dark," I attempt to explain. "I can hide from my true calling—and the unknown world of myself as a writer—and use debt as an excuse for why it's not time to write yet. Sometimes there is a comfort in hiding and allowing myself to live in self-delusion. Even though it is dysfunctional, I guess sometimes I *want* to live in the darkness inside my Box, away from the light."

It is as if God hears my confession and decides to do for me what I cannot do for myself . . .

My customer that had the multi-million dollar deal I almost

postponed my trip for receives funding. I win the deal and make enough commission to pay off my debt. Next, my company makes the formal announcement that it is selling our sales division. I have no more excuses to hide behind. God has flung the door to my Box wide open.

I will have to shelf learning to treat a job as an opportunity for service until later. Right now, the time has come for me to step out of my Box again and go after another dream. It's time to explore the world of Michelle Bain: Professional Writer!

Chapter 17:
Trusting Intuition—Portugal Return

"You know you can do this right? You're going to be a fantastic writer and I'm so proud of you already for going after this dream!" Chris says as last words of encouragement and support as she hugs me goodbye.

"I believe you," I reply with a huge grin and a gigantic hug, ever grateful for my best friend. She is dropping me off at my beloved LAX International Terminal so that I can fly overseas to Portugal to start my future as a writer. After six months in California trapped back in Box mentality, I am free again to enjoy the exciting new possibilities my future may hold.

I have about a million butterflies fluttering around in my stomach! Ah, the lovely country of Portugal awaits me ... the place which captured my heart only a year ago. I remember when I set foot on Portuguese land and instinctively knew I would return again someday and when I returned, it would be for a significant reason. I was right! Here I am, heading to The Algarve, the beautiful Southern Coast of Portugal, where I will spend a month writing my very first book.

Quitting my old job the second time was much easier than the first. Partly because I wasn't facing a dilemma over a huge potential sale, but also because leaving allowed me to run from the whole "work as service" idea which I was failing at. For now, my focus has shifted to how I might help others through books.

The big win and sale of my division were much needed reminders about the existence of God, an important thing I forgot when I returned to California. With renewed faith, I leap into the unknown again with God by my side.

My plan for the next thirty days incorporates what I learned in Ireland; while I have a writing schedule typed up, I do not have a list of selected cities or sites so I can be flexible and go with the flow about travel.

I have to pick up where I left off on my trip around the world and learn to balance and adjust old and new ways. It's the balance that makes all the difference versus the extreme tendencies I default to. Things like schedules can be good but flexibility has to be the predominant factor.

A few weeks ago, I did an online seminar themed *How to Write a Book in Thirty Days,* which is how I came up with my thirty day overseas writing deadline. Tucked away in my trusted travel suitcase is my Book Schedule (September/October month-at-a-glance calendar pages where each day has a designated chapter title filled in that corresponds with my book outline). If I stick to this schedule, I will have a completed book by the time I return to Santa Monica.

My initial idea is to travel along the Algarve Coast and hit as many cities as possible, starting in Faro. After landing, I catch a cab to my hotel, throw down my things and head out to explore the town. I quickly realize my old way of city-hopping is not going to work.

"Day two: here I am with some great information to tell people about the city of Faro, but I haven't even opened my laptop to work on my book. Now, I'm on a bus on my way to Albufeira!" I write in my journal. "Changing cities and exploring isn't going to work; not if I want a completed book."

I guess my go with the flow challenge has shown up differently than expected. I thought it would be about which cities to visit, but instead it is showing up as a big decision: to travel or to write!

"The Algarve will have to wait for another visit," I say as I decide to plant myself in Albufeira for the rest of the trip so I can focus on writing.

"This place is ideal," I declare the minute I enter the hotel. "Exactly what I need for undistracted writing," I think as I look around the small, plain room with only a double bed, old wood desk and chair, bathroom and small balcony. An unplugged television is mounted in the corner (which I intend to keep that way) and there is only internet access in the lobby.

What the room lacks in décor, it makes up for in view. From my little balcony, I can see the city and the turquoise waters beyond. The rooftop pool has a spectacular view of the ocean and the hotel sits in a quiet, residential part of town. The icing on the cake is that since I am here after tourist season and staying a considerable length of time, the hotel manager is able to negotiate a much lower rate for me.

Now settled, I quickly develop an informal, non-written Daily Agenda to go along with my Book Schedule. Every morning, I rise early to the warm ocean breeze that softly enters the room. I sit up in bed and bask in the tranquility of my quiet surroundings. Then I meditate and visualize for a half hour.

A forty minute run along the hilly, cobblestone walkways of Albufeira starts my blood flowing as I explore Old Towne or the Marina. On the way back, there's a quick stop at the small family owned grocery around the corner, where I pick up my daily breakfast of yogurt and bananas. I eat and drink tea on my balcony before heading to the pool to catch an hour of sun. After that, I stop and grab a fresh meat-filled pastry from the local deli to eat later for lunch.

I return to the hotel about 11:30 a.m., flip open my laptop, plunk down at the desk and write for the next 10-15 hours. This is a simple way to live for almost a month but it is glorious.

"Writing is glorious too!" I say from a heart brimming with joy. As the words flow like water from a fast running spout, I gain confidence.

I really am supposed to be a writer!

Each day, I start fresh with a new chapter and a little prayer, "God, please let the words flow from You to me, so that I'm able to pass Your messages along to anyone who reads this book. It is with complete thankfulness that I write this. Faith is what made it all happen." I feel my connection to God again and the serenity that was missing in California wraps around me like a warm blanket.

"I'm so glad I decided to listen to all the people I ran into throughout my trip and write a book about my travels," I think with gratitude. "So many memories; they are clear in my mind, fresh as if they happened yesterday. What an incredible trip," I sigh as I reminisce about those months. "The stories and events formulate almost by themselves into great lessons for me to pass on. Like each chapter is a mini story of its own!"

"Gosh, I get what Chris meant when I told her some of these stories. Some sound almost unreal. Yet, it all really happened to me. I'm so lucky!" I smile and say as I type.

Sometimes as I write, I wander down a wrong path and get into too much detail but it seems I almost instinctively recognize when I head off track. Something guides me back and I quickly delete the section and move onto the next thought that enters my head.

Each evening, I review what I write, make minor changes and adjustments, and close up for the day between 11:00 p.m. to 1:00 a.m., happy and content. Then I wake up the next day and start all over again, filled with excitement and joy.

Every once in a while if I am ahead of schedule for the day, I take off for a few hours in the afternoon or early evening and wander around Old Towne or go down to the beach. An occasional gelato break is essential sometimes to rejuvenate the ol' travel taste buds. Portugal has the absolute *best* banana-chocolate gelato—highly addictive.

Old Towne Albufeira has a quaint feel. As I look down at it from the bluff, the white stucco buildings and terra-cotta tiled roofs look like piles of seashells tumbling toward the ocean. Proud, bright blue chimneys jut out from each one, as if to break up the monotony. Narrow cobblestone roads wind between a variety of tourist shops and restaurants in town. All these roads look similar to me and it's easy to get lost. Fortunately, the town is not large and the ocean is always handy as a southern guide point.

The shop owners I meet are very hospitable and extremely friendly, especially since it is late September. They tell me that in August, every seat is taken, every room is filled, and every spot on the beach is occupied as Albufeira transforms into a very hectic European vacation environment. It's hard for me to visualize because there is such a relaxed atmosphere here right now.

One day in town, I happen across a fruit smoothie stand where an energetic man from Ireland is busy cutting up apples, oranges and strawberries. He has a contagious smile, so I decide to take a little longer break than usual to enjoy a smoothie.

He introduces himself as George, and we start with small-talk about smoothies and such. Within three minutes we catapult straight into deep, heartfelt conversations about following dreams. He is an unguarded man, open and willing to share his experiences with me. George explains that after fifteen years of marriage, he is recently divorced. Through the process, his perception about life changed and he decided to quit the job he worked for 20 years so he could move to Portugal to open this stand.

"One thing I realize is how short life is. There are so many things I put off until the future because I wanted security in the present, but how secure is life really? Life can change in an instant," George explains. "Today all I want to be able to say is, 'I gave it a try,' instead of, 'I wish I would have'. It's hard for most people to understand. My family thinks I'm crazy but I had to have a-go at it. Do you know what I mean?"

Boy, do I ever.

This conversation with George plants many seeds in my mind, new seeds of possibility I hadn't considered before. The main seed really taking root during my runs is this burning desire to live part of the year right here, in Albufeira.

Automatically, old thoughts try to jump in to squash the idea. My gripping fear of commitment reaches out, "That is crazy. You move every year and don't even own a place in California because you can't commit. How in the world are you going to bring yourself to commit to something in another country?"

I sprint faster up the hill as I attempt to outrun the arm that is about to clamp onto me.

Stop the negative. Play a "what if" game instead, Michelle. Fantasize about positive outcomes!

"What if I throw away the word 'crazy' and consider 'possible' instead?" I ask on the run back. I have an odd sense of déjà vu. My run feels familiar today, like I am back in time when I had another big decision to make involving risky dreams.

"What do I see if I look through the eyes of possibility?" I continue. "I see a city where I feel serenity and joy, where written words flow freely from me. A city that is by an airport that flies to many places in Europe. A city that has a large tourist market."

A city that has my heart!

"So let's say I bought a place, how would that work?" I ask as I continue my run along the coast. "Well, I could live here part of the year when I want to write, and then maybe rent it out or something the rest of the time. Or house swap with people around the world so I could stay in other countries." The excitement of these ideas gives me instant goose bumps!

"I'm sentimentally attached to Albufeira because it's where I started my writing career. Besides that, it just feels good here—like home. I can easily see myself returning regularly to write many pages for many years. There's no coincidence that I landed here to start my dream. I think it's meant to be!" I exclaim.

"You've never owned a house before! You have no clue how much houses cost here or about the buying process in Portugal!" my mind strikes out with obstacles and challenges.

"I don't care. It feels right so I'm going to explore the idea," I fire back from behind my shield of enthusiasm. "I don't have to buy this trip, but I *can* research and explore. My rough draft is on track with only a couple of chapters left, so I have a few hours per day I can afford to spend gathering data. If I find a realtor's office, I can at least glance at some postings to get a general idea about cost. If cost fits, I can return home, save some money, and come back later to do some serious house hunting."

"I'll have to look for a real estate office tomorrow. Right now, I need to finish my run so I can start working on today's chapter!" I remind myself.

After my jog through the marina, I head up the hill. I pass the Centro Commercial, a small block of businesses facing inward toward a central square. I always skip the center because I'm all sweaty, opting to jog around it instead. Today, I see something that stops me short. At the bottom of the stairs leading up to the square is a sign that says "Realtor."

How many times have I passed this same sign in the last few weeks?

Sweat and all, I decide it's worth a few minutes to start the investigation, especially since my first task *is* to find a real estate office. I venture up the stairs and sure enough, there is an office with postings spread across the window. My stomach jumps.

A block from my hotel! What are the chances?

The photos of the exteriors are beautiful and there are a variety of prices.

This dream could really happen!

"Excuse me, I see you are looking at the postings. Are you visiting Albufeira?" I hear a voice say.

I look up and see a dark-haired Portuguese woman dressed in a slim skirt and white blouse standing in the doorway. Suddenly, I am very conscious of my tight stretchy workout shorts and my shirt that is drenched in sweat. "I was going to sneak up and take a quick glance at the postings," I think in embarrassment. "No one was supposed to see me."

"Um, yes—I'm visiting," I answer. "Actually, I'm here to write a book. I don't really know if I'm interested in houses. More curious I would say."

"Why don't you come in for a second? We have many houses in our office catalog, in case you decide you might be interested," she offers in a friendly, non-threatening way.

"Oh no, I could never come in like this!" I protest, very aware of how dreadful I must look and smell.

"Please," she persists, "do not feel uncomfortable. My name is Nalia. I'm the only one here in the office and I'm the office manager, not a sales person, if that makes you feel more comfortable."

It doesn't make me feel any more comfortable, but I decide to go in anyway. "I'm in a foreign country and will probably never see this woman again," I reason with myself. "Why let ego stop me from gathering the information I need when it's standing before me, ready to be passed along?"

We take a seat and I inform her that if I were looking, I would like the place to be close to Old Towne and that it needs to be on the lower end of the price scale. She pulls open the book and one of the very first photos I see is a bungalow with brick arches and an old wooden door with a wrought iron knocker.

I can't believe my eyes! That iron knocker and those beautiful arches are things I always visualized that my future dream home would have.

"Tell me a little about this house," I ask calmly, trying to keep my poker face in place so that I don't reveal the excitement I feel after seeing those beautiful arches.

"Why don't I show it to you?" she recommends instead. "It's very close. Come, we can walk and I will tell you about it on the way," she smoothly suggests. I find myself following her down the cobble stone sidewalk. Eventually, we enter a small gated yard and take the cobblestone walkway up to that gorgeous old wood door with the wrought iron knocker.

Nalia cranks the brass skeleton key and pushes the old wooden door open. Before I even step foot inside I see a beautiful wood burning fireplace and the layers of brick archways which grace the entry and kitchen. Off in the distance, an ornate wrought iron banister leads up to yet another brick archway.

I don't even need a tour beyond the front door to know this bungalow is my dream home . . . and that I will do whatever it takes to make it my own.

# # # #

"If something is meant to be, it will happen effortlessly," I remind myself as I reluctantly leave the bungalow.

If this house is meant to be mine, it will happen effortlessly, just like my first trip abroad.

The number of things accomplished over the next few days is nothing short of miraculous. It turns out that the home is actually owned by the realtor who runs the office. The place has been in his family for generations. He inherited it upon marriage but unfortunately, there was a divorce. The house has been tied up in litigation for almost two years and it just became available, which missed tourist season.

Desperate to sell so they can finalize the divorce, he is willing to knock down the price. As the past owner, he is able to give me specific details about plumbing, construction, electric wiring and appliance installation.

It is a beautiful place with plenty of room for family and friends. It is also over my original budget, but as visions of the arches dance before me, I vow not to let a little thing like *money* stop me.

The office deals with many out-of-town home buyers and is able to easily explain non-resident purchase requirements. I secure a wonderful lawyer, meet with a bank and file initial paperwork all in a single day.

The next day, I hit local stores to see furniture options and prices so I can estimate cost. While shopping, I run across another real estate office and do a little extra investigating to confirm the information I received is valid. Prices are accurate, especially for the area and so I grow more excited than ever.

Solutions seem to be everywhere at this point. It turns out my realtor/seller is part of a family business. His sister runs the rental division and supplies me with rental rates and places to advertise, should I decide to rent. They also offer property management so I leave with these fees as well.

I sit on my bed that night, exhausted but completely giddy with excitement, sorting through stacks of information and rapidly plugging numbers into spreadsheets.

I never thought it was possible to accomplish so much in so little time!

I calculate different scenarios and the numbers seem to work. "I think I can really make this happen," I conclude in joy.

"But you don't even have a job to go home to and only have a little buffer left in the bank. What if this is the biggest mistake you ever make?" my head chimes in as I pace the room.

Maybe it's time to break out the cell phone that hasn't been turned on yet this trip, and make a few calls home. But first, I need a moment to myself. I need some fresh air!

I throw on my shoes and head out for a walk . . . directly over to the gate of my house-to-be. I swing open the wrought iron gate and sit on the tiled patio bench, my head feeling heavy with the decision I face. Leaning back, I gaze up at the cloudless night sky filled with a million twinkling stars as the cool ocean breeze blows softly across my skin.

This is a defining moment in my life. One I will never forget.

"God, thank you for making things so effortless," I pray. "Deep inside, I feel that despite this being one of the bigger decisions of my life, things are falling into place. I feel like this house is meant to be mine and that it will bring me years of happiness. I'm willing to do whatever it takes to make this dream come true. I'm willing to take a risk and see this through to the end, knowing that You are here with me, and that everything will be okay, no matter the outcome."

It feels so good to whisper these words up into the twinkling stars on this quiet night.

"My little casa," I say as I look around, "My little casa with no name. All the other houses in Albufeira have beautifully tiled signs built into their front walls which proudly announce who they are. What will be the name of my home?

"It is the house of Michelle. Maybe the House of Shell for short? I'll have to ask the girls at the hotel desk what the word for shell is in Portuguese. Actually, that would be fun to do right now. Visualizing this house will be much easier if I see it proudly stamped as mine. The House of Shell—I like it!" I declare.

I quickly head back to the hotel and ask the girls at the desk, who inform me the word for shell is Concha. Casa da Concha. Right or not, this clicks with me and I run to my room and start scrawling out drawings of the tiled sign I will someday have imbedded into the wall of my new home. It works.

Casa da Concha—my little place in Portugal—is firmly imbedded in my heart.

I decide it is time to call back to the States and tell my parents, Chris, and Karen that I am attempting to buy a house in a foreign country. With my casa name in place, the doubts and questions about the decision seem to evaporate, replaced by a knowing that this is going to happen. My confidence must carry across the ocean because I do not get the resistance I expect when I spread my news. I drift off to sleep with visions of my Casa da Concha sign proudly hanging outside my new house as my family and I sit in front of a roaring fire inside. Peaceful dreams.

The next day, I meet with the appraiser, who appraises the home for slightly higher than my purchase price. I head to the bank with this essential information. Since I am a non-resident, they are only able to lend me a portion of the value, leaving me with a required down payment of twenty percent. I have absolutely no idea how I am going to come up with that money, but I don't let it discourage me.

If it is meant to be, it will happen effortlessly. I guess more will have to be revealed in California on how this deposit situation will work itself out.

I head back to the States floating on a cloud of excitement. On my computer is a finished rough draft of my very first book and about a hundred digital photos of Casa da Concha. My happiness and gratitude seem to surround my entire being for the twelve hour flight.

Life is good and people of the world are still helpful and good. No matter what the final outcome on both of these huge projects, thank you God.

# # # #

Note to self: next time I use the statement 'If something is meant to be, it will happen effortlessly' as my guide, I absolutely must define 'effortlessly' a little more clearly. I have a feeling that I am about to learn the hard way that while things may fall into place effortlessly, the end result may require an incredible amount of sacrifice.

Take for instance the house loan. I need a job which pays a certain amount to secure the Portuguese loan. I get a job offer the week after I return which pays the needed amount. *Effortless.* Yet, this job puts me right back into the career I just escaped. I have no desire to do the job because it is technical, complex I.T. equipment and I have to sell to a market I am not established in. My best intentions are to be a success there, yet the only reason I take it is for the house. *Sacrifice.*

Then there is the down payment. There is a fluctuation in euro to US Dollar exchange rates, so with estimated furnishing costs factored in, I now need six-figures down to make it happen. I have exactly one-tenth of that. My bank gives me an unsecured loan which covers a fraction. Limited in options, I decide to apply simultaneously for maximum credit with six credit card companies to make up the difference. Within four days, I have the amount I need at promotional interest rates lower than the average bank loan. *Effortless.* Yet, I will also take on minimum monthly payments that total thousands of dollars for a house I am not even living in. *Substantial Sacrifice.*

"So it boils down to: how much do I really want this house? Am I willing to throw logic to the wind and sacrifice for many years to make this new dream of writing and living overseas a reality?" I think as I contemplate the beyond-dollar costs. "Am I willing to work hard and pay every ounce of money I earn toward the debt I incur from this decision, or is it better to walk away and wait until I am more financially prepared?"

I gave up everything before. I traveled the world by myself. I stared into the eyes of a hissing cobra. I faced the depths of the unknown. I went for it. Why not stay in faith and roll the dice again? After all, it's only money, right?

I roll the dice.

Chapter 18:
Service to Others—PSI and Homeless

Although my time in Portugal was short, returning to the reality of California is no easier this second time.

What is it that actually happens to me while I'm away that I never seem to be able to hold onto when I get back to the States? I go from euphoria straight into depression every time.

The excitement of the house helps, especially when my parents agree to come to Portugal at Christmas so we can use our family do-it-yourself skills on the house. Traveling with my parents is a dream come true. I never thought I would get them out of the country, but they are more than willing. With our combined skillsets, we are able to furnish and decorate the entire house in a week. The fun we have and the gratitude I feel about the dependability and loving support of my parents fills my heart.

The house turns out beautifully—better than I ever envisioned. I have my book ready to edit. I am back in Santa Monica, with the beach only a few blocks away. "Life is good!" I tell myself.

So why do I feel so alone and so incredibly sad? Like all this goodness doesn't matter much because now that I am back, so is the void. Something is missing!

I'm sure some of the loneliness is homesickness because I enjoyed spending time with my parents. More comes from acknowledging that I haven't done anything to build a life in Santa Monica. I haven't reached out to make new friends, like I said I would after the PSI *Basic* event. My existing friends seem so far away, especially since Chris decided to move out to the desert to build a new territory.

"Karen always says, 'Grow where you are planted,' but instead of planting new roots here, I continue to choose isolation," I admit. "Returning back to this apartment feels so lonely."

My plan to move away to escape commitments and my old Box sure backfired. It reminds me of when I tried to outrun the rain in Ireland only instead of rain pouring down on me, loneliness pours down on me now. There are so many people who love me back in Redondo Beach.

"It doesn't help that I am back in a job I have no interest in. It was necessary to complete the house purchase but the dread in the pit of my stomach is only too familiar," I think with a sinking feeling.

Am I strong enough to suck it up since I have new inspiration backing my cause, or am I selling my soul and happiness in trade-out for material things once again?

"It doesn't matter now. I already made my choice," I realize with dejection. "Payments start soon and I am substantially in debt. I need income."

The rough draft is done for the book but *something is missing* and I am not quite able to identify what it is. Karen and Chris's advice is, "Let it rest. I'm sure more will be revealed," but insecurities start to develop.

"What if I never figure out the gap and it remains in draft status forever? When am I going to find time to work on this with my new job? It is my dream to be a writer. What if I have to postpone my writing dream again, in sacrifice of a new dream to live overseas? What if I never finish the book at all?" discouraging thoughts cry. I hear the *Splat. Splat. Splat. Splat* as each one strikes the blob of darkness.

"Reality! I just can't take all this reality!" I yell out in frustration. The empty hole in me grows larger by the second.

"Maybe if you eat, it will fill that hole just a little. Maybe if you eat, it will bring you a little moment of joy," the voice slithers. I reach for the unopened package of Oreos . . . within minutes they are gone. Only remorse and a few crumbs stare up at me from the bottom of the empty tray—not joy.

Such an empty promise. No outside fix ever works to fill the hole. It might patch it up for about five seconds, but in the end, the darkness remains and I always feel worse. What will fill this void?

# # # #

"Baby, you know the best way to get out of depression is to help others," is Karen's recommendation to escape the darkness that surrounds me once again.

Yes, I do know this. I have so much past proof—every time I take the focus off me and help others, the blinds go up and I see light again. Flopping on the couch in self-absorption might be easier than driving to a shelter or picking up the phone to talk to someone going through a difficult time, but it sure doesn't lead to a positive end result.

"Where is the selflessness you learned, Michelle?" I ask myself. "Think back to Chris and France and how good it felt to put someone's needs before your own. Think how good it felt to help others during your travels. Why are you choosing to go back to self? Get into action and help others!"

Plus, involvement with others gives me perspective. How can I complain about my job when there is someone in front of me begging for spare change? Someone who has no job, who only has one set of dirty clothes and sleeps in an alley?

Opportunities to help surround me. The staggering population of homeless people living in Los Angeles number in the hundreds of thousands. There are thousands in Santa Monica alone.

Dressed in worn, filthy clothes with maybe a backpack and a blanket as their sole possessions, these men and women pass the days sleeping in the parks or along the beach until forced to move. Perched in front of grocery stores, convenience stores and stop lights—hands extend, begging for change. The "slam" of dumpster lids echoes throughout the city, as homeless people wander the alleys and scrounge for things to recycle for money or for discarded food and clothes.

Early each morning, I jog past at least a dozen homeless people on my way down to the ocean, asleep in tattered sleeping bags in stairwells or on park benches.

What would it be like to sleep outside every night, exposed to the elements—with little control over your situation, limited options on ways to better your life, no hope left in your soul? Just existence—a day-to-day transient, hungry existence.

As I run, questions float in the air, "What might cause a person to be on this path? A path where he might no longer believe he deserves more. Is it simple misfortune? A life of abuse or addiction? Insanity? Loss of faith and hope? Or is it by choice? The choice to be free from a life of possessions?"

It's entirely different but I remember how free I felt with only a small bag of possessions when I traveled. I also know how easy it is to cave to fear instead of faith. Imagine if I had to face the horrible challenges these people face! How much harder would it be to keep faith in their situation, when life seems to deliver one blow after another, when meeting basic needs seems impossible? I witnessed this in impoverished countries, but now it is being revealed to me in my own back yard.

"So, what are you going to do, Michelle?" I probe myself. "Are you going to continue to take the easy, self-based path where you jog by this situation or are you going to take a step in a new direction?"

It is time for me to take action. Action that requires more effort than doling out change to an outstretched hand in front of the supermarket.

I start to develop a new vision in the skies during my morning run. In my daydream, I see myself giving each homeless person I pass a bag of food.

Why not make this a reality as my first step?

"You don't have enough money to make that happen," my mind immediately protests from its invigorated state of financial stress.

Instead of listening to it, I do something I have not done since my return to California. I stop on the beach, sit in the sand with my eyes closed and get quiet as I listen to the waves. "You have enough for this, Michelle, it won't take much," the waves seem to say.

I do have enough. Maybe not enough to feed everyone, but enough to feed a few.

All of a sudden, this need to help feels urgent. "It's Saturday morning. If I prepare today, I can deliver bags of food tomorrow morning," I realize. After my run, I drive to the Dollar Store to pick up some essentials. Then I will go to the grocery store for the rest. My plan is to make fifty bags.

Heading to the register, I unload paper lunch bags, bottled water, breakfast bars, juice boxes, bananas and bags of Tootsie Rolls, because everyone needs a little candy. Behind me, a pleasant man with a friendly smile winks and says, "Boy, you really like bananas!" I explain that it is all for a little project I have planned for tomorrow.

"What's the project, if I may ask?"

"I'm going to put together a few bags of food for the homeless and drop them around my area at dawn," I explain. "Nothing big, just a little movement in the right direction where I'm concerned."

"You don't say. My home is in Nevada but I'm a huge advocate for homeless and whenever I am here I do a lot of work with various organizations in Los Angeles that help the homeless. If you're interested, I can give you some great organizations that could really use your help," he responds.

Here it is, happening again. Whenever I chose the right path, I am sent confirmations that support my decision.

I quickly jot down a few websites the man provides before I leave with a "Thank you" to go pick up additional fruit and sandwich supplies.

I already feel the light starting to peak in!

Once home, I set up an assembly line and get ready to start

making my little breakfast bags. I stop for a moment and close my eyes in a little prayer, something else I realize I have not done often since my return to California.

"God, thank You for allowing me the means and desire to do this and thank You for helping me choose a different way. Thank You for the little 'sign' from the guy at the Dollar Store that signaled I am on the right path," I pray. "Please help these children of Yours have renewed faith and remember that they are loved by You and that this is from You, not me. Thank you again," I end as I wipe tears from my eyes.

How can I let them know this is from God? It is so clear to me now that this can't be about me at all. It needs only to be about God giving to them. I am just a conduit.

I instinctively hop up and grab some colored markers from my closet and write "YOU ARE LOVED" with a big heart under it on every one of the brown paper bags. I don't know if they will feel God's love through these simple words, but at least my heart knows who is delivering this message.

The next morning before sunlight, I drive my car to the park by my house, take one of the plastic bins full of lunch bags, hook it onto my little two wheeled pull cart and head off to deliver some breakfast and messages of love.

I am met with disappointment. "Where are all the homeless people I always see?" I ask in confusion. At this strip of the park I picked for my starting point, there are usually many homeless people asleep on benches. Today there appear to be *none*.

This isn't quite what I had in mind.

"I didn't think to check if there was a soup kitchen or something today. I assumed the homeless would be here seven days a week. Maybe they are at the other end of the park. After all, this stretch is at least a mile long. Maybe the police got everyone moving early," I say as I attempt to reinvigorate my earlier excitement and enthusiasm.

"Whew, there is someone over by the bushes," I see with relief as I walk over and give him a bag. "One bag down, forty-nine to go. Hey, there's someone else over there on the bench." I head over and place the bag next to the shoulder of an outstretched sleeping man.

He flinches when I set the bag next to him and tightens his grip on his backpack. My heart beats with compassion.

Everything seems more real now as I stand close to this live person. I can't imagine sleeping on a bench out in the cold all night. What causes this life? Why do people have to live like this?

I continue on down the path but there are only a few more homeless people there. Undesirable thoughts start to grow inside my mind, especially after I hit a curb and flip my cart. As I pile the many bags back into my bin, I battle my frustration about not having investigated other homeless events taking place today.

"There is no room for thoughts like these today, Michelle," I tell myself and continue on. Not seeing many people in the distance, I decide to head in the opposite direction. I walk back by the bench where the outstretched man is so that I can give him another bag since it appears I might have a few extra.

The man is sitting up this time, facing my direction, and I can see now that he isn't a grown man. He's actually a young teenage boy. As I walk toward him, I notice his shoulders shaking beneath his ragged sweatshirt. "He's crying!" I realize and without thinking, I sit down next to him on the bench, take his hand and ask him, "Are you okay?" His hand is dirty with broken nails but what I acknowledge more is how cold it is in my own hand.

He raises his teary gaze up to meet my eyes and with tears still flowing he says, "When I saw 'YOU ARE LOVED' on the bag, I don't know what happened. I've been out here on the streets for a year and I haven't cried once. When I read that, it was like I couldn't control myself. I started to cry and I can't seem to stop."

The pain I see in this poor young soul's eyes reaches inside of me and breaks my heart wide open.

He's just a boy, this is so unfair.

I start crying with him and reach my arm around his shoulders. It's like a dam breaks within him. He starts sobbing, huge wracking sobs that shake his entire body. I sit there holding him on that park bench as he cries and cries; two complete strangers, there on a bench.

How could I have let myself forget that we are all one, here to help one another? There is no aloneness, only oneness.

After a few minutes, he pulls himself upright, a sheepish look on his face, and starts to apologize for his breakdown. "I'm so sorry, I don't know what happened. I'm usually so tough. I smell horrible too! You have to be completely grossed out. I am so sorry!" he repeats.

"Don't worry about silly stuff like that," I say with a smile. "It's more important that you're okay. My name's Michelle. What's your name?" His name is Noah and he is nineteen. We sit there and talk for at least fifteen minutes on that park bench.

Noah tells me his story about how he grew up in a small town, headed to Los Angeles with dreams of acting, got nowhere and eventually ended up living on the streets. Although he says that his mother will let him return home, his pride keeps him from going back. His mother did not want him to go after this dream and he dreads the thought of her saying, "I told you so," if he returns. His fear of failure and ego cause him to choose this life over one filled with comfort and love.

I point this out to him, hoping that maybe I can be the *voice* for this poor boy; the voice that comes to me through others when my connection is not strong enough for me to hear it myself. That voice which speaks truth louder than the false truth in my head.

"Please God, let him hear any words that may help him understand," I silently pray as I speak. We talk about ego and how it can make us chose the tougher path, if we let it. We also dig into the words on the bag and why they might have triggered the dam to break open. God touched his hardened heart when he least expected it. He was reminded that he IS loved by a family that he refuses to return to because he is choosing to let ego run his life.

I share a few of my experiences, so that he understands that I face this same head-battle almost every day and how I end up locked in my Box, listening to its false messages in agony and pain. I tell him how my perfectionism and need for approval had become so powerful once that it became deadly and almost resulted in me ending my own life.

I also explain that choosing ego as our leader is an option. That we have the choice of love or pride and many times we go with ego because it has tremendous strength after we have fed it for so many years. I also share how God speaks to me through people that are more connected than I am, and that maybe right now God could be sending him a little message.

There are no coincidences. Everything I tell Noah is a message I also need to hear. It slowly dawns on me how clear God's messages are to me when I am in my heart. No other voices are required when I am there, only a quiet conversation between God and myself.

This is my problem. This is what I lose in California—my connection to God and to my heart. I turn off prayer and meditation here and the ego-driven voices in my head become so loud and strong, I remain trapped in my Box. Just like Noah hearing truth when he let go, I see my truth now, when I am in a heart filled with compassion for him. The 'mysterious place' where the positive messages, the soft voice and my connection all sprout from is my heart!

Noah continues to talk, and tells me that his only friend here was put in jail the night before, and how last night was his first night alone. We talk about some options; as sad and lonely as he is, not having his friend around gives him some freedom. As one person, he actually has enough money for a night at a hostel, which means a hot shower and a peaceful night's sleep. Being the traveler that I am, I know there are three hostels here, one of which is only a mile down the road. I draw him directions and after another hug, he heads off toward the hostel. I continue on my path to distribute more bags.

Bag Number Three. I will never forget Noah and the message that bag delivered to both of us!

Further down the path, I meet more homeless people. My worry about having too many bags is quickly replaced by my original fear of not having enough. Fifty bags last me about a half mile. I need at least another hundred to complete the stretch.

Many short conversations take place as I deliver bags that day. Sometimes these are comments of gratitude, other times they are about general things like the weather. I have another lengthy conversation with a beautiful French woman, Alecia, who at age 74, is homeless due to a lifelong gambling addiction. Alecia has two grown children she abandoned in France in their preschool years in search of a better life in the States. Landing in Las Vegas, she quickly developed an addiction she could not break and every penny she made at work went back to the tables. She has not seen her children in France in over forty-five years and talks about how much she hopes that she gets to see them one day before she dies.

Despite being homeless, Alecia is a well-kept woman with a lot of energy and an upbeat personality. Her hair is curled and styled and she has a beautiful complexion, complimented by a small amount of make-up to accent her face and eyes. But behind the perky exterior, I can plainly see the sadness in her eyes about the choices she has made in her life.

I ask if there is any hope for a reunion and she replies, "There was a few years ago. A relative of mine in France offered to buy me a plane ticket to return home but I refused. I was too embarrassed to meet my children with teeth missing. I couldn't do it. Isn't it crazy what pride will do to you, Michelle?"

Yes it is and I know this only too well.

"Please promise me you will never let an addiction to anything run your life or let vanity make decisions for you. You are a beautiful girl. Love life and be smart!" she begs me, like she is talking to her own daughter. "Oh, and take your vitamins every day. I may be homeless but I have healthier skin than many people!" she adds as parting advice. I have many experiences like this, often without instigating the conversation.

People are all searching for heart. We all want to know that others care. I am linked to the people on the streets like I am linked to family and friends and to people around the world. We are all connected to this big universal energy, God, which orchestrates our paths so that we all can continue to grow as souls through love. WE ARE ALL ONE.

As my synergies continue to align with this idea, I join Agape Singles Group the next week. Their very first community project is the annual United Way Walk for the Homeless. I enlist the help of my family, friends and co-workers and raise thousands of dollars for the cause. The day of the walk, tears brim in my eyes as I see hundreds of people joining together to help this section of our population. Fifty bags might not have been enough to meet needs that day, but the walk set records for the amount of money raised for this cause. It is amazing what we can do as a group of individuals joining together with a common goal.

I also check out the organizations my Dollar Store friend recommended and start working at a Santa Monica food shelter once a week. Even if it is only for a few hours a week, it is time I commit to reaching into my heart so that I can be reminded that we are all interconnected.

# # # #

"My book is making me crazy. I hate it!" I cry to Chris in frustration. "I now call it 'my stupid book'. How did it go from a thing of joy to something I despise and want to throw away?"

My intention was to lightly edit the draft I completed in

Portugal, which I wrote in a state of bliss and connection, but many months have passed.

After my revelations about God, heart, service and oneness, the mechanical arms start to flail madly in every direction. My ego is not about to let me go. The powerful arm of financial insecurity latches onto me in a horrific way. Machine mode is back in full session.

I quit the technical I.T. job and take a position working for yet another information technology company. "You cannot fail. Stay focused, work harder than ever. Get out of debt. Make this happen!" are the thoughts that bombard my brain each day as I run from account to account.

My mind formulates an idea to speed up the debt payment process, "Sell books—lots and lots of books. Finish this book right now and sell a million copies to get out of this debt!" In this frenzied state of mind, I come to believe another idea: a book that talks about God won't sell enough copies to make it all happen.

"All this God reference is going to cut out a huge market section," I explain to Chris. "I can't afford for that to happen. The book *has* to be rewritten!"

"So basically, you are pulling God out of the entire book?" Chris questions in complete disbelief. "I don't think this is the right move, Michelle. The entire journey is about you and God and living in faith not fear. I just don't see how removing God is going to work."

"I will *make* it work!" I declare with complete determination.

Every night, I come home from an exhausting day in the field to sit and stare at the computer screen. Not a word flows. Hour after hour I stare at complete blankness. My frustration grows, but so does my determination to make this book happen.

"Your financial life depends on it. You need the money!" I hear the voice boom so I begin to take what I have already written and start to modify it; chopping it up into pieces and stripping out any reference to God.

Night after night, I sit at my desk and chop away. I read what

I write and know it is pure crap—words without essence and empty sentences. I blame it on writer's block, which sends another arm out to latch onto me, one of self-judgment and doubt. Soon, I am into another whole tailspin where I second guess if I am really supposed to write if writing is this difficult for me.

"I am never going to finish this book!" I cry in complete exasperation to Karen over the phone.

"Maybe it's not time, Baby," Karen advises. "Maybe more is supposed to be revealed and the time isn't now. Maybe you should put it down for a while and come back to it later."

"I have to make this happen, Karen," I reply as the arm of control latches tightly on. "I have to get past this block and work this all out. I have to push through this and make this book happen! I sit here every day and stress about income and the fact that I can't seem to make this book right. I'm going to lose my mind!"

"I know what I'll do," I say as my mind suddenly comes up with an external quick-fix solution. "I'll play that PSI ninety-day goal setting game, *PLD*. If I proclaim to the world that I am going to make this happen then I'm sure I will," I declare. "Pressure and commitment will help me break through this writers block, I know it."

"Whatever you think, baby, but I think you should set it down for a while," Karen reiterates.

"I can't, Karen, I need it to be done!" I state. "In my time, not God's," I add to myself.

In follow up to PSI weekend seminar, *The Basic*, PSI offers additional seminars. The one I now plan to do is a ninety-day goal setting game called *PLD*. You are on a team with fifteen people and the program is designed to show you what habits or restrictive thoughts prevent you from achieving goals through a series of weekly meetings, personal and team exercises, and group activities.

To my surprise, I cross paths with Paul, the vulnerable guy from the stage. We say hello as we sit next to each other at the *PLD* orientation meeting. My stomach jumps when I see him. "It must be the accent," I conclude, since I know I am only interested in guys with chaos-free lives.

"So how is your divorce going, Paul?" I ask as a way of reminding him that I remember him and his story from *The Basic*. "Still in the works and still causing me heartache and stress," he replies with a mixture of excitement and sadness and then starts to tell me about a few of his ideas for *PLD* goals.

"Maybe I can put Paul on the *Friends* shelf at least," I think to myself as he talks. "Close enough to learn more about, but far enough away to stay clear of any potential mess. That's the place for him."

Orientation starts and they tell us two mandatory dates we must attend, one of which I cannot make. They inform me that I will have to wait and start with the next team.

Why do I feel disappointed but at the same time feel like I might have just dodged a bullet?

A month or so passes and the next *PLD* session starts and I am able to join this one. Each week, Paul and I pass each other at team headquarters and say hello. I make sure there is a lot of distance between us, determined to stay clear of potential hazards so I can focus on my own obstacle (which apparently is myself, based off initial *PLD* results).

One thing that becomes immediately obvious to my *PLD* team is that my need to control runs my show; my way is the best way. My lack of faith in others leaves me in situations where I am then forced to do a majority of the work.

In spite of my fear of failure, I also soon realize how often I set myself up to fail by creating too many impossible goals to be achieved in too short of a time period. I over-commit, over-promise and under-deliver with myself. It is the high bar and expectations once again. My goals are huge compared to others on the team, and I add an extra one just to ensure I face more challenge.

My goals to achieve in ninety days are: 1) lose 20 pounds so that I weigh the least I have ever weighed 2) pay off $100,000 of debt

3) finish my book and have it in print 4) find the love of my life and 5) I don't even remember what this one is because they make me drop it a few weeks in. All of this might be achievable for someone else, but when I factor in my procrastination issue and high-stress day job, life becomes an exhausting, frustrating nightmare.

One coinciding trip in the elevator, Paul asks me what my goals are. I tell him my goals and he laughs in disbelief, especially as I mention the one about "finding the love of my life." Since this one is hard to quantify traceable movement toward, I set that I will go on fifteen dates (1-2 per week). "Well, if you get in a pinch or short on time, make sure and call me. I will be your emergency date," he says with a smile as he hands me his phone number.

"Thanks for the offer, but I should be just fine," I reply nonchalantly, as I stick his phone number into my wallet and wave goodbye. Stories have surfaced that he has moved into the rebound stage of his break up. "Glad I am keeping my distance, but someone really needs to help straighten that poor guy out. I hope someone steps up to the plate for him," I think as I head on my own way.

Because of my procrastination and over-extension, the last few weeks of the program are pure hell for me. I starve myself, date every man I meet, write until the wee hours every night and sell off things I own to raise cash for debt . . . and I hit NONE of my goals. My attempt to push myself to succeed through pressure and commitment does not work.

I learn a lot over the ninety-day period, but my issues could have been summarized in six seconds by anyone who already knew me and in six words. When I am trapped in my Box as Michelle the Machine, I AM MY OWN WORST ENEMY.

One substantial positive which comes from playing *PLD* is that we are required to put together a community service project. There are no guidelines, except that we need to involve at least one-hundred volunteers and the project needs to be completed in a single day. I am not the only procrastinator on the team. Three weeks before the event, we still don't have a project because everyone is focusing on goals.

Being the controller that I am, I step up and find a project—only to have it not pan out. Frantically, I make phone calls looking for anyone who needs the help of at least one hundred volunteers for some type of renovation or rejuvenation project. One lead turns into another and I find myself at last meeting with the principal of an elementary school in Los Angeles. This school is over 100 years old and in a not-so-great part of town. It looks worn and uninspiring, but there are no district funds to improve it. We decide this is our project.

"When something is meant to be, it will happen effortlessly," proves itself true once again. While there is a tremendous amount of effort involved with this project, it goes effortlessly as all the pieces fall into place over a few weeks. Plans are quickly coordinated for one of the largest renovation projects ever completed by a team playing the goal game (of course this would be the case since I am on this team).

In a nutshell, it includes numerous inspirational "I AM" murals inside and outside the school, new paint everywhere, landscaping, renovating a back area and turning it into a landscaped teacher's lounge, mosaic tree planters, murals on the large backboard dividers, repainting all the benches, finding 100 volunteers and someone to donate lunch.

We divide up the parts and set out to make it happen.
- Phone call after phone call, begging for supply donations.
- Trips to paint, tile, carpet and supply stores to pick up donations.
- Arranging for 5,000 pounds of donated pavers to arrive and be unloaded.
- Posting flyers around the neighborhood asking for community help.
- Dropping off extra flyers for the kids to take home.
- Emails and phone calls to friends and families.
- Donations of money to pay a food truck to provide lunch for the many volunteers.

- Donations of trees, flowers and wood chips from environmental groups.
- Approvals from corporate level on the school side.

The list goes on and on—all while we still continued to work regular day jobs and complete personal goals.

On daily conference calls, we cheer with joy when one more part falls into place. Everyone is doing their best to make it happen because we can clearly visualize what a difference it will make in the lives of these kids.

"Here it is, morning of the big day. What if no volunteers show up? What if the environmental organization doesn't show up with the trees? What if the paint gets spilled? What if no one can paint murals? What if we don't have enough time to complete it all?" as I drive, my mind races through all the things that might go wrong.

When I arrive, I resist the urge to jump out of my car and head straight into action. Instead, I sit alone and admire the sunrise for a few seconds before I walk over to meet the team.

However it goes, it will go perfectly. Don't worry about the "what ifs." Everyone put a lot of heart and effort into this event and all the footwork that can be done, has been done. The results are beyond my control.

It is an amazing day. Not only do all the supplies and food arrive as scheduled, but over 150 volunteers show up, ready to work hard and do whatever needs to be done. To my surprise, Paul is one of the volunteers. Every volunteer is given some fun task to do to help make the day complete. Even toddlers paint and plant.

People on ladders paint wonderful "I AM" messages while others kneel below them working on colorful murals. Beauty covers both the exterior walls and interior halls of this once depleted school and it now sings with inspiration.

Mosaic dolphins and underwater scenes appear on tree planters and bursts of plant life shoot out around the trees and in the gardens. Soon, color is abundant everywhere and a breath of life flows across the entire school yard, replacing the drab grey/blue surroundings from before.

The commitment of this community to help better the lives of their children makes my heart swell with gratitude. Suddenly, the self-anger about not hitting my personal goals is non-existent. Once again, helping others has pulled me out of my head and gently returned me into my heart. In this moment, *I AM LOVE.*

Chapter 19:
The Business of Dating

"We are getting married!" Chris exclaims in joy. I am so excited for her, I have tears in my eyes. As a heartfelt, loving person, Chris has always been open to true love and because of this, she is often in a relationship. This is the one we have been waiting for—Doug is her man. They are wonderful together and plans start for a big wedding up in Oregon, where they both are from.

I, as usual, will be attending this festive event alone. I am the most single person I know. For a head-driven person like me, connecting with true love is not about love at all; it's about finding a man who I can place the most check-marks next to when it comes to *The Ideal Man List*.

The Ideal Man List has its own little space in a room titled "Men/Relationships" inside my Box because there is so much judgment and structure built around and woven into it. I am almost guaranteed safety from ever having to deal with things like commitment and relationships behind the protection of *The Ideal Man List*. It is pages long and, as the organized business woman that I am, it even has categories: interests/hobbies, income, assets, physical traits, career, spiritual beliefs, travel knowledge, dreams/goals and—last on the list—personal values.

I compare every man to *The Ideal Man List* and if a potential candidate appears to have a shot at rows of check marks, I go on a date with him. After the date, if the list isn't filled with check marks, I move on to the next candidate.

I remember one guy exposing the truth of it. We were on our first phone call and he said, "I feel like I'm on a job interview." He was falling short on the list anyway, so I decided not to waste any more time on him, but he nailed it; I operate my search for a mate like I would operate a small business.

Karen calls me on it all the time, "You treat your love life like a business, Michelle. How are you ever going to find love that way, when it has no heart?" She is right. I have no room for spontaneity or random encounters when it comes to love. No opportunities for romance, only check marks.

Others may hate it, but online dating is a dream come true for me. With this type of dating, I can quickly skim a potential candidate's profile, compare their answers to *The Ideal Man List*, count the checkmarks from a distance and narrow down prospects without meeting any live men. It's a very efficient system for someone like me.

In theory it should work, right? All boxes checked means he's the One. So why do none of these matches-on-paper ever seem to work out? Most likely because, after checkmarks, the next move is dating—where real people are required. Unfortunately, one of the people involved in this next step is me—Michelle the (Sabotage) Machine.

I sabotage because I still approach relationships in the same way that I used to approach self-love; with a tough, judgmental hand and unrealistic expectations. I might not expect perfection from myself anymore, but I definitely expect it from any man I would ever trust enough to date long-term.

I am elated that Chris has found love, but this entire situation with her does make me stop and take a look at my own track record. High school and college were all about fix-it cases. One five-year failed marriage in my late twenties, a fix-it also. One brief chaotic relationship after that. Then about another five years of scattered short-term relationships and more dates than I can even count.

As I complain to Karen about yet another failed first date she candidly asks me, "Michelle, can you meet your own list?" "Of course I can't Karen," I reply. "There are only about two people on the planet that could 'X' out the entire list: Superman and Batman (and maybe Gerard Butler on a good day). So what are you getting at?" I say, knowing very well what her answer is going to be.

"Maybe it's time to stop using *The Ideal Man List*," is her answer—the exact answer I expect.

"I might be willing to put it away for a while," I decide to myself, "but it doesn't mean that *poof* all of a sudden, the room in my Box labeled 'Men/Relationships' will cease to exist. There is way too much unknown concerning all this true love business to toss aside logic for *crazy in-love*."

# # # #

While I am in the process of retiring *The Ideal Man List* and my business approach to love, there is a solid friendship evolving at a rapid pace with Paul. After the community service project, we start to talk frequently on the phone. I decide that despite the mess, I like this guy and I'm okay developing a friendship with him.

We talk about his pending divorce and I ask if there are any last possibilities of a reconciliation now that the rebound attempts are over. He doesn't think so. A week later, I get a phone call from him telling me that he tried to reconcile but it ended after a few days. I console him and praise him for at least giving it one more try so that he would never second guess his decision.

Paul asks if he can come over so we can talk about it. My stomach jumps. I have kept a safe distance through the phone until now. "Yes, but I need to take you up on your initial offer after all, so how about if we go to the movies so I can check-off another date for *PLD*? I am down to only a week left and have two dates to check-off still," I admit with a laugh.

Strolling the few blocks to the theatre under a sky full of stars,

I impulsively reach over and squeeze his hand and tell him, "It's all going to be okay." He smiles like he believes me.

"I am just supporting a new friend," I say to myself as I brush away the alarm bells that ring in my head. After the movie, we come back to my apartment and sit on my sofa talking for hours about our dreams. For such different backgrounds, it amazes us both how much we have in common when we talk about what we want for our futures. Travel comes up often.

I mention my need to downsize my apartment due to finances. "I'll go with you to look at new places," Paul offers. "We can make it a fun day." I agree since I am not looking forward to it and company might make it less agonizing.

Then we lay head-to-head on the sectional couch, each extending off toward opposite ends in a just friends kind of way. Soon, I feel him running his fingers through my hair.

It feels so soothing and relaxing. It has been a long time since someone has played with my hair.

I usually have a look-but-don't-touch demeanor, but Paul is only a friend so I let my normal defenses relax.

Mmmmm, this feels good.

He stops after a while. "Thank you, Paul. That felt so wonderful!" I say in a half-dreamy haze. "I'm sorry, Michi. I thought you were asleep or else I wouldn't have stopped," he responds as he starts stroking my hair again.

What kind of man is this? Can he really be this thoughtful?

Yes, he is that thoughtful of a guy. Paul proves this a week later when he helps me move about ten streets down the road from my current apartment, to the new place we found on our fun day of searching. I have never in my life let anyone help me move. I think moving is annoying and that one of the heaviest requests you can place on a friendship is to ask someone else to suffer through this. Paul insists though and in the end, the two of us move the entire apartment so I can save money on movers, an unbelievable feat. More unbelievable is that we actually have fun doing it, and pull off the day without a hitch through complete team work.

I call Chris because I am still unable to believe how we were able to get the move done, without issue, in a single day. "Why are you two just friends again?" Chris asks. "Moving is something that can break up the best of couples. You two completing a seamless move is an amazing thing."

"You know why, Chris. I want easy; a guy who is stable and drama free. Not someone who is going through transitions and divorce, who has ex-wives and kids and a mess of other issues. This is right just the way it is, as friends," I reply again to this frequently asked question. "You know what other interesting thing happened? You know how we have Secret Angels that gave us gifts during *PLD* and how I'm always saying how my angel gets me the most fitting gifts and cards? Well, it turns out Paul has been my angel all along! They revealed it at our closing event. Our team had to get on stage and cover our eyes and then open them to see who it was. Paul was standing there in front of me. He was all decked out in a suit and he looked really handsome."

I do not tell her that in my surprise of seeing him as my angel, I hugged and kissed him. I also do not tell her that the kiss between us lasted a little bit longer than it should have. That would just spark more comments from her and I am still processing the shock of how I felt like I melted into a puddle in those few moments. I need to stuff those events away, not explore them—which I know Chris would push me to do.

"Michelle, you are my best friend in the world. I only ever want the best for you so I just have to point out that you compare every guy you date to Paul," Chris replies. "'I wish he was handy like Paul or thoughtful and giving like Paul,' are your regular critiques about other men now. You no longer compare men to *The Ideal Man List*, you compare them to Paul. When are you just going to let it be Paul?"

"I just can't Chris, so don't press it. You, my parents, Karen, my sisters—all of you just need to let this go. We are meant to be very close friends. I can't even check off fifteen things on *The Ideal Man List* concerning Paul," is my comeback.

"Friendly reminder—you gave up *The Ideal Man List*, Michelle," Chris counters. "Paul has what counts: integrity, honesty, dependability and a loving heart. Those are the things that matter in the long run. You need someone who is in-touch with his heart."

"He is so thoughtful too!" I add, "Did I tell you that he showed up with flowers when I got back from my birthday? And that he drove all the way over the other day when I was having a rough day just to give me a hug? I just need to find someone LIKE Paul who doesn't have all the mess."

"Michelle, did you ever stop to think that this is what God has planned for you or will you at least keep your mind open to it, please?" Chris begs.

"Sorry Chris. Not an option. Too illogical and messy. Besides, he's dating other women so it's just friends from his perspective too. That's what makes it so easy," I quickly reply. "I'm going to pay him back for helping me move by cleaning out his old garage. I can use the pictures as organizing business references if I finally quit I.T. once and for all to focus on writing again and start that as a side business."

"Oh," I add quickly, "Paul and I decided we are definitely going to Argentina soon though. He needs friend-support to face some things back home there and I've always wanted to see South America so we decided to go together."

"You two are going to make me crazy, but I'm glad he's in your life," Chris comments before hanging up.

"I solidly believe I am in full control of the situation," I say to myself with confidence. "I enjoy the security and comfort of his friendship but I am focused on my future dreams and plans. There is no room to get sidetracked. I value Paul for sure, but he is *not* the guy for me with all of his chaos. It's nothing personal, just a better decision on my side to stay a loving support, but at a distance. That's the way

I look at it. My top priority is figuring out why I still can't break through this writer's block. No room for potential mess or heart stuff. The only love I'm going to invest time in finding right now is the lost love for my book."

Even if it does feel so wonderful whenever he holds me in his arms.

"Okay, back to business."

LAP III

FAMILY LIFE SHOWS ME THE WAY

Chapter 20:
Unconditional Love

"Just friends. Paul and I are just friends. It might be easy for someone who doesn't know the two of us to be confused because of how close we appear, but we are just friends. Two good friends, on an airplane together, flying all the way from California to Argentina. One friend emotionally supporting the other, while also traveling to a new country as a bonus. That's what friends do, right? Spend thousands of dollars on a flight to another country because a friend needs support?

"This might be something I normally wouldn't do, especially for a guy friend, but that doesn't mean that there's some driving force behind my action beyond friendship. It sounded like a logical win/win for both of us, since traveling with someone who grew up in Argentina and who speaks the language would be an easier way to see the country. Mutually beneficial for us both. Just two friends on a journey together," I sigh as I silently run through these thoughts again.

Paul continues to run his fingers through my hair as I lay sideways across the seats, my head resting on a few pillows in his lap. The chest cold I caught a few days before we left is draining me, but I feel uplifted and content right now from the comforting gestures of my good friend.

# # # #

Buenos Aires, Argentina is fantastic, full of energy and good times. We stay with Paul's old family friend, who welcomes us with open arms and her home is warm and inviting. Paul shows me many places from his childhood including the house where he grew up and the schools he attended. We also visit some tourist attractions and go to a few evening shows with his old high school friends. All the while, we mix in more of our heartfelt conversations about values and dreams.

I am there to hold his hand as he stands over the grave of his father for the first time. I give him words of encouragement and am by his side when he faces his mother and family after decades of separation. I wipe away his tears of joy and sadness later as we talk about good and bad times from his past, including the feelings of failure he has over three ended marriages.

Mostly, we relax and have fun. There is one surprise that he arranges which catches me off guard. In one of our first conversations in California, I nonchalantly mentioned to Paul my childhood daydream about riding horseback through rolling green meadows. His surprise is a horseback ride for the two of us through beautiful polo pony fields. I think about The Law of Attraction and Karen's statement, "In God's time," as I look over and smile at my friend riding next to me, so grateful that he turned this daydream into reality.

My favorite part of the trip are the late night conversations between the two of us. As we lie in our single beds shooting stories across the safe gap between us, we laugh into the wee hours of the night. Tears of laughter stream from our eyes as we hop from one humorous story to the next. Intimate dreams, fantasies and past mistakes: there are no boundaries in our conversations, but there is always a feeling of joy, even when we discuss painful memories.

"I have not laughed like this in so long," I think as I wipe away more tears. "I never thought I would relate to a man like this on such a deep, trusting level. Is it because the pressure is off since we are just friends? I have dropped the defensive wall and allowed him in to relate to the true me. Is it because I trust him? Is that why I have let go of prim-and-proper Michelle?

"Paul is so happy and full of confidence and joy here, surrounded by old friends who knew him before wives, family and divorce. He is relaxed," I acknowledge. "I feel so comfortable traveling here with him. Like I can take a back seat to planning and agendas because he has things under control. *It feels so nice.* Our conversations about travel dreams and creating financial freedom through businesses and other ideas gel seamlessly.

"More important than all that is how I feel around him. I *feel* his heart always wrapped around me and I feel like my heart is safe around him. So safe that I drop all my normal defenses and conditions with him. I know that Paul would never do anything to hurt me. His only offer to me, even as a friend, is unconditional love. He is a man who truly lives from the heart, so unlike me."

I look over at him on the other bed. That same respect which struck me when he was vulnerable on stage rushes through me again, along with the envy of wanting to be like that.

He opens up your heart, Michelle. He brings out the best in you. Admit it, you love this man.

"Paul, I think we should be together as a couple." The words come out of me before I have a chance to think about them . . . or stop them. It's like in Spain when I said, "I'm supposed to write." The words just shoot out of my mouth. Only there is no lightning bolt this time that jolts me with energy. Fear strikes me instead.

What did I just say?

"What did you just say?" Paul asks, like he read my mind. The look on his face is one of surprise, because before I blurted out my statement we had been talking about the Argentine government. He also has an element of shock mixed into his expression, like he can't believe those words came out of my mouth.

You and me both!

After throwing myself into the deep-end, I panic and start

treading water as fast as I can. Words of logic and proof start flying out of me, almost like a sales-pitch, "I think we should be together, as a couple. We are so compatible and have so many of the same dreams. We have fun together and I feel safe when I'm in your arms. We can build such a great future together where we help each other grow and support each other as we go after our big dreams.

"All my business experience, ambition and strength at moving things forward will help you as you rebuild. You are great for me because you live in your heart and have such a helpful, giving nature. I really think that we are meant to be. Everyone keeps telling me this and I didn't want to believe it because I was too scared. Now, I know it in my heart, so I'm saying this aloud. I love you," I finish with a big splash after my frantic rush.

I want to run and hide. As fast as the words fly out of my mouth, equally as fast anxiety about possible rejection flies in, bracing me to be spurned. My body is completely stiff as I hold my breath in anticipation of Paul's response. There is total silence on the other bed. Seven seconds of torturous silence. Seven seconds of space for me to start looking around inside my mind for ways to rebuild the defensive wall around my heart. I am still holding my breath.

"Michi, I am so surprised!" Paul responds slowly, "This does not seem like you." I look up at Paul. I need to look into his eyes for whatever comes next. I will not hang my head in embarrassment or shame. "There's no crying in baseball," flickers into my mind as I prepare for the rejection. I realize I am still holding my breath but I don't let it out. I can't yet. I will drown in this deep pool I have thrown myself into if I breathe right now.

We look into each other's eyes from across the space between the beds. I am grateful for the few feet of physical distance between us as I struggle to decide if I should stay in my heart or run.

"I can only tell you," he continues, "I feel the same."

He feels the same. It's okay to take a breath now, I'm not going to drown.

I let out a shaky breath and feel my body soften slightly as the tension unclenches. "Honestly, I have for a long time—since the moment I met you," he continues and instantly I know that he truly means this because his eyes send a message of love and reassurance across the distance straight into my heart. I immediately bridge the gap and hop over to his bed so that I can be in his arms. I curl up against his chest and he wraps his arms around me. That protected feeling washes over me.

Paul will not break my heart. I can trust him. He knows how to love. He will teach me the way. He loves me.

"I don't know what to do," he says, only this time I hear concern in his voice and notice conflict in his expression. "After this divorce and my rebound phase, I made a vow to myself that I would stay single for at least a few years. My life is a mess. I don't want to drag anyone through that. You deserve more. I don't have a lot to give at this time," he reminds me. "Plus, I have been in marriages my entire adult life. I don't even know who I am. My life has always been about wives and kids."

"I can handle it—all of it. I am a strong, capable woman who is able to rise to all challenges and I love you, Paul," I assure him with a solid voice as I give him a tight hug. "I really feel that I'm supposed to be with you to support you through all of your rebuilding and transitions. Plus, we both know how much I love my independence, so there's plenty of space for you to explore who you are. You couldn't ask for a better girlfriend for what you're going through."

"Someone needs to save this man" floats into my head in my own haunting voice from the past but I quickly brush it away. "So what if I turn out to be the one to save him? There is no better person to fix issues and clean up messes than me."

"But when we get back, reality will be there with three young kids, an unstable ex-wife, pending divorces and all the rest. It is a totally different story than the one here on vacation," Paul points out. My body tightens a little, like he struck a nerve. Returning to reality is never my strong suit. He instantly feels this from my position against his chest and adds, "Let's think about this for a few days while we are each alone when you head up to visit Iguassu Falls. That way, we can both decide if this is right," he suggests.

I agree. This sounds logical. Then we kiss and logic suddenly does not seem so important. After a bit, I return to my own bed and quickly fall asleep.

This business of heart and emotions is exhausting. Way more exhausting than any seventy-hour work week I ever put in!

A few days later, I fly up to Iguassu Falls. These waterfalls that border Brazil and Argentina are some of the most magnificent in the world. I've been to Niagara Falls in Canada, but people said to be ready for the dramatic difference in size and quantity of Iguassu Falls, and they are not mistaken.

For as far as the eye can see, there are roaring falls (two-hundred seventy-five to be exact) which wrap for miles along the country border. The sound of crashing water is almost deafening as some falls drop almost three-hundred feet. Small rainbows arch all around as the sun's rays bounce off the mist. Surrounded by acres of lush, green forests and fast running rivers, these falls are majestic.

As the powerful waters rage, so do the thoughts in my mind and the emotions in my heart. I feel the familiar jabs of anxiety whenever I think about the word "relationship". Like when a doctor whacks my knee with the little hammer and my leg automatically kicks out, as soon as I think the word "commitment" my thoughts kick out in defense.

"Paul understands this part. He knows how to commit. He can show you the way," I counter, yet thoughts about the unknown fly through my head on the train back to the main entrance. Hundreds of butterflies fly along and surround the open train. I look around at all of the butterflies, bedazzled by their beauty and mystified by how something so small can fly as fast as a train. Chris always says, "When you see a butterfly, you are on the right path," and in this moment, it seems like those butterflies are there just for me; flying ever so quickly so that they can latch onto one fear after another and flutter away with them.

I am on the right path. The path of love.

Two days later, Paul meets me at the airport. Rainbows and butterflies disappear as my stomach clenches in a knot. "What if he decides against us? Now that my heart is fully open to love, what if he says no?" I think as the knot tightens and grows.

Paul wraps me in his arms and kisses me like the long lost lover I recognize him to be. "I love you, Michi-fus," he whispers in my ear. "Let's make this happen."

# # # #

We fly back to California that Saturday, a new couple in love. Like Paul warned—reality is there to greet us before we even step foot off the plane. It comes by way of a text from the ex-wife. Trouble is brewing and I feel like I'm heading straight into a storm.

As I drive off to my apartment in Santa Monica, while Paul drives off to the Valley, I feel relief. The safe space between the beds is back temporarily.

I am capable. I just need a little time to acclimate to reality…

For the time being, I decide not to think about the relationship. Instead, I'll go home, unpack and get together a new game plan to solve issues in my own world. I still have a book that I need to force myself to write, and a boring job that I need to perform on Monday. My own reality is plenty for me to tackle right now.

I call Chris, Karen and my family and tell them I returned and that Paul and I are officially a couple. Comments include: "Of course you are" (Chris), "Baby, I am so happy for you" (Karen), "We love Paul!" (Sisters), "Well that's good news" (Dad) and "Great—now you won't be alone forever" (Mom). With proof-of-approval in place, I let the relationship rest on the back burner and move onto resolving my other dilemmas.

Over the next several weeks, I attempt with all my might to force myself to grow past my writer's block, even though my track record shows that forcing myself to grow has not worked in the past. My ego will not surrender and it throws out the usual arsenal of thoughts. "You aren't pushing yourself hard enough," it yells, so I double my efforts; which results in more wasted time staring at a blank screen, and more useless chopping and cutting of the old version.

The next excuse is, "It isn't writer's block. It's an unhappiness block caused by your sales job. You can't be creative when you're miserable. Yes, that's the problem! It doesn't matter what it pays, you need to escape the misery. Think about it—it has already been a year of suffering through product tests, account changes and all that crap. Escape the job!"

"If I get rid of the bad energy from this job, then I will write freely again like I did in Portugal," I tell Karen on the phone. "It is the job causing me my issue, not writer's block!"

"Baby, you said this before and where did it get you? It isn't the job. It's your attitude again," she reminds me.

"No, I am absolutely sure it's the job, not my attitude. It is just too stressful and uninspiring which sucks away all my creativity," I say with confidence.

"I don't think that's it but you seem pretty sure. So what are you going to do about it? You always have a plan so what's your plan?" Karen asks. I know she is holding out hope this minute that I will admit that she is right and reveal that my plan involves asking God for help to change my attitude.

"I'm retiring from Information Technology," is my cop out plan instead. "I am throwing in the towel when it comes to working in this industry, Karen," I continue, but add, "There's only one company I will come out of retirement for and only if they call me.

Besides that, I am officially retired from I.T."

Negativity wins again. I am just too tired of battling energy-sucking thoughts every day while at work. It is pure torture. I have to fight with myself just to get out of bed every morning, and I complain about it non-stop, especially to sympathetic Paul.

Karen sighs with disappointment, "Okay, Baby, if that's the best idea you've got." I assure her that this is the best solution. With the pessimistic job attitude out of the way, I am confident the words will flow freely again. I quit my job and cash in my 401K to cover living expenses, intent on writing full time.

During this time of decisions and transitions, I collect a broader view of Paul's reality. At first, his choice is to focus only on fun as a couple—to fuel positive energy into our new relationship. Whenever I ask questions, he diverts and spins the conversation to me and avoids any discussion about what is happening in his life. My work and writing frustrations seem to give us plenty to talk about, so I don't pressure him about it.

When his look goes from handsome to haggard (like he hasn't slept in days), I have to draw the line and insist that he fill me in. More insight about his reality is definitely revealed—a full avalanche of it. Financial issues, bad living arrangements, trouble with the kids, chaotic arguments with the ex, business downslide—it's all there.

Using his behavior with me as an example, I hold him, console him and offer ideas, but behind the scenes, I start to feel my own panic growing as well as my old beliefs. "Chris, this guy has some very serious stuff going on," I say with concern. "It might take a while to sort this out. I hope I can do this! Right now, I feel like I want to run really fast in the opposite direction. His life is a disaster!"

"Michelle, I dealt with similar things with Doug. It's all about acceptance. When you decide you love someone, it should be unconditional love. No obstacle is too big. God will work it out for him," she replies from a voice of experience before switching the topic. "How's the writing going?"

"No better than before, unfortunately," I sheepishly reply. Quitting my job did not deliver the writing solution I hoped for. The energy-sucking job is gone, but my writing still isn't flowing with this cut-and-chop version. Now that I have nothing else to focus on, my frustration grows tenfold as I face blank screens and no words day after long day. Fear of failure has its talons imbedded into my shoulder, as it perches and stares at the same empty screens with me each day.

To escape the screeching voice of failure, I divert my attention to helping Paul fix his world instead, since I know I'm good at that. I get deeper and deeper into his issues and focus less and less on my own. Instead of writing, I put together budgets and financial spreadsheets to help him get a grip on his financial situation. Then as overwhelm hits him, I hug, console and wipe away tears.

Unfortunately, the more involved I get, the stronger my urge to run grows. "What a mess! What is your future going to look like with this man? There are way too many variables involved," my head says. This unknown is huge and it feels like there is no element of control to me.

Unconditional love—that has always been (and still is) my ultimate goal—to know I am capable of breaking from my past ways and can love a man unconditionally without judgment despite any mess. That is the grand prize I hope to achieve. Karen has it mastered. Chris has it mastered. Paul has it mastered. I want to master it too.

"I need to commit and commit big or else I'm going to cut and run soon," I think to myself. "I can feel it. This situation has more challenges than I have ever faced in one relationship. The unknown is huge and there are too many external variables outside of my control, with not enough guarantee."

What if this is my only chance to find out if I am capable of unconditional love? Right here and now, in this relationship with someone who understands it?

"I have to stop myself from running. I have to force myself to commit so I push myself to reach this goal of unconditional love. I have to prove I am capable, like I professed to Paul, and I will never find out how capable I am if I run. I feel myself pulling away and judging more each time another issue from Paul's reality surfaces. If I don't lock myself in somehow, I will run!"

The frantic thoughts race through my mind as I get more and more entrenched in Paul and his life. I shut down memories concerning my past failures at forcing myself to grow with the excuse "This is different!" while I feed the belief "Something has to happen soon or else I will be gone."

About a month later, Paul announces that he found a small three bedroom home to rent in the San Fernando Valley. As we unload the last boxes, I look around. The place is barren; he barely has any furnishings, and I know from preparing his budget spreadsheet that he has no extra funds beyond current bills. This empty house will be the place he will attempt to raise three young children every weekend.

This is my chance to lock myself into commitment so I don't run.

"I think I should move in with you," I say to him as we stand in the empty living room. My voice is calm and even. He looks at me with the same shock and surprise as the day I said that we should be a couple and then it is slowly replaced by that same look of conflict from before.

I had thrown myself into the deep end again so I quickly start to tread water like before. My sales pitch flies out of me. "Paul, it makes sense. I have everything you are missing: furniture, dishes, TVs, décor—everything it takes to make a home. Plus, we won't ever see each other living so far apart geographically."

"Then there are the kids," I continue to tread. "What's your plan? You will have more than you can handle as you try to rebuild your business and manage three young kids every Thursday through Saturday. They will be here on your busiest work days. What are you going to do? You can't afford a sitter and do you really want to leave the kids with a sitter anyway, when they are already vulnerable and in shock about all this new change? You need me to help you."

"Also, my lease is up soon and it would be great for me to reduce expenses while I work on my book since I'm living on savings. This is a logical decision. Total win/win," I conclude as my sales pitch draws to an end.

Plus, I have to force myself to commit like this or else I am going to run!

I can see from the concerned expression on his face that he has not thought through many of the issues I brought up. There is a small visible struggle with Paul as he realizes he is further breaking his vow to himself, but all the points I make are too logical for him to argue with.

The very next day, the moving truck pulls up to my apartment. I had to act fast before one of us changed our minds, but when I explain the urgency to Paul, I use the excuse, "Don't you want to have a beautiful, inviting home ready for the kids when they arrive in a few days? We need to start all this now!" I don't mention my compulsion to run.

"Are you sure you want to do this Michi? We have only been dating for six months," Paul presses. "I know we are here with the moving truck, but you can still change your mind. You were very spontaneous yesterday when you said you should move in with me and this is not the normal you. You create lists, you call friends. This doesn't seem like you. You have a lot to think about and didn't give yourself an ounce of time. After living at the beach, moving to the heat and smog of the Valley is going to be a shock. Living with three kids who are all under the age of six every weekend is going to be a huge adjustment too. The house isn't that big you know."

I fight back the concerns clenching my gut and resist the urge to call it all off. Instead, I put on my "got it together on the outside" persona and reply, "This is a logical decision and it will be best for everyone involved. Besides Paul, I loooovvvve you," I add with a wink and a hug.

"Okay, let's get moving then," he says with a big smile. Love flows through him to me, which gives me strength.

It is all going to be okay. I am going to be okay. I am capable of handling challenges. I am capable of commitment in the face of uncontrollable elements. I am capable of unconditional love.

And my life as the other half of a committed couple, complete with an instant family, begins.

Chapter 21:
Do-overs via Parenting

The best way I can describe the first week of my new life is to compare it to when I first stepped off the plane into that airport in Mumbai, India... overwhelm, overstimulation and complete overload of the senses. It seems like there are suddenly people everywhere and there are so many loud sounds and voices and unusual smells. Everything seems to be in a flurry of constant movement so that the small three bedroom house almost bursts at the seams.

Similar to what people warn when they say, "Nothing can prepare you for when you first enter India," there is also nothing that can prepare you for three young kids and a man entering into your life virtually overnight. Even for the most capable woman, it is still a total shock.

The kids are a riot, in every sense of the word. We all take to each other instantly. At ages two, four and six I know that they are looking for more people to love them and play with them, so I do my best to make their transition smooth by adopting that role. They are all over me, following me, sitting in my lap—which I eat up.

I prepare for their arrival by using my do-it-yourself skills to buy necessities and to decorate their rooms in fun themes. I also buy games and toys. Their welcome could not have been any smoother or more enjoyable.

Of course this is the case, I am Michelle—the get-it-done and do-it-right woman!

Every time I look at Paul, his eyes are brimming with tears of happiness. "Thank you so much Michi," he mouths over to me as we sit on the sofa with three kids piled on us. His arms are filled with a sleepy two year old but I can feel his gratitude reach over and hug me. My heart fills with joy.

Am I on my way to unconditional love?

"The kids are fantastic, but there's just so much noise!" I tell my mom on the phone a day after they leave. She laughs, having had three kids of her own. After living alone for over six years it is a constant shock to me how much noise is suddenly in my life. I jump from enjoying it: laughter, movies, music, songs and dance; to a state where I am about to lose my mind over it: fighting, yelling, general loud volume.

For someone used to quiet, there sure is none on the weekends anymore!

I have events and activities planned for the kids almost every weekend for the first many months. It's a chaotic change for me but it's also fun to have all the energy around. Plus, Paul is gone for work during a portion of their stay each weekend, so I feel like they *need me* to be a solid pillar of support for them as they adjust to a new split-home life. We bake cookies, go for walks and play games at night. I set up a curtain like a stage so the kids can perform skits and sing songs with costumes. These are very bonding times. During the week, I take care of all the food and clothes shopping, cooking and cleaning.

I am turning into a regular Susie Homemaker, something I never knew I had in me. This is such a contrast to my old roles as lone-wolf traveler and success-driven business woman!

I handle it all how I would handle anything; with organization and a degree of structure, only this time there is *heart* mixed into the picture. And mess . . . there is a lot of mess mixed into the picture too. My apartments have always been orderly and neat. Every weekend, it looks like a tornado touched down at the house. These kids are so loving and full of energy, but they haven't been provided with many examples of order.

Karen had given me some stellar advice before the kids arrived for their first weekend. "This is a great opportunity at a do-over," she said. "Think about what you wish would have been different in your childhood and make it happen now." She also told me to look for the love when things get hectic.

I like this do-over idea!

While I had a loving, remarkable childhood filled with laughter, activities and support, there are four things I wish would have been different:

1) Calm reason with explanations versus "Because I said so"
2) Communication where I felt heard
3) Stronger bonds between siblings at a young age
4) An unconditionally loving family dog

I decide to put the first do-over into effect when I confront the messy house issue by focusing on calm reasoning with explanation. Instead of saying, "Clean your rooms . . . because I said so," I paint a vision of all the advantages they gain from tidier surroundings: toys will be easier to find, less hurt feet from stepping on things, and no sadness over broken or lost toys—simple ideas.

Since they are so little, I add fun to the mix by introducing the Counting Game. The game is that everything has to be put away by the time I count to ten. There are lots of dramatically elongated numbers (especially the niiiiiiiiiiiiiiiiiinnnne's) while everyone rushes, but there is also a lot of laughter and I pitch in and help. Then there are hugs and kisses as I yell "TEN" because everyone always meets the deadline. There is little resistance because the kids have fun with it.

I try to be consistent with explaining why to the kids for almost everything that happens. They love it. You can tell by their respectful responses to me that the kids recognize that I have respect for them. I take the time to either sit or kneel so I can look them in the eye and calmly and lovingly tell reasons. It makes all the difference in the world in our connection.

This leads into my second do-over: communication where kids are heard, not yelled at. There is a fighting incident and so I call our first Family Pow-Wow, where everyone sits in a circle and I ask,

"What's going on?" or summarize the issue as I see it. Each kid gets to tell their side, which is so cute because they raise their hands and take turns. The kids came up with that. Then I ask, "Who has an idea to make this better?" and they all raise their hands and say their solution, which gets creative and funny. We laugh quite a bit, but I make sure that we all move toward a solution and that things get resolved.

I only call Family Pow-Wows for major stuff but it dramatically reduces yelling and fighting. We all have a voice that is heard. Even the little two year old raises his hand (he gets a hug and a "great job" although we don't quite understand his baby babble).

Wow, think about how much resentment and anger would have been spared in my young mind had I experienced things like the Family Pow-Wow! All those harmful feelings of not being understood or heard would have evaporated if I had known reasons and felt that my opinion was being heard and that my voice mattered!

My third opportunity for a do-over (sibling bonds) presents itself within the first month after a physical argument breaks out between the two older kids. Siblings will always argue, I get this, but to hit, yell, call mean names, and tell each other they hate one another is a bad path these three are on since "What you feed will grow."

I wasn't the best older sister and treated my young sisters like crap growing up. I missed out on a lot of fun times with them when we were young and it took me a long time to repair those bonds later.

These kids have a great chance to learn a different path, especially since they are so close in age.

I call a Family Pow-Wow. "What's going on here?" I calmly ask no one in particular. "He kicked me," she cries. "Because she took my toy," he retaliates. Then they immediately start to do the "Nu-uh, Uh-huh" thing back and forth.

"Okay, everyone stop for a minute," I say calmly and wait for the accusations to die down, which they quickly do. "I have a question for you. Is this how you think family should act toward each other?" Silence, so I continue. "Family is so important. If you become friends, your brothers and sisters will be the people that will always be there to love and help you. I talk to my sisters every week and love them to pieces!"

"Instead of hitting and yelling, what can you think of that we could all do to show love for each other? Give me some ideas," I ask. Hands shoot up in the air. Ideas like "watch TV together" and "eat ice cream together" pop up. The ideas start to get sillier and everyone is laughing.

"Great job!" I respond enthusiastically. "These are all great ideas for things we can do together! How can we also show love and appreciation to each other?" Silence again. I lead with a few ideas, "Could we help someone when they need it? Could we tell them that we love them?" Heads nod yes but there are looks of doubt.

"How about if we go around and each say a couple of good things about everyone else?" Instant protest. "Come on kids! You can do this! How about if I start?" I go around the circle, say good things about each one and write them down so they each have their own list. They all say things about each other and I add it to their lists.

"That was awesome! Now, next time you get mad at someone, before you do or say something to hurt them, you might want to remember the good things that person said about you." There is a massive reduction in yelling and fighting.

To grow trust between them, Paul and I ask them to go to each other for help instead of to us all the time. This one is touched on lightly since they are so young. We do family projects so that they can learn how to work together too.

It is important to me that these kids feel a lot of love, especially while they shuffle back and forth between homes, so I read *The Five Love Languages for Children* by Gary Chapman and Ross Campbell and then start to speak each kid's love language to them. Small gifts (like stickers and notecards) greet the "Gifter" each week. I always seem to find a little love note of thank you on my desk each weekend from her. She feels my love and gives it back in return.

For the "Quality Time" kid, I focus a set amount of time for undivided attention to do whatever he wants, just the two of us. We build things with Legos or sometimes I sit next to him and watch while he explains the video game he is playing. He feels the love too. It is evident when he asks, "Is it time for you and me?" and when I say yes his face lights up into a mega-watt smile.

With the "Physical Touch" kid, I shower him with hugs and kisses and he laughs and giggles in return. It is easy to see that he feels loved because he always snuggles into my lap with a smile.

It might only be a few days a week, but I do the best I can to make sure they look forward to it.

The final thing I wish was different about my childhood is that I always wanted a pet. Pets teach a level of unconditional love as well as responsibility. Even though I feel overwhelmed much of the time with the new "insta-fam" responsibilities, I decide after about three months that we need a dog.

There is a selfish twist in this. Besides all of the good this will be for the kids, I really need something that is *mine*. The kids act like they are mine almost instantly, but I need something that I get to pick out as my own. Paul is a hard sell on this one, but I win when I point out how much the kids will enjoy having a dog in the house.

We find Jake the Wonder Dog from an ad in the paper. He is only eight weeks old and he is a golden retriever mix with a white chest, speckled stockings and a white tip on his tail and nose.

"This is the dog I have always wanted!" I exclaim. He is adorable and I instantly know that he is the right dog. Paul, on the other hand, is not so sure since the first thing little Jake does is throw up all over him, but he warms up to this sweet bundle of love within hours. He is totally sold when the kids arrive and they are so excited about the new family addition and about the fact that they all get to help train him. We all talk to Jakey-Wakey in baby voices, especially Paul, who calls him Puppy Love because he's an eager-to-please, easy to train puppy full of love.

These chances for do-overs and the opportunity to give and receive love through my new little "insta-fam" definitely add a new dimension of love to my life. All this change is still overwhelming after living such a self-based life for so many years, but I feel so grateful to have the opportunity to experience love while helping bring positive paths to the lives of these sweet kids.

Chapter 22:
The Battle—Head vs. Heart

Now that I live in the same house with Paul and the kids, our lives are fully out in the open and intermixed. There is no more space between the beds. Instead, every day I'm confronted full force by the chaos of his reality. While I enjoy the love of Paul and the kids, I cannot get into acceptance about the rest of the mess.

"Every day, there is just so much damage and wreckage to fix, with new issues added on a weekly basis! Did I make the wrong choice? Life was so much simpler when it was just me. Am I exhausted because I'm a square peg trying to shove myself into a round hole, or do I just need time to adjust and grow into this experience?" I immediately start to question.

"Don't worry about square peg/round hole yet, Michelle," Chris advises when I call her to voice my concerns. "You and I have many of the same issues going on. Your situation might have some added extremes but I have found that if I just get into acceptance, I have a great deal more happiness each day. Everything is part of God's plan."

"Acceptance: an action centered in faith, love and heart. Not my strong point," I think to myself, "but I am in this to learn to love unconditionally from the heart. I can do this!"

"You might be able to," the voice in my head responds, "but it sure is a lot of effort. Look at how exhausted you are! You should just run away," it says, "where you are safe from the chaos. Run from this mess!"

But I don't want to run, I am tired of running. I want to change and live in love and in my heart! What if this is just a rough patch on the road to my destiny? I will never know if I run.

Judgment strikes, "But he is clueless when it comes to money! You put his entire life into a spreadsheet and he hasn't even looked at it! Are you just going to accept that?"

Focus on writing and the organizing business and weekend plans, Michelle, not on Paul's finances. God is back in your book at long last! Be excited about how much better writing flows now. Think about fun with the kids too.

"But why is he so emotional? The man is too in touch with his heart!" the voice critiques. "He lets emotions stop him from moving things forward, like his business!"

I wanted an example of someone in touch with his heart so I could learn to live in mine! Yes, there are tears but be supportive instead of judgmental.

"And why did he ever agree to such a bad divorce settlement? It's like he didn't even look at it. Just signed on the line! Are you going to accept that you will have a life of struggle with him while she gets more money than he even makes?" my mind accuses when new realities surface.

He is a man that puts happiness above money, and love above logic and strategy. I knew it in Argentina and in Santa Monica also. So why am I acting like this is all new information when these are the exact things I found attractive about him?

The arm of judgment continues to wave about, as it searches out and finds more targets to scrutinize, more ammunition against acceptance. I attempt to deflect it again and again, but it is a strong voice determined to find more and more things that are unacceptable. Soon, the arm has latched on and I feel myself being pulled back inside my Box.

"You can fix it!" my ego promises as it pulls me the rest of the way in. "You are capable of *that*. You can fix all this mess. This is *who you are* and *what you do*! Get this ship sailing straight, put it on the path you want it to follow!"

I hear the battle call and cry back, "I will! I will get everything on path and then I will love unconditionally!" I immediately start to shift the ship's path. "What do you think we should do Michi?" quickly transitions into, "Ask Michi what she wants us to do," and control is surrendered into my hands.

What my mind is not at all prepared for is a new force in the equation: the incredibly counteractive power of other people's love. This love has a beautiful, non-evasive strength to it, a joy that draws me out of my Box like a magnet. My life starts to resemble the Hokey Pokey Dance:

"You put your whole self in. You put your whole self out.
You put your whole self in and you shake it all about.
You do the Hokey Pokey and you turn yourself around.
That's what it's all about!"

During the week, I put my whole self in my Box, where I plot and manipulate ways to change all of the non-acceptable elements. Then the weekend rolls around and I find my whole self out; drawn into my heart by the rambunctious, contagious, unconditional love of three adorable kids. Camping trips, family games, and bonding, loving times consume my heart each weekend.

The week starts, and I am yanked back into my Box again, where I shake it all about as I devise new plans to stabilize the chaotic elements and get the ship and its passengers on a path acceptable to me.

When I am in my Box, one thing becomes clear: Paul's consistent response, "Whatever it takes, Michi," is not acceptable because it is never backed by enough action. "Paul just isn't producing the desired results in any area," I conclude as I sit there stewing over the state of affairs. "Maybe he needs an example. I will show him how success is done."

With this as my new plan, six months after we move in together, I pull myself out of retirement and go back into technology sales. I allow it to happen because the number-one company calls me to say that they need someone to be the first-hire for a new division; a person who can prove a new tiered-system is smart so they can expand it across the company.

"We need a superstar who will blow numbers away and based off of your record, we think it is you," they say at the interview. "Of course it is," is my mental response, "I always succeed at business!"

But I also said no more I.T., only writing and organizing.

"Yes, but the number-one did call me! That was my disclaimer when I retired so it *must* be fate," I quickly point out to myself. "I will get this entire ship on track much faster if I set an example of how to achieve business and financial success and debt-free living. Plus, driving 3-5 hours a day all over Southern California will be a much needed adventure to break up the monotony of this domestic life. It's a solid, stable company so it will probably add a level of calm to all this chaos. Chris and I will be at the same company, so it will be fun this time. I get to be a superstar again, and I need to feel like a superstar right now. It's decided—I will take the job," I conclude after listing all these positives. "Michelle Bain: Professional Business Woman, is back to show them all how it's done!"

# # # #

"What do you think about me working, Paul?" I ask as we sit eating frozen pizza together one night. I have been on the job for several weeks and it is our first night together because I have been traveling out of town. "It sure feels better than I expected to be back in a professional corporate environment."

Paul looks slightly hurt at my comment but says "Michi, you know it doesn't matter to me if you work or not. I would love you whether you sat at home all day eating bonbons or if you made a million dollars. I am in a relationship with YOU—the person, not you—the doer," he replies with his usual stance of unconditional love.

"That attitude is exactly what put you into your mess, Paul," I point out. "If you pushed people to have a little self-sufficiency in your past, we might not face all the issues we face today."

"He is not following my example and his situation is no better than it was before," I think with resentment. "Paul has to change. If he were more like me, all of this would be so much easier. Examples aren't working. How can I get him to be more like me?"

The solution comes the same day when this discussion turns into an argument and I yell, "Paul, I'm tired of all this crap. I'm leaving you if things don't change!" His face has a look of pure panic. Fright about being alone. Apprehension about managing life on his own. Worry about losing me. Anxiety about failing at another relationship. I see fear of every type written on his face.

"You've got him," the voice of victory trumpets as it latches onto Paul and pulls him into my Box. "It will be much easier to change him to be more like you if he's inside. Keep him here and things will move much quicker in an acceptable direction." I shove Paul into the room marked "Men/Relationships" and get back to the business of directing the ship's course.

A few weeks later, I come back with the demand to move to a bigger home. "I've complained about this for weeks and I am done. I am going to leave if we don't move. I cannot reach maximum productivity when I have to shuffle into the corner of the bedroom every Thursday night when the kids arrive so I can work on Friday."

"If that will make you happy Michi, and if you are willing to pay the added cost. If you're happy, I'm happy," is his auto-response.

"If I'm going to pay even more, then everything else gets taken off my plate. I am no longer responsible for cooking, grocery shopping, cleaning or watching the kids every Saturday since I work about twice as many hours as you! It is time you come up with a system to manage work, kids and house without me doing *everything*," I declare.

"Whatever it takes, Michi," I hear him call out after me as I head to my work desk.

# # # #

Moving turns out to be fantastic for the entire family. Not only do I find a house with a beautiful office upstairs for me to work and write, it also has a heated swimming pool and huge rooms on the main level for the kids. It even has a fenced yard with a dog door for Jake.

My weekends become filled with even more heartfelt fun as we all swim and play water games and bounce on the trampoline. We hold bake sales and lemonade stands to learn about value of money while also earning money for new pool toys.

Almost like a fresh start, Paul and I take advantage of this new place and add some heart to our Sunday times together. We go on long bike rides around the park or on the trails. We even take a trip to Puerta Vallarta. This trip brings us back in time, to how we felt in Argentina, as we enjoy a horseback ride, zip-lining, parasailing, and romantic strolls on the beach.

"Ah, Michi, I knew your heart was in there," Paul says, rejuvenated by our loving time together. Upon our return, we attempt to hold onto that joy, to foster and nurture this fresh, unconfined love.

I feed it by listening to inspirational audio-books while I travel to all parts of my territory. Driving becomes like a daily vacation. During the long drives across Southern California, I soak in the variety of scenery: sparse desert, gigantic mountains of golden rock, serene ocean, rolling green hills. Every day is different and I listen to endless hours of books on tape as I take in the views.

Words of inspiration fill my ears and sooth my soul. Deepak Chopra, Esther and Jerry Hicks, Michael Bernard Beckwith, *The Secret* and my forever favorite, Dr. Wayne Dyer, all speak the words I need to hear as I drive along. *Change your Thoughts, Change your Life, Excuses Be Gone, Making the Shift* and *There is a Spiritual Solution to Every Problem,* are all audiobooks by Dr. Dyer that I listen to while on the road.

My heart starts to expand as I listen to the messages: "God is within. Your highest self is within. The answers are all within. With God, all things are possible. Let go and let God. Meditate."

I think back to times years before, as I traveled alone and listened to similar messages.

What inspirational times! I felt so connected to God back then. The only time I really feel connected now is when I am around the kids and occasionally around Paul. The rest of the time, I feel too exhausted by all that needs to be fixed to have the energy to focus on God!

"I should do service work again," I say to myself as I think back to the happiness it brought me. I make a silent vow to look up old friends and see if there are any projects going on.

"I also need to meditate again," I admit, as I suddenly realize that I have not meditated since I moved in with Paul. "There always seem to be too many distractions, with so many issues and so much noise. This new house has space. I will start meditating again," I vow, instantly feeling a calmness in my heart that I have not felt in a long time. "My new office will be my quiet place of solitude to recharge!"

# # # #

My commitment to staying in my heart is short-lived. As success shows up, it fuels the desire for more success and family is quickly pushed aside. It takes me seventy hours a week with almost five hours a day spent driving, but I win a stack of sales achievement awards my first year and blow out every quota they set for me. Every penny I earn beyond bills goes straight toward my rapidly decreasing debt.

"I am so much better at this than I am at love," I think as I see my name in work headlines again for another win. "This feels so good. My hard work is paying off!"

Long hours cut down on my time with the family but Paul steps up in my absence and takes over most of the household responsibilities. He also hires babysitters to cover the kids when he is not able to be there. "I have taught him well," I pat myself on the back in congratulations. "Even if it did take tough love and threats to leave, Paul is following all of my examples and is turning into a really good father. Now, if I can just get him to follow my financial example—more work required there!"

The kids tell me that they miss me when I don't make it home for dinner or family movie night, but my mind says, "They're fine. They have Paul. At least I'm setting a great example for them of how someone can be productive and successful, which they desperately need!"

"The only downfall," I acknowledge, "is that I'm exhausted and feel depleted all the time, but the financial payoff and decreasing debt is worth it. I have to continue to set this as the bar. I might not see Paul and the kids often, but there is only so much one working woman can do!"

# # # #

"Michelle, when this job is all said and done, do you think they are even going to remember that big sale you brought in, or even remember who you are? Those kids will be there for you for the rest of your life and they will remember the fun times at dinner. You have to realize they only want you there because they love and miss you. Don't forget that," Karen cautions when I call her on a drive to tell her about yet another fight Paul and I got into over my lack of family participation.

Paul keeps telling me that they all miss me and that I need to cut back on work and be part of the family again. I tell him that I don't have a choice, that this is an active job and it is hard keeping my head above water as it is. I can only handle so much! This fight has become a regular issue as I am away more or locked up alone in my office.

"Karen, this is good for Paul. He is taking care of his responsibilities completely now, and I am focusing on mine," I respond matter-of-factly.

"Okay, Baby. Just remember what I said. The job might not always be there but the family always will be if you are there for them."

"I promise I will remember Karen," I reply as I rush off the call with her so I can take a work call that is coming in on my cell phone.

"Michelle, it is a JOB!" Paul yells two days later as he flings the bathroom door open. I had slammed it shut a second before, annoyed that he would expect me to come all the way downstairs to say good morning to everyone as they leave for school, when he is very aware that I am late getting ready for work.

"I am through being last on the list. I am through hoping things will get better and that you will get a clue that family comes first. We do not matter at all compared to your precious job. You are always tense and tired when you are here and you are gone most of the time. Well, I am through. I am done trying to fight for us because I cannot win against money and your job!" he continues to yell.

"You know what, Michelle? I think you should leave! I think you should move out. You don't want to be here. We are something hanging around, aggravating you and your busy work life. We deserve more than this from you," he bellows and then stomps down the stairs to where the kids are waiting to be herded off to school.

They all leave. I stare down the steps from the bathroom in shock. There is only silence in the empty house. A silence so loud, my ears ring. My hands start to tremble.

"What the hell just happened? Paul doesn't break up with me. I break up with him! He has never told me to leave. Just the opposite, he always begs me to stay. What just happened?" I ask myself in total bewilderment.

"I don't know how to handle this situation. I'm the one who has the power! This can't be happening," I say. "What do I do now?"

Suddenly, I can't think straight. I look down at my shaky hands not quite sure what they are for, like I have never seen them before. It is like my brain is broken. I can't move. I am numb.

I look up at the clock which reads 8:05 a.m. and realize I'm late. I walk over to my desk and sit down. My hands start to move toward the keyboard. I start to open an email. My thoughts starts to click into place as the gears of my mind start to grind into motion again pulling me out of my temporary stupor.

"I am late. I need to start doing emails. Business as usual, put on my game face and get on with the day. I have issues to take care of and people to email. Another day in the life of Michelle Bain: Professional Business Woman. There is no crying in baseball. The show must go on." *Clackety-click, clickety-clack.*

One email, two emails . . .

It hits me square in the forehead like a huge sledgehammer right before email number three. "Oh my gosh, Paul just ended things with me and here I am emailing customers because 'it's my job!' He is right! I do put work first, even before my own self! Stuffing down emotions when I feel like crying and focusing on the task at hand instead. This is the repeat story of my entire life!"

I want to cry. I want to cry so much that I feel my hands start to shake again because of the tension caused by my restraint.

So cry for once Michelle, feel the feelings, release the pain.

"But you already have your makeup on and you have a reseller lunch scheduled in a few hours," my head counters, "YOU DO NOT HAVE TIME FOR A BREAKDOWN RIGHT NOW!"

I sit there in my desk chair, staring at the screen but not seeing any of the words as my hands continue to shake. I force back the tears while the battle rages on between my head and my heart. My head is suddenly so heavy. I can't take the tremendous weight of it any longer and rest my forehead on my desk in front of the screen.

I am so tired—so, so tired. I am so tired of trying to keep the ship pointed in the direction I think it should be on. I am so tired of working so hard every day. I am so tired of being me.

And then I break. My emotional restraints start to snap one by one, like metal bars which can no longer hold back the thousands of gallons of water pressure pushing against them from a caving dam; my restraints snap free and tears start to pour from my eyes onto my desk. Soon, wracking sobs shake my entire body as the rush of emotion bursts free and releases itself from my tormented soul. I cry for half an hour, my head still resting on the desk. I can't control the tears or make them stop. They keep pouring out of my eyes as I sob in pain.

I don't want to be like this anymore! I don't want to be someone who puts money and success over love. I want to be someone who loves, someone who is about family and life. Someone who opens her heart and actually FEELS!

The flood of emotion sweeps through me and I move to the floor, afraid I am going to be swept right off my chair. I lay curled in a ball there by my desk, sobbing tears as waves of regret wash over me.

All that unconditional love I shunned, as I hide behind work. Focusing on something I knew I could win at, versus giving my heart to the unknown of relationships and love. All the pain of non-acceptance. All the excuses of setting an example.

Heavy sadness takes over and new droves of tears start to flow as I realize I have lost it all, and that it is my own doing. My heart breaks as the pain of loss rakes over it; this feeling of loss is so excruciating, I have to clutch my heart before it bursts.

Suddenly shame floods through me as I think, "Is this how

Paul feels every time I break up with him? Did he feel this disparaging sadness each time I threw the threat of leaving in his face? He couldn't have. There's no way that someone could have endured this pain over and over again. It isn't possible. No one has enough faith in love to withstand what I am feeling right now."

I am so engulfed in these waves of emotions that I don't even realize that Paul has returned from dropping off the kids and has raced up the stairs in alarm after hearing my racking sobs. He crosses the room and kneels down beside me and instinctively folds me into his arms.

I shake and sob as he holds me tight against his chest, stroking my hair and murmuring, "It's okay Michi, you are going to be okay," again and again as I continue to cry. Finally, when the flood of tears subsides, I look up into his warm brown eyes and see that they are filled with anguish over the pain I am in.

He is hurting because I am hurting—because Paul is a man of compassion, heart and love.

"Is it true?" I ask as dread grabs my heart over the truth that is about to be confirmed, "Every time I threatened to leave, did you feel this much pain?" I need to hear the answer. I need to hear it from his lips.

He looks back into my eyes, tears cloud over his own as the question triggers the painful memories. "Yes, Michi," he answers, staring into me. "Every time you say it, I feel like my heart is being ripped right out of my body."

I see this truth; like the woman in the mirror, I see down into the depths of his eyes and see the scars of pain on his soul. I grab hold of him, so tightly like I am never going to let him go, as my body wracks with uncontrollable sobs once again. Only this time, these tears are not for me, they are genuine tears of compassion for Paul.

"I am so sorry, so, so sorry that I caused you so much pain. This is not the woman I want to be for you, and I will never make threats like that again. You are worth more than that. I'm going to change. I'm going to put love first, and I'm going to value love, all the love, starting this second."

And I vow to myself that I would rather die than ever pull someone else in and make them a prisoner in my Box.

"I believe you, Michi," Paul softly replies as he strokes my hair while I lay in his arms, weak from my release and realizations. "All the pain was worth it, if that is what it took to finally open your heart so that we can live a life based on love," he affirms from his place of faith.

He does believe it too, because he has that much faith in love. This same faith is what kept him with me, surviving each threat. This is the incredible Power of true Unconditional Love.

# # # #

I take my commitment to Paul very seriously and stop any threats of leaving. The realization of the pain I can cause when I pull someone into my Box as a prisoner is a much needed slap upside my head.

The first thing I do is become an active part of family life again. The kids have missed me terribly and are so excited when I tell them that, from now on, I will be home for dinner when they are at the house. I also make sure I am there for family movie night on Friday nights. Each evening, I tuck them into bed. It is a ritual we had developed, but one I neglected in my unwavering focus on work. I swim with them in the pool, play games with them and build Lego castles—all of the things I once did to show them how much I loved them.

Like Paul, there is some trepidation. When someone gives you love and then yanks it away by absence, there is always going to be a lack of trust. I have to prove to the kids, like I do to Paul, that I intend to stick with this family first philosophy. I keep at it, hoping I can stick to it myself.

I take on duties involving the kids again, like grocery shopping, making dinner and watching the kids while Paul is at work on Saturdays. I do everything I can think of to show that I am serious. Slowly, the air of caution starts to shift slightly with them.

I begin to pray and meditate again every morning, starting my day with connection to God as I did on my worldly travels. I involve the kids in meditation. Each one gets a pillow to sit on and we all pass around the singing bowl so everyone gets a chance to make it sing. Then we all close our eyes and say "Aum" for one minute. It is so adorable! I always peek to see who else is looking around. Sometimes there is no one, they are too busy with their "Aum" to worry about anyone else.

Paul and I decide to attend Agape on a weekly basis, a spiritual center run by Reverend Michael Bernard Beckwith, who I had watched for so many years on *The Secret* video. Reverend Michael's consistent message that "Potential happiness and everything you need all comes from within" resonates with me. I realize how off-track I'd become in my quest to have things be the way I think they should be. It nearly cost me a family of love.

"All of your needs are met," Reverend Michael preaches from the stage one month, "and only through gratitude and appreciation for what is, will you ever attract more of what you want." This is a loud message directed at me, I believe, because I have lacked gratitude for so many things in this relationship. Gratitude starts to blossom again from my newly compassionate heart: gratitude for so many wonderful basic things in my life, like love, food and shelter. Memories of the poverty of India flash back into my mind, forgotten reminders of how abundant my life is.

Service—I need to get back into service work. This keeps me on path. I call Sharon, the current Vice President of Childhelp—an organization I had joined many years ago. This organization helps abused children and it is dear to my heart. I had all but abandoned any involvement. I was too busy. "It's so good to hear from you. We miss you!" she exclaims, excited to hear my voice on the phone. The warmth of the love extended to me after my neglect causes me to choke up momentarily.

"It's so good to hear your voice too," I reply. "I've decided it's time for me to be involved again, but I'm still working this crazy job so I don't have a lot of time to dedicate. Can you think of anything for me to do?"

It turns out, she can. There is a new national education campaign going on for abuse awareness in elementary schools. They want to get posters hung in schools for the abuse hotline. I have eighty-six school districts as accounts at my job. I pick up supplies and deliver them to districts every day as I make my work rounds.

I clean house, literally, and pull together bags of clothes to donate. I call Homeboy Industries to see if they take donations after reading a fantastic book, *Tattoos on the Heart: The Power of Boundless Compassion* by Father Gregory Boyle. They are ecstatic when I tell them I have clothes. It turns out, they are in desperate need and are often not thought of when people decide to donate.

"Give me three weeks," I say, "and let me see what I can do." I make a few calls and start spreading the word and within weeks I have seventeen bags of clothes to drop off for them.

Writing—I need to reconnect with writing so I stay in touch with my dreams instead of tunnel vision focus on work and money. I also need to recharge my batteries with a good dose of God. It's time for a trip to Portugal!

I take off for my blessed home and for the next two weeks, I frolic in the waves and write in a state of bliss. "I am back where it all started—the writing, the dreams of a happy future," I say with a sigh. "When I breathe in this fresh air from my secret cove and stare out at the expansive sea, my soul is at peace.

"Thank you for this moment and for this experience," I pray. "Thank you for this wonderful weather and for this blessing of a few weeks alone in Portugal to work on my book and to rejuvenate."

After a long slumber, my dream of living part-time here and part-time stateside is re-awakened. I feel the joy of that dream burst forth from my heart with excitement.

One recurring set of thoughts invade my vision, "How can this dream all work out so that it includes Paul and the kids? Family trips? Am I just gone for months alone? They weren't a factor when I first bought the house. Would I give up the dream for family? Is it my true desire to live a domestic life for the next fifteen years? What if I decide that I am a square peg in a round hole after all? My renewed efforts with love are moving in the right direction, but what if I find that this life, with all its continuous bombs of chaos, isn't what I want in the end?"

I can't see what's around the next corner. I need to trust and have faith that everything will work out exactly how it is supposed to. I need to have faith that more will be revealed and focus on the NOW.

I let go of my concern about the future and return back to Paul and the kids with my passion for writing reignited. When the kids are busy swimming on Saturdays, I type away on the pages of my book, as I continue to add God back in. "So much energy wasted struggling to push myself through writer's block when my only real block was keeping God out of it," I admit as I think back.

Removing the God Block seems to create an avalanche of words. I type as fast as I can, attempting to keep up with the flow during my Saturday sessions. I stop to catch a breath a few months later and realize that another entire section has poured out. I stare at the pages of Lap II in awe and wonder, something I never envisioned when I started the book almost four years ago.

Karen was right. It is about God's time not my time with this book and more definitely was revealed to me!

My technology company holds a computer sale for employees

and Paul and I buy the two older kids each their own computer so that they can write books of their own. Now, I have a new heartfelt way to bond with them. It is fun to sit next to them as they read their stories aloud to me.

As my writing flows, a wonderful event occurs to add more positive energy to my true calling dream. During my visit to Portugal, I make a vow to do whatever it takes to hear Dr. Wayne Dyer speak in person when I return.

"I will fly to any country, spend any amount of money—whatever it takes. After all those hours of listening to his audiobooks for the last five years, I want to hear him live. I am sure that meeting my mentor will impact my life forever. It is time to make this Dr. Dyer thing happen!" I say with determination.

It's a Wednesday night a few days after my return; I jump onto the internet, type "Wayne Dyer events" into Google and prepare for anything. I stare at the screen. I blink and stare at the screen again.

"This website says he is coming this weekend to Pasadena, only fifteen minutes away from where I live, and tickets are still available for the 'I Can Do It' weekend conference," I say with glee. The synergy of my dream turning to reality so quickly is astonishing. "If I had waited another two days, I would have missed it."

But you didn't.

Paul and I show up to the event and I am so excited I can barely stand it. "I feel like I'm going to cry," I say to Paul, who is sitting next to me. "I have read every book Dr. Dyer has ever written and have listened to him for over five years. This is a defining moment in my life right now!" Then Dr. Dyer takes the stage and it is exactly like I dreamed.

The last day of the conference, I see a mob of people and head closer to check out the commotion. In the center is Dr. Wayne Dyer, who has been absent from the conference since his lecture. He is signing autographs and posing for photos.

What if this is my only chance? Where is Paul?

I rush over in time to hear Dr. Dyer say that he's expected upstairs and has to leave. He starts to break away, peeling bodies off of him as everyone surges toward him for a last minute photo. Soon, he is walking up the stairs to the safety of the secured room they have waiting for him.

I missed my only chance!

Disappointment and frustration flood my body. "I was so close!" I think back, full of regret that my spiritual mentor was only a few feet away and I was not able to meet him.

"I missed Wayne Dyer," I inform Paul as he joins me empty handed after his coffee hunt.

"I am sorry, Michi," he consoles, understanding what a huge disappointment this is to me, "but we should get on our way." The entryway has totally cleared because it is time for the next breakout sessions.

As I agree, still dejected, I see Anita—the main speaker with Dr. Dyer onstage—standing alone, as if waiting for someone. "I want to go introduce myself to Anita really quick, we can be a few minutes late. I have to tell her what an affect her story had on me." Paul follows, a little disturbed that we might be late.

I approach her with a big smile. "Anita, you did a fabulous job up there," I say and give her a big hug. We face each other, conversing like old friends. "Your story had a huge effect on me. I've been going through my own personal struggle with deciding my path in life and you really brought it home to me. I should really live in authenticity to myself and let the rest be revealed. Would you mind if I take a quick picture with you so I don't forget the message?" I ask.

"Absolutely! Thank you for saying all this too, it gives me confidence that my story is supposed to be told," she replies as we huddle together for a quick photo that Paul snaps for us on his cell phone.

I hear a voice behind us speak. It is a voice I recognize only too well since I have listened to it for endless hours over many years.

"Anita, I've been looking for you. I thought we were supposed to meet upstairs." I turn around, and there he is . . . Dr. Wayne Dyer, and for a few precious minutes, I have him all to myself.

"He has the same eyes as me," I immediately think to myself as I look at his face and his smile. We pose for a photo together and he laughs when I say, "Now I can replace the photo on my vision board with one that has my real face in it versus one I had to photo shop in." I tell him how much he has affected my life both while traveling and driving.

"No wonder you're so vibrant and beautiful," he replies, and I feel myself blushing from the compliment.

"Thank you so much for all you do," I say before we head off in the opposite direction toward our workshop. I float through the rest of the conference and return home, my mind racing with thoughts.

"'Don't die wondering,' Dr. Dyer says, but there are so many things to wonder about! So many constant choices to make in life," I think. "I wish I had a crystal ball to see the answers so I would always know the right choices!"

Sorry—there is no crystal ball, Michelle. Just like Australia, the depths of the deep blue unknown will always face me, but will I remember that the Guide will always be there to support me and take my hand?

Shortly after the conference, the unknown shows how unpredictable it can be when we are blindsided by devastating news. "Doug has ALS," Chris tells me over the phone between broken sobs.

"This can't be true," is my instantaneous thought. "Doug and Chris are only in their early forties. This is a fatal, non-curable disease that only has a life expectancy rate of a bleak two to five years. No, this can't be happening! Not after all the years she waited for him to arrive in her life. Not right before their second anniversary. Not to Chris, a constant source of love and support. This is not happening." I continue to deny, unwilling to accept the news.

Chris explains the overwhelming evidence, confirmed by doctors and tests, which supports the diagnosis. My heart breaks into a million pieces for my best friend and her true love. "What are you going to do?" I ask dumbfounded.

"What can we do?" she replies. "With this disease, there's nothing we can do. We have to accept it and figure that God has a bigger plan."

I sit there with my jaw hanging. This is not an answer I would expect from anyone who received this information, yet here is my best friend, already in full acceptance about this horrible news. It is then that I realize the depth of Chris's unwavering faith and her willingness to accept all events that she knows she is powerless to change.

At the same time Doug is diagnosed, Karen calls to tell me that Bill's health is declining and that if he doesn't receive a liver transplant, she might lose him. Their life is also filled with a great amount of unknown and yet Karen's response is, "Baby, even though I'm scared, I have to stay positive and turn it over to God." Again, an example of such faith and trust when facing potential loss.

"How can this be happening? How can these people I love, who are so good, so giving and so loving suddenly be facing death? How can this be?" I ask myself repeatedly.

Confronting the truth about mortality has never been on my radar. I operate under the assumption that I have all the time in the world. What if this isn't true? What if my time is limited? What if I waste more days trying to change things to be the way I want them and it never happens?

How often am I not really present in any given moment because I am trapped in my Box, tied up by unhealthy thoughts? I live in constant distress about the future not going the way I think it should. What if there is no future?

The depth of my attachment to Paul grows instantly as my heart fills with gratitude that he and the kids are in my life. I am grateful for the example he has provided to me of unconditional love.

I commit to letting go of my need to control so that God can control the outcome instead of me. I am going to relinquish control and live in the moment so that I can focus on appreciation and gratitude for life.

# # # #

My heartfelt declaration that I am ready to "Let go and let God" run things in California is met with a very loud, "No, you are not!" from my head. The battle wages on. My faith in God's management abilities is squashed down by old fear and logic so instead of letting go, I do what I always do—amp up my efforts to control all external factors.

"I am the only one capable so the more control I maintain, the better shot I have at keeping all of the plates balancing on their sticks," is my driving belief. I continue to burn the candle at both ends as I strive to be Wonder Woman at family, job, writing and service work.

"Well, at least my job is stable," I laugh with Karen, "Since the family life still has drama and chaos. I can be grateful for that!" I might as well have knocked the job plate off the stick myself with that statement.

I wake up a few mornings later to a phone call from a friend. "So do you still have a job?" he asks.

"What are you talking about?" I say into the phone as I jump out of bed and head into my office. My heart starts to race. "Did I do something wrong?" I automatically ask myself. "Of course it didn't. I am a superstar. I win. I succeed."

"Haven't you heard the news?" he says in astonishment. "This morning, they announced that your company is considering spinning off or selling your division. The entire industry and stock market is going bananas over the news. Oh, and the product you were excited about booking four million dollars in sales for last week—they announced they are killing the entire product line."

As he speaks, my stable career and my solid company comes crashing down around me without a word of warning. "I have to go,"

I say in a stupor and hang up the phone. I jump on the internet and see that the wire is alive with all of the news.

My initial shock turns to anger, "How could they not have warned us? We are their employees! Why are we the last to know, with the wire announcing it before we are informed?"

My mind leaps over to another massive new concern, "What if I don't have a job and income soon?" I call Paul in a panic and relay all the devastating news.

"What will we do if I lose my job?" I question as visions of us living on the street start to catapult through my head.

His response is light and casual, "Well, you said you wanted to work less so this would definitely do the trick! Relax Michi, it will all work out. Think about it. You could write more."

"His tone is way too cheery about all this," I think with frustration. "I have to call someone else who will understand the potential crisis I face." I call Chris, since she works for the company also. "Chris will understand my panic."

Chris picks up the phone on the first ring, "Don't panic," are her first words, before she even says hello. "I talked to management the minute I heard the news and this is going to be a mess, but we are not out of jobs." I let out a shallow breath of relief.

"Michelle, when I told you to pray for a solution for the over-working thing, this isn't exactly what I had in mind," she jokes. I laugh back, feeling lighter now that I know I'm not going to be unemployed by the end of the day. We agree to keep in touch about anything that we hear and hang up the phone.

Is God intervening and showing me something I refused to see: that if I place a job and corporation as my foundational source, it can quickly turn into a pile of instability?

"No, this is only a coincidence and you're caught in a horrible dream," my mind counters. "You can figure this out and straighten out this mess too. Save the customers and save the sales. Get on it!"

Damage control is the new path for each day and it is a

hundred times more exhausting than my previous excessive-hour-work-weeks. Plus, my faith in the company is destroyed. "I invested a great amount of effort into this company, which didn't think for a minute about my welfare when it decided to upend my entire life."

Is this what Paul and the kids feel like about my love? Is this Karma for my past behavior for all those times I threatened to leave?

I brush those thoughts aside and focus on my new do-or-die mission: maintain work success in spite of insurmountable obstacles.

For the rest of the fiscal half, I apply all of my efforts toward saving sales. As hard as I try, sales keep declining and my attitude declines with them. Quarter after quarter I am behind in numbers. The shooting superstar I used to be descends across the black sky farther and farther away, until I fade into a small flicker of light in the distance.

"No more superstar . . . no more success. I am failing . . . I have failed . . . I am a failure," is my new mental mantra. "I don't know how to survive this. I have never failed before at work. I am always a success, one any company can count on to build a territory and deliver. How do I live through this? How do I survive failing the one thing in life I have always been exceptional at? How can I be trusted to fix all the other messes colliding in my life if I fail at the thing I am best at?" I feel the foundation I have built my entire life upon starting to crack.

"I have to quit," I tell my manager. "I can't take failure. Plus, how can I work for a company I no longer trust? I have to leave. I'm not willing to wait and see if the other shoe drops." I have a very down-to-earth manager whose strength is definitely his people management skills. He is a laid back guy who also calls it like he sees it, regardless if it fits management script or not.

"Michelle," he starts off in his matter-of-fact voice, the one he uses with me that has a get-a-grip undertone to it, "this is just a job. Do you believe that I think less of you because you are not hitting quota? This job is not who you are. This is something you do to pay the bills, or else it should be. You're not a failure," he tells me in the matter-of-fact voice again.

"One thing I've learned over the years," he continues, "is that you never go out on a low. You'll regret it for the rest of your life because you drag it around with you. Stick it out. Things will change. Get back on a high and then decide if you want to leave."

"Can I do that?" I ask myself. "Can I get over my anger and resentment at this company and find a way to stick with it as it struggles to rebuild? Can I face possible failure on a daily basis and still stay with something and have faith that things will change? Can I reframe my personal perception so that I do not see myself as a failure, but instead as someone doing the best they can?"

"It is crazy how similar this mirrors my exact situation with Paul," I realize. "Maybe if I master this resentment and fear of failure about work, it will give me the strength to overcome my resentments about Paul's chaos!"

I can run away and never know the answers or I can stay to see if I am able to overcome resentment and also love myself in spite of my fall from superstardom. I have to stay. I will always wonder about all of this if I leave.

So I stay. I stay and I work harder than I have ever worked in my entire life to create change. Unfortunately, what I become obsessed with changing isn't me and my attitude: it continues to be *it* and *them*. Instead of diminishing, my resentments only grow as my ego brushes off failure with a new defense . . . blame.

"It's *them*, not me! *They* are causing me to fail. *They* are causing the ship to rock out-of-control instead of turning in my direction. *They* are the ones making me miserable! They don't think I am capable of changing everything but I will show *them*!"

My mission is one of pure overdrive, fueled by the ugly dark coal of resentment. "I'll show *them*. I will make this ship turn or I will die fighting! *They* cannot defeat me!" Every thought lasers in on the one and only acceptable result: fix it or die trying. I work around the clock and drive endless hours to beg accounts to stay with me.

"I cannot accept this company's instability! I will create

stability. I will fix the damage this Fortune 100 Company has caused in my life! I will stop all of the chaos!" are my battle cries every morning.

All of the plates are still spinning in the air, in spite of my focus on changing and fixing the mess of my work environment. They might not be spinning as fast, but they are all still up there to some degree or another. "I will get it all under control—I can do this," I say with pride and determination. "I might do it while filled with anger and resentment, but I will keep these plates spinning and keep this ship on track."

It is right about this time in my plate spinning act that I hear slow, heavy footsteps coming up the stairs to my office one morning. Paul is standing in my office doorway. "Michi, we need to talk," Paul says to me as I sit at my desk in my office. Usually, he comes in and sits down on the couch and starts talking when he has something he wants to discuss with me. This little preparation is not good. My stomach clenches up.

"God, please don't hit me with anything else. Not right now while I'm still in full battle to fix the chaos at work," I say in silent prayer. "I don't have that fully under control yet. I haven't fixed it yet. Please don't hit me with more."

"Yes, Paul—what's on your mind?" I reply as I spin my chair around. He has crossed the room and is sitting on the couch. He looks extremely anxious and even nervous.

"She's been evicted again, Michi," Paul hesitantly tells me, "The kids have to come live with us seven days a week through the summer—most likely forever."

And there explodes yet another atomic bomb. My life passes before me in a few seconds like I am on a speeding train watching scenery fly by. Constant struggle for money, dinners every night, toys everywhere, responsibility—never ending responsibility—never being able to travel or go anywhere, babysitters, noise—so much noise—and bombs, always more bombs.

I am never going to be able to get <u>these</u> ship passengers on path. They are beyond my capabilities. I cannot change them or fix them . . . and I cannot accept them.

All the feelings of gratitude and love I had been attempting to feed for the last three years seem to evaporate in an instant and only my dark resentment about the out-of-control status of someone else's life constantly affecting mine is left. *Square peg, round hole.*

I look at him with a blank expression on my face and reply in an emotionless voice, "Paul—I'm out. I cannot accept this constant level of instability for the rest of my life. Since you can't afford this house on your own, you need to start looking for a new place for you and the kids to live," and then turn back around to my computer.

Later, he comes upstairs in tears and attempts to talk to me. He breaks down in complete panic about what he is going to do. "You said you wouldn't threaten to leave anymore Michi," he accuses.

My resolve starts to waiver as I see his pain, but my mind takes possession of my actions and says, "This is not a threat. I am done." He brings up his bad credit and how he won't be able to get a place and I feel no compassion or love, only judgment, "I guess you should have followed my advice. I am no longer your clean-up crew. You will have to figure this out on your own. No more bombs for me."

And with that, I take the relationship and unconditional love plate off its stick, firmly into my hand, and send it flying up against the wall so that it shatters.

# # # #

That night, he sleeps downstairs in one of the kid's beds while I take the bedroom. Remorse sets in as I review all that happened. I think about the kids and how much they love me.

Is this who you are, Michelle? Someone so run by control and resentment that you are willing to throw love away?

I get out of bed and walk down the stairs. Paul is wide awake and gazes at me with eyes filled with a sadness I have never seen. I immediately start to cry. No words need to be said, our looks communicate what we both know. Paul continues anyway, like he needs to say it aloud so that it is real.

"You are never going to be happy with me. I might always have situations like this sprung on me and that is not a burden you should have to bear," he starts to cry, like a beaten man who faces the impossibility of overcoming situations beyond his control. "It is time we go our separate ways Michi," he says.

I thought I was capable of rising to the constant challenges and of fixing it all, but I am not. I'm unable to accept without judgment. I am not capable of unconditional love. I admit defeat.

"We can act like roommates for a while; this house is large enough for that to happen," I offer as some type of consolation.

"I don't know what I am going to do," his voice cracks as new waves of distress arise; he starts to sob. The fear I used against him now consumes him before my eyes. Suddenly, I want to shield him from it and make him realize that he will be okay. Like the times he held me and stroked my hair, telling me it was all going to be okay.

I have to protect him!

I reach out and take him in my arms and rock back and forth softly as his body shakes with racking sobs; my heart breaks into a million tiny pieces. For him, for me, for us, for a love that was and a love that might have been.

Why couldn't I rise above? Why did I let myself stay trapped in my Box, listening to what was not right instead of all the good? This man is all love and only wanted love in return. Instead I judged him because he did not think and act like me.

After a while, I go back upstairs. There is no sleep as my head and heart collide. Memories and solutions swirl around in massive balls of darkness and light.

There is no solution. That time has come and gone. The solution was acceptance and love and I chose control and non-acceptance instead. I am the one who shattered the relationship and love plate beyond repair.

We split the king-sized bed down the middle and manage to operate as roommates for weeks. We exchange sad smiles in passing and try to coordinate bedtimes so the other is already asleep.

I hide in my office most of the time, especially when the kids come, since they don't know. They think I am busy writing or working. This is fine with me. I have to have space so I can detach. I need time to separate from my heart so that I can handle the pain of never seeing them again. As I listen to the laughter down below, I silently cry upstairs, alone. Tears of pain and heartache as I realize how much I will miss them all, what a big part of my life they have become. How much I loved and learned from each of them in their own little ways.

The day we finally tell the kids, I call my last Family Pow-Wow. We all sit in a circle, like we always have, and I break the news as gently as I can but I am crying the entire time. There are no hands raised this time, only tears and hugs as they try to stop this reality from coming true. These little souls love me and cry and grasp onto me when they find out that we will no longer be a family. I make promises to see them if they still want too, but it does nothing to console their bleeding hearts, nor mine.

This is a mistake! I can't let them go! I am wrong. I'm supposed to choose love!

I cling to Paul after the kids leave and plead that I will change. "Please, please don't go through with this," I beg. "I will find a way to reach some level of acceptance with all this. I promise, Paul, I will do whatever it takes. Please don't leave." My words mean nothing- only my past actions can be heard. My promises are too little and too late.

"I can't take that chance Michi. Not with my children's welfare at stake. I have to make sure they have a home," he says with sadness in his voice, but with determination.

I am not going to win. I can't change his decision. The actions dictated by my controlling mind can't be undone this time. I took the beautiful gift of love offered to me by this man and these children and I destroyed it beyond repair . . . only to realize too late how much I want and need it.

Yes, I chose to follow my head instead of my heart and the payoff I get is a sad, lonely world where my obsession over control drowns out any joy and where my lack of faith kills love.

Dejected, I stumble over to the stairway as the overwhelming pain of failure and loss tighten their grip on my heart. I pause and stare down into the darkness. No light awaits me, only a blackness filled with despair and sorrow. Step after step, I descend alone. With each step, I feel myself sink further into hopelessness as the light from above grows dimmer and as the weight of my past mistakes grows heavier. By the time I reach the bottom, I am so lost in darkness, only one solution seems to exist that would end both my heartache and the constant struggle with my mind.

After a detour to the kitchen, I lay on the sofa under a thick blanket. Tears softly stream from the corners of my eyes.

I am tired, I am done. No more striving, no more learning, no more lessons. I am tired of living in fear of the unknown. I am tired of living in the anguish of non-acceptance. I am tired of always needing to be in control. I am tired and I don't want to play God anymore. I thought I was capable, but I am not. I am only capable of being sucked back into my Box, not living in my heart.

The blade of the sharp kitchen knife feels so cool against my wrist where it rests, ready to free me once and for all from the inescapable prison of my mind.

All those beautiful life lessons I have been given, yet I always end up back in my Box facing the same issues over and over. My Box—My Will—is just too strong and I am just not strong enough to escape it. I am never going to change. I have tried and I cannot make it happen and now I just don't have the strength to battle my head anymore. I throw in the towel. I admit failure and defeat.

God, I surrender!

And with that, the entire foundation of my Box begins to crack and all the walls come tumbling down.

Chapter 23:
Ultimate Surrender

I sleep deeply that night, deeper than I have in many weeks, maybe even months. So deep I do not even hear Paul leave for work in the morning. This is a good thing, since I suddenly can't seem to put thoughts into words and it would have been hard to explain the knife at my side.

My mind doesn't feel like it is in slow motion. It just feels like it is a thick, dense cloud of nothingness. Like I can't think at all.

Have I lost connection with reality as well as my connection with God? I don't know what to do.

"I need help Chris," I say into the phone. My voice is calm, alarmingly calm. There are no more tears, just numbness and a low ringing in my ears. "I killed love, failed at playing God and now my head is broken. I almost tried to cut and run last night and now I can't think. I'm scared, Chris. I can't think straight and I can't find God," is all I manage to pull together. It is enough. "Stay put, I'm on my way," she replies. I sit on the floor by the bed, numb-minded and rock back and forth.

Back . . . and forth . . . back . . . and forth . . . back . . . and forth. Three hours pass as I sit and rock in a state of numbness. Only the ringing in my ears lets me know I am still conscious. Then Chris arrives and we decide it is best to involve professionals since my mind is still a complete fog of numbness.

Soon we are in the waiting room of Adventist Medical center. Inside the examination area, there is a small room with a tilted chair where a nurse and a psych attendee ask a few pages of questions. After my interview, we all decide it might be best for me to stay a few days until the fog clears.

My first time in a psych ward is not at all what I expect. I think this one is nicer than most. It has a courtyard with flowers and trees and many windows with light streaming in. Most importantly, every hour a soft voice comes out of the speakers by the head of each bed with messages such as "God loves you" and "You are special to God."

I sit there in a ball on the bed in my gown and socks and listen to that soft voice, and let it seep into my soul.

I love You too God. I am sorry I let You down. I thought I would be able to rise above all the chaos and choose faith and love, but I just wasn't strong enough. I failed. I am so sorry.

God doesn't respond but the little voice in the speaker says, "God loves you" again. I lay in bed, waiting for the voice to come back.

My mind is so foggy and numb . . . I am so tired . . . I just need a few minutes of sleep . . . I will try God again later . . .

When I wake, a priest is there and asks me if I would like to take a walk in the courtyard and talk. I agree and pad out in my gown and socks to sit next to him on a bench.

"Do you believe in God, Michelle?" he asks by way of starting the conversation.

"I do, but I tried to take over God's job and failed miserably," I respond.

"Did you really think that you could play God, Michelle?" he asks.

"Yes. I thought I was that capable. I thought I could run lives and control things and make everything go in the direction I wanted it to go. I thought if I tried really hard, I could make it happen but I botched it all up," I reply with a laugh. *It feels good to laugh.* He laughs too, "Obviously!"

"Why are you here, Michelle?" he asks next.

"Because I am so, so tired . . . of who I am. I can't battle my ego and thoughts anymore and I can't let them continue to run my life so I decided it might just be easier to run away—for good. I want peace and love, not anger and resentment. I want to accept people and situations, not always judge them or try to change things. I want to live in my heart, not my head. I want to be unconditionally loving, not a machine."

"Most of all, I want a life of faith. To be led by God, not BE God. I can't handle the battle against my fear and ego alone because alone, I always lose. I need God to run my head and to add strength to my heart so it is more powerful than my mind," I cry.

He pats my hand. "Why don't you go inside and get quiet for a little while and see if you find what you're looking for," he says with a wink.

I go back to my bed and start to pray for all those things that I said to the priest. I lay there in silence for ten minutes, then twenty.

I truly surrender God. Only You are powerful enough to change my mind. I surrender my ego and my mind to You, God. I can't do this alone.

The voice in the speaker comes on again, it is a male voice this time, soft and smooth. "God is always with you," the soft voice promises me. "You are never alone. Never lose faith."

A warm glow spreads throughout my body and I close my eyes and drift off to sleep. When I wake, I notice the fog around my brain has lifted a little.

I feel so much peace.

A memory of a soft voice whispering through the crack in the window floats into my head.

It is all going to be okay. There is no more Box.

"There is no more Box," I repeat aloud. "There is no more Box. My Box has been torn down. That's why my head has been a numb fog." Tears of relief pour out as this realization sinks in while my heart overflows with gratitude.

It's all going to be okay. I am going to be okay. I am going to stay free. I will continue to surrender and have faith so that I do not rebuild that prison. I won't play God again.

Thank You for being here with me, God. Thank You for loving me in spite of myself. Thank You for breaking me down to the point where I would be willing to do anything, including die, to no longer be a fear-driven headcase.

Please strengthen my heart with Your love and guide my mind. I know where love is now. It is in the place where You reside, in the space where You are. You will help me to be unconditional love some day because although I do not have the strength, You do and with You, all things are possible.

Thank You for life! I am sorry I lost all hope and faith and was ready to run. I will make it up to You somehow, someday, I promise I will. Tell me how and I will do it. I am willing.

I promise You I will find a path that will guide me closer to You and that I will stay on that path so that I am connected to You here, there and everywhere for all the minutes of the days. Please help me to better hear Your voice in the silence. My will is Yours, my acceptance is Yours. Thank you!

They call us in for craft therapy. I climb off the bed and head toward the room. I know exactly what my project will be the instant I see it on the table. Throughout my travels, I collected a religious symbol from each country, like crucifixes and such. I have so many beautiful symbols displayed in my office, all with the country and year written on the back.

The craft I choose to make is a small, simple wooden cross only about six inches tall which I glue rows of colored quarter-inch square tiles onto. I select the tiles randomly with closed eyes to insure it's not perfect. When I'm done, I write "Psych Ward" on the back as a lasting reminder of where my destructive old ways lead me.

I will hang it on the wall with the others. My memento of the painful journey to ultimate surrender and faith.

If it takes a complete mental break down for me to break free so I can have a lasting, heartfelt connection with God, I am willing. This experience is a small price to pay in trade-out for a life of freedom and joy. I am willing to accept what God has planned and to truly let go and let God be in charge.

"And acceptance is the answer to all my problems today. When I am disturbed, it is because I find some person, place, thing or situation—some fact of my life—unacceptable to me, and I can find no serenity until I accept that person, place, thing or situation as being exactly the way it is supposed to be at this moment."

"God, grant me the serenity to accept the things I cannot change, the courage to change the things I can, and the wisdom to know the difference."

LAP IV

DIVINITY WITHIN SHOWS ME THE WAY

Chapter 24:
Honoring Commitments

"I never would have been able to swim alone before because of my shark phobia, especially at night," I think as I swim another lap in the lit water of the backyard pool. "I have grown so much, and overcome so many fears, especially after my ultimate surrender. I have faith that I will survive this recent loss and grow from it too."

Nighttime swims have become a regular thing for me since Paul and the kids left. It is a therapeutic new activity for me, instead of only running. The warm water during my nightly laps seems to wash away the stress of my busy work days while it rinses away lingering thoughts of sadness as well. After my laps are complete, I often float on my back for a while and stare up at the dark night sky and its millions of twinkling stars.

"Stars, do you know what my future may bring?" They do not answer but continue to twinkle down on me with all their glittering glow as if to say, "Look at all of us watching over you. Do not feel lonely, we are here with you, Michelle." The vastness of that night sky makes me and my troubles seem so small and insignificant, yet the pain of heartache is still there, never-the-less.

While I was away finding God, Paul had been busy finding a new place for himself and the kids to live in. He was able to get a smaller house in another city and he and the kids moved out shortly thereafter. I decide to stay in the large house alone for a few months while I work out the details of my new position with my company, the one good thing that resulted from the company chaos.

In all honesty, it isn't just the job transition keeping me here. I'm not ready to let go of this past and move on, not quite yet.

Although the emptiness of the big house haunts me with memories that keep the pain of heartache alive, I am not willing to sever the cord.

Paul and the kids stop by every week or so to see me and Jake, but I am sure if I move, this will end. I say that keeping a cord intact is for the kids and that my staying close gives the kids time to gradually adjust, but I am the one who needs time to adjust to my loss and time to digest all that has taken place. I find comfort in Paul living close and in spite of all that happened, we still have love for each other. This soothes my soul as well.

I'll know when it is time to cut the cord completely. The time is soon. We all have to move on.

There is a lot of silence in the empty house . . . too much silence. It makes me think back to all the times I complained about the excessive amount of noise. I want that noise today in a way. There has been a great amount of reflection in this silence though. Time will heal the wound, but clarity helps keep me moving in the right direction.

In spite of all my surrender, my resentments toward certain people and work still linger. They were not all instantly removed. Resentment is *the most* powerful soul strangler I have ever encountered. I don't let it run me or control me though, I just continue to pray every day that my resentments are removed so that I have peace.

Looking back, I realize how I ignored, "If something is meant to be, it will happen effortlessly." Many signs, including my immediate doubts and unhappiness, said that this relationship was not meant to be, yet I tried to force it to happen anyway. Paul should have been allowed the space his instinct initially told him that he needed, but I overrode his inner voice when I took on God's job. I tried to force Paul to be someone he wasn't. I forced myself into a commitment and into a situation that had more challenges than I wanted, so that I could test my abilities.

I might feel lonely, but now that I have space from it all, there is a huge sense of relief and peace in the absence of constant challenges and unexpected tidal waves. Even my chronic lower back pain and skin rashes went away a few weeks after we separated lives. Heart/head contrast aside, we probably had too many other core differences to make it work long-term.

Even though I believe God's Purpose was for me to come to a place of surrender, acceptance, and willingness to change, I can see I was a square peg trying to cram myself into a round hole. It never would have worked with my dream to live overseas, we have different dreams.

This newfound clarity makes the ending of the relationship easier to accept. I feel sad that I never achieved unconditional love, but I also know that there will be a day when unconditional love will flow effortlessly from me.

# # # #

"It's time for fresh starts!" I declare. The territory transfer came through about a month ago and so it feels like a good time to make the final break with Paul and the kids and start fresh in a new home. My search across the Greater Los Angeles area for a new place for Jake and I has *not* been a success. This is my first time in California with a dog and *No Dogs Allowed* is the standard rule eighty percent of the time.

Sometimes, after a disappointing day of searching, the frustration in me says, "If only I didn't have him." Then I return home, open the door to that big empty house and there is Jake to greet me— a sweet bundle of unconditional love with joy so intense that his entire body wags in happiness. My heart instantly melts.

"It's you and me, Jakey-Wakey. I'm in this for the long haul. I'm your person and I'm committed to you. You can count on me.

Even if it takes me months and I have to look at two hundred places, I'll make sure we find a happy home where we can make a fresh start," I promise him as I toss aside feelings of defeat and hug my happy pup instead.

It still ceases to amaze Chris that her commitment phobic best friend, who previously could never comprehend Chris's deep love for animals, is now a dedicated, loving pet owner herself.

That little love puppy is my trainer as he teaches me about commitment and unconditional love!

"'Baby, go where the love is.' That is the advice Karen always gives me and love, for me, is back in Redondo Beach," I realize. "That is where my entire journey started and it is where I want my next journey to begin. It is time to go back to where I am loved and build deeper bonds—to commit to these friendships. To set roots and grow where I am planted on a much deeper level."

It is time to return home.

Shortly after I commit to this decision, I find a great little house by Redondo Beach that is newly remodeled and has a back yard for Jake. It is central to my new territory, which reduces drive time significantly so I should have more time to dedicate to living life. I am instantly back in the mix with old friends and live right down the road from Karen again.

It feels so good to be back!

I remember my promises to God in the ward when I vowed to somehow make up for my loss of faith and for taking my priceless life for granted. Using my personal experiences with downfalls and challenges, I start to help other women. I make sure to help through sharing my experiences versus attempting to fix anyone or by playing God. Instead, I give unconditional love and support as these women struggle to overcome their own fears and issues.

It is amazing how much my heart is growing, God!

Another way I keep my vow is by helping kids. I commit to another school renovation project with my same group of PSI friends who start Operation Project Hope, a non-profit organization. Similar to the other school beautification projects, there are hours of painting, planting, cleaning—all done with love by hundreds of volunteers who want to show these children how much they care.

Tears of gratitude stream down my cheeks as I walk the campus reviewing the final result. What once looked like a grey prison, the school and yards now brim with life and positive energy.

God is everywhere here!

Beautiful murals cover the walls, with "I AM" messages filling every barren space. Walls of colorful handprints decorate the halls, to convey the message that "we are all one." Outside, new flower gardens, trees and greenery brighten acres of barren cement lots.

Such an impact this makes on young lives. I am so grateful to be a part of this!

I also do not forget my vow to find a guiding path so that I continue to foster and grow my relationship with God. While on my travels, I had read *Autobiography of a Yogi* by Paramahansa Yogananda, a spiritual master from India who followed his calling from God, which was to bring the practice of Kriya Yoga and Raja Yoga to the Western world. His foundation, Self-Realization Fellowship, has beautiful centers in California with meditation gardens and weekly services.

Based on the concept of daily meditation as a method to reach deeper connections to God within, the Sunday services pull teachings from Jesus and the Bible, and Krishna and Bhagavad Gita, into messages that help followers overcome obstacles to achieve closer connections to God. A melding of East-meets-West in a God-centered, non-denominational, non-religious way.

This path combines much of what I have learned and studied globally and fits around me like a warm cashmere blanket, both gentle and comforting with an air of peace and tranquility. It is how I always wanted my path to God to be. I commit to twice daily meditations (which I do in the quiet meditation area I set up in my home) and to the actual lessons which arrive to me every two weeks. I read many of the books and attend service every week, so that my new relationship with God can flourish from my growing connection with my heart.

The security cord that ties Paul and me together remarkably stretches all the way from the Valley to the beach, over an hour and a half away. He comes over and helps me with some plumbing issues one weekend and then swings by for dinner a few weekends after that.

"Are we ever going to cut this cord all the way?" I think to myself after he leaves. "I need to stop this because we have no intention of reuniting. This is just a crutch so we don't have to move on!"

Isn't it interesting how we hang onto something that doesn't fit: jobs, relationships, bad habits; simply because we are familiar with them? We escape the unknown but have to live with the knowing that this isn't our real path.

Thankfully, God does for me what I can't seem to do when Paul informs me the next week that he has found someone new. My ego pops back into the picture and I throw into his face that he is repeating his same old issues.

I cannot fall prey to all that negativity ever again or else my Box will start to rebuild. It has to stop once and for all. It's time to move on—past all of the resentment, anger, sadness, guilt and regret and move into the unknown future.

So instead of feeding the negative, I pray for acceptance. I tried this in the past when I actually lived with him, but my prayers were really only lip service. Back then, I didn't want to let go of the resentment. No way. I wanted to play the victim and the blame game instead. My prayers were words, but my mind and ego were fully in control. Choosing the lower, easier path of bad behavior pounded those old prayers down into dust.

Today, I pray for acceptance from a place of truly wanting the best for him, and the best for myself. A place of wanting to evolve past my old judgmental, resentful self so much that I am willing to take any action required to change. I pray from a place where faith and freedom flow instead of venom and entrapment.

This time, my prayers come from my heart. They come from a heart totally willing to surrender to God for help because I can't do this through my willpower alone. I already tried that and failed and now I know I need God for the strength to rise above. This time I pray with a level of willingness that comes from a desperation that someone only feels when they know they will become a prisoner again if they don't stay on path with a new way.

My sincere prayers are answered, but not right away. It actually takes months and I am grateful for that. If they had instantly materialized it would have been too easy and I might have taken the results for granted, which would have set the groundwork for me to repeat the past instead of changing for the good.

These prayers for acceptance are answered through the freedom I feel after I take action to change. I write down lists of all the good qualities of Paul and for the first time, only allow myself to focus on the good. I talk about the good, tell friends about the good, and allow my heart to remember all of the good, instead of the negative I used to feed.

This brings another wave of deep sadness for what I took for granted but the sadness helps me grow too. I openly admit my part in our downfall so that I focus on my own behavior, because this is what I want to change—me not him.

The biggest, most ego crushing action I take is that a year later, I write two letters to Paul, each one about specific lacks or wrongs that I demonstrated in our relationship. I ask for his forgiveness for my lack of faith in him, controlled emotions, playing God, and even my inability to reach a level of unconditional love. These are heartfelt apologies, not lip service, and over the distance Paul feels this and recognizes that I am apologizing with a genuine heart. After some time, I ask him if there is anything more I can do to make up for all the damage and pain I caused.

I receive a short reply. "We are all good Michi," is his five word response. Five simple words that set me free from who I used to be.

The interesting thing is that, through this process of willingness and only focusing on the good, a transition has taken place. Somewhere between Point A: resentment, Point B: remorse, Point C: willingness and action, Point D: acknowledgment of good to Point E: acceptance, my heart has transformed as well.

I feel true, deep, unconditional love for Paul. I only see the good in him and only want happiness for him with all my heart. I know we're not meant to be, but I can accept that with total contentment and have faith that things are the way they are supposed to be. My heart loves him unconditionally, for the man he was, is and will be—not the one I expected him to be. This gives me such faith!

I am capable of unconditional love!

About six months after this, I receive a letter from Paul's nine year old daughter. It is filled with love and gratitude for "my helping her grow and discover the person she is meant to be." Tears flow freely as I soak in her loving words and look at her drawings of horses and read stories about her friends as she tries to catch me up on the past year or so of her life.

The next one has a letter about how much she misses me. Inside, there is a medallion made out of cardboard and ribbon that says, "I 'heart' you, #1 stepmom forever!" but what is really says to me is, "We felt your love, Michi. Don't let yourself think you were all bad. You might not have been capable of acceptance, but you did a great job in some areas and did the best you could in others. Now, you have done everything possible to change. Next time, if you stay in your heart, you will do even better."

Related to this letter writing episode, the ex-wife reaches out to me to see if there is a way I can be a more permanent part of this young girl's life. I open the email and realize that all the terrible, crushing resentment I had toward Paul's ex-wife has completely evaporated as well. It is gone. No bitterness or blame, only gratitude for the fact that she is trying to find a way to help make her daughter happy.

We all decide it might be best to let the past be the past, but I'm able to pass on last words of inspiration to this little girl and this opportunity fills my heart to bursting. It's a chance I never imagined I would get. I tell her, "We might not be able to see each other, but we will always be in each other's hearts. Remember, what you think, you bring into your life, like people who love and support you! It might not bring me this time, but keep your eyes open to see if God puts someone else in your life to fill my space. Make sure and thank God when they arrive!"

I will never forget again, God. I will never forget that for any point in time, we are all doing the best we can for where we are, both spiritually and mentally. I will never forget that acceptance is my key to happiness, while resentment is my path to misery. I will never forget that love is the answer and to be so grateful for the love I receive. I will never forget you again, God, or try to take on your role.

The next day, I go to the tattoo shop to get my first tattoo: two lines in a simple font, nothing fancy or dramatic. **Love ~ Acceptance** and **Gratitude ~ Bliss** with bliss representing the joy that comes from my conscious contact with God. Four words that mark the cornerstones of my new foundation of life, forever etched as a constant reminder, right where I can see them many times throughout the day . . . in the exact spot on my wrist where I once held a knife, ready to throw it all away.

Chapter 25:
Final Barrier

On the job front, I am working my new territory and my drive time is reduced dramatically since my new territory is within two counties. The downside of my new territory is that it comes with a gigantically huge quota. I mean gargantuan! It isn't an unfair quota; I now manage some of the largest accounts in the territory so big numbers are expected.

"Balance, balance—I will maintain balance this time. I really mean it!" I tell Karen on the phone a few days in. Balance lasts about thirty seconds. After that, I am back into eighty-hour work weeks as I work myself to the bone.

Well, I wish I could say I work myself to the bone. I actually gain about fifteen pounds from eating comfort food and not working out. I also spend most Friday and Saturday nights at home on the sofa in a tee-shirt and sweats in a semi-vegetative state in front of the television. After dressing in meeting attire, conversing in business slang and dealing with major issues all week, I am drained by the weekend and find myself too exhausted to make any attempt at social conversation.

To my credit, I do have a fabulous motivator this go round—and it isn't success. Nope, this time I am not driven by fear of failure *or* the need to be a superstar. This time my dream is to save up enough money to take time off to write full time. I see this new territory as a golden opportunity to get the rest of my debt paid off and put money in the bank so that I can focus solely on writing for a while.

This is so exciting! Words still flow . . . when I find time. Who would have thought a Lap III would evolve with this first book? Now, I have a new writing project with Chris's husband, Doug, which I want to research and explore. I need to wrap up this first project so I can dive into the next!

In my excitement, I get slightly off course with the amount of work I am willing to take on to make this future happen. It appears my willingness here knows no boundaries. Week nights, weekends, holidays—all spent strategizing plans to increase business, answering and sorting emails, preparing proposals, finding product to send to customers—while the normal work hours are spent in front of customers, dealing with issues and closing sales.

"Big quotas equal big stress" is my new mantra, forgetting for a short time that what I feed will grow. Soon, stress on a magnitude I have never experienced before keeps me up in endless hours of thought every night, as I worry about if a needed sale is going to come through and if product will arrive by customer's deadlines.

"But the payoff is worth the stress and effort," I justify, as my debt grows smaller and smaller.

I increase sales twenty-five percent in my first year, which is millions and millions of added revenue. I am once again the superstar, back on top, a total success . . . and this time I couldn't care less. My goal is not ego and success; it is money so I can be free from it all!

"Fantastic job!" I hear from management to which I reply, "Thanks. So how can I make more money?" Although fear is not my motivator like in the past, the drive for more, more and more money so that I can move onward to my dream starts to build the old walls back up. Even with my new foundation, my Box is once again under construction!

It's on my birthday that God jumps in and takes control of this. I decide that since it's my birthday, I will actually take an entire weekend off to go snowboarding out of town with friends. The day is beautiful; warm and sunny with a good level of snow. I joke with my friend about how heavy my head feels from the new helmet she insisted I buy that morning. I usually snowboard without one.

We are on one of the last runs of the day because the sun is about to start its descent behind the mountain soon. Since this will be one of my few opportunities to snowboard this season, I tell my friends to go ahead without me because I want to squeeze in one more run. The plan is that the two skiers will go straight off the lift and head down that path while I go right, so that I head down another path. The end of the lift is in sight, only fifteen feet away, so we all prepare to get off.

I don't remember getting off of the lift. I regain consciousness with no clue who I am or why I am at the top of a mountain. I sit up in a daze and attempt to get my bearings. Many minutes pass as I sit there, looking around in complete confusion. I am only about thirty feet around the bend from the lift. My board is strapped on like I am ready to head down but I have no clue how that happened either. I have a slight headache in the back of my head, under my protective helmet, but have no memory of ever falling or hitting my head. *My mind is a total blank.*

A man skis up and asks me if I'm okay since I have not moved. "I don't know," is my shaky reply as I look around and attempt to remember what happened. "Do you know where you are?" he asks. "A mountain," I answer. "Do you know which mountain?" he continues. "No," I reply. "Good thing you had a helmet on!" he comments.

Yes, good thing.

This goes on for a few minutes as I continue to look around and attempt to connect to my thoughts and memories together as he phones the ski patrol. I start to tear up as the realization settles in that I have no idea what happened.

"Don't worry, I won't leave you," he says and holds my hand.
I have heard that message before.

"Thank you," I whisper and lay back into the snow to wait for the ski patrol to arrive.

Chris was right about one thing in Switzerland, the idea of riding down the mountain strapped inside a sled being pulled by the ski patrol is petrifying! I want to walk down. Unfortunately, they don't give me a choice since I have some degree of amnesia and a possible brain injury.

The ski patrol has to physically pin me down for a few seconds. When the neck brace goes on and then the confining straps on the sled tighten to hold me in, I have a claustrophobic attack and almost flip the sled. Since they can't tighten the straps without me hyperventilating after that, it is a long, slow ride down.

The good news is, by the time I'm at the bottom, I remember who I am, my friends' names, and where I am, but still have no clue what happened. It is a complete blank . . . total white out. The person in the office tosses me a couple of aspirin, tells me to watch for a few warning signs and sends me on my way.

Back home, I get an MRI because my speech is still slow and I am informed that it is a slight concussion and that this slowness might last for a week or so. The doctor tells me that I really need to take it easy.

Take it easy. Slow down. I get the message behind your God Whack loud and clear. No more Sermons on the Mount required. My head is Yours again, God. You have destroyed the rebuilding of my Box. Thank you!

I take action. I have conversations with management about ways to reduce my workload by hiring extra support help. At first I approach the subject from a fear of loss angle, which gets me nowhere. I switch my approach to what they will gain if they move forward with my plan and I get approval.

Remember, fear is never the best motivator.

It takes a while, but my plan for added support falls into place. Unfortunately, I end up with more stress and work than before, since my job involves training new help on top of volume.

"Well, I got what I asked for at least," I say to Chris, "but I'm only a flicker." Chris and I have this joke between us about "being the light" since I went to an energy shifter once and her advice was, "Be the light, not the darkness, in every situation."

Since sharing this info with Chris, we gauge our attitude toward things by if we are "the light" or not, and end calls by telling each other to "be the light" before we hang up. When we can't quite get there, we call it "flickering flame" mode. I am a flicker right now.

"'Ask and you shall receive,' well I asked and I received," I say to myself, "but I asked for what *I* thought would fix the situation and I asked the wrong Source!"

Sorry God. I tried to control things again. I need relief, however that may come. You know my plan is to save up enough to write. If it is Your plan for me also, so be it. If it is not Your plan for me, I will wait for Your plan to be revealed.

In the meantime, I decide to try an experiment. It goes back to the hard work mentality from many years before, and the fact that I never attempted to discover if it is fact or myth when it comes to jobs.

I do something completely contrary to my norm: I cut down the number of hours I work to fortyish. And then I hope for the best and pray to have faith that it will all still work out somehow.

Turning this over is difficult for me, but I do it. I stick to normal hours and start delegating and escalating instead. The stress it initially causes is twofold: 1) I have to accept that people do not work like me and that everything is not always done the way I think it should be done 2) I have to let go of control and have faith.

I look at my wrist every ten seconds for the first few weeks. "Acceptance, Michelle. Accept people and situations and be grateful that you are not working horrendous hours anymore. Have faith in people and know that you are putting forth all your effort to make things successful during your hours and so are they," I say out loud to myself as I see yet another issue pop up in my inbox.

I keep turning issues over in complete surrender. "God, if it is your will, then the shipment will make the cutoff. If it's not your will, then at least I feel clean that I did everything I could," I say. "God, if it is your will that we win this big deal, then so be it. I again feel clean that I did everything I could to help it be ours." So on and so forth for weeks and then months, all while I continue to stop myself at forty hours per week.

What I find is that, about 98% of the time, everything is working out to my favor. As long as I put forth the best effort I can and feel I have done everything I can to move something toward resolution or success, this is all I can do and the rest is up to sources beyond me. Sure, there's a lot that falls to the wayside, like e-mail filing and such, but I find more efficient ways to do things so that I do not waste time with petty things. I delegate more, even though this means the risk of mistakes. I surrender it all.

I realize with work that while I want to have integrity and feel confident that I always do my best, I also want to have peace of mind and not go crazy overworking myself in the process. Simple . . . yet profoundly effective. I am finally at the place where I provide the best service I can as an employee for my company, in exchange for pay.

I let go of all attachment to the outcome. If we win, it isn't about me succeeding, it is about things aligning for a win to take place. Same with losses. I don't take things so personally: I do my job the best I can and leave the results up to God.

It might have taken me decades, after many failed attempts but I am no longer my job. I am someone who is simply of the best service possible to her employer. I am finally there!

I call and thank my old manager for his words of wisdom. If I had left on a low instead of staying until things were on a high again, I would have missed out on this miracle, as well as the financial miracle that next takes place.

Not only do things work out with this new attitude, they work out beyond belief. In a matter of months, I am debt free and have hit the financial marker I set that allows me to leave to write.

To put it into perspective: It took me two years filled with seventy to eighty hour work weeks to earn what I earned in about six months of forty hour weeks where I do my best and turn the results over to God. My stress levels are at an all-time low as I put forth my best actions and detach from the end result.

If only I had learned this sooner! Think of all the hours of life I would have had for fun, relationships, and joy of living. I loooooove my new ways of thinking and living! Thank You God!

My mind swings over to Chris's husband, Doug, who has ALS. No one can guess when the last day might be. I never want to waste time in stress and worry about a job again; stuck in a rut of anxiety where my last day on earth might be wasted as a fifteen hour work day instead of spent on family, friends, and joy of doing what I love.

"It is time for me to go, Chris," I say one morning to her on the phone. "The boxes are all checked on my 'when this happens, then I can quit' list. I know you understand this better than I do, because you live it each day as part of your reality with Doug, but life *is* too short and it is time for me to do what I love." Then I call Karen and my parents and tell them the same. Cheers of support meet me, for we all know that it is time.

On my other wrist, I stamp these new lessons so I don't forget all I have learned. Same font, same two lines but a few more words. *Heart ~ I AM ~ Faith* and *There is only Now*. Heart—so I remember to live in my heart, never my head again. Faith—so I always remember Faith not Fear. I AM—to remember I am one with God and all creations. There is only now—because there *is* only *now*, only this second—there are no guarantees, as dear Doug and many others realize. I want to choose to spend this NOW more wisely than before and hopefully going forward, I will.

I am glad I got this tattoo when I did because taking the final leap of faith to quit again seems a little harder this time after I set a personal income high. To counter this, I meditate more often and look down at the word "Faith" on my wrist. "When something is meant to be, it happens effortlessly" was already proven by the quick financial accumulation; there is no reason for me not to take these last steps forward. Yet the hesitancy is still there.

As usual, when I need a push, one is delivered. This one comes as a painful sales loss which I recognize as God saying, "Okay, Michelle, the list is checked, that was the deal. Take the leap off the diving board. You know how to swim. Don't worry, if you start to drown, I will be there to help you float."

I am able to accept things so quickly now, and so willing to let go of control! Living in faith in my heart is so exhilarating . . . and so much easier! I fully understand now the place where Karen and Chris come from and why they choose to live there. I am so glad I choose to live there now too—life is so much less stressful in my faith-filled world.

I put in my notice, with a smile about how wonderful it feels to be so connected to God and to recognize lessons and direction. Work thinks I am resigning because I'm upset over the loss, but I assure them it is not the reason. The loss was just a push I needed to jump and take action toward my dream.

After many conversations, management finally believes me and sees my future vision. I offer a longer leave time than normal so that no one is in a bad situation. I wait for someone to be hired and train him to take over my territory. They divide up my territory, so I prepare account history documents for hundreds of accounts/departments so that each rep inheriting the accounts knows who, what, where, when and how and I pass along all contacts. I take reps around and introduce them to their new customers. I explain contracts and tell future happenings. I make sure all big issues are resolved so no one walks into a mess.

My manager and teammates thank me daily for working hard until the end so that they can succeed. "Thank you so much. I have such a better shot at success from all the information you gave me," one says. "I am so grateful that you took the time to introduce me to everyone," another says. "It's so rare to have someone work with such dedication and diligence up until the end. Thank you," management says.

Each thank you reminds me how much I have changed as a person as the result of my many life experiences.

I smile and respond back to him, "No problem *(Central India)*, my only motive *(France)* is that I want everyone to have the best chance at success *(Kids)*," and I mean this, from my heart *(Paul)*.

I leave with grace and integrity *(Italy)* because that is the woman I am today *(Psych Ward)*.

A woman who can stare into the next door *(Portugal)* that holds her true calling *(Spain)*, but who still has the patience *(Ireland)* to put others first *(Switzerland)* and to help others *(PSI)* with the knowledge I have before I shut the last door.

A woman who treats others how I want to be treated *(Scotland)*, because "we are all one" *(Santa Monica)*.

A woman who no longer lives in a Box run by fear *(Battle)*. One who will take the time to inspire and support others *(Fiji)*, like others have done for me *(Chris and Karen)*.

Regardless of the hardships *(Rajasthan India)*, I appreciate this company and all the growth lessons I have learned and am grateful for this "vehicle" which came into my life when I needed it to *(Greece)* so that I could finance my dreams.

For all these reasons, I stay . . . until their third extension request. Then I remember that sometimes the cord has to be cut but that there is growth for all involved on the other side of that too *(Paul)*.

Yes, this is the woman I am today because on the journey to becoming my ideal self, I have been shown The Way (God).

# # # #

The first day of unemployment, I wake up with my stomach clenched in distress about the unknown, but recognize this as an old habit and quickly realize that it will pass.

The second day, as a writer following her dream, I wake up and cry with joy.

The third day, I wake up to stress rearing its ugly head. Stress about finishing the book, about not getting up when I said I was going to, about completing my agenda for the day.

Each day after that, I wake up with a new agenda: to live the day in bliss. The bliss that comes from inner joy when I am in conscious contact with God. I return to living in the excitement about the mystery of what the day will hold, like I did while traveling the world, only today I embrace this from my heart—right here where I am.

Yes, I'm finally able to wake up in my own bed in total excitement about the day and in total joy about life because my search has ended. I no longer need to seek the answers. What I need to keep on path to my ideal is right inside of me. It is in the sacred space of my heart where God and love reside.

"Where ever you go, there you are." This is so true and it fills me with strength to know this today because this means where ever I go, God goes too. So in essence, the ideal *me* is the ideal *we*.

I still listen to God's message in the voices of people God puts into my life. Now, instead of asking what they would do in a situation, many times I cut to the chase and ask, "What would God have me do?" and pick the action that follows faith and results in love. And if I still can't quite connect with which action, I have patience and trust that the silence within will whisper a soft answer and that I will be shown the way.

The choice of who I am is always mine to make, but after the examples I have witnessed, the situations I have experienced, the pain and the joy I have encountered and the clarity God has provided . . . who else would I really *want* to be but the ideal me?

Conclusion

I find it fabulously interesting that after this eight year journey I have come full circle so that I end almost exactly where I start. I live in the same area, drive almost the same cars, had the same type of job, have the same single status, same friends, same family, same, same, same . . . yet I couldn't be more different than the woman who started this journey.

As I walk through my next door, into the adventure of the unknown as a writer, I have a different mindset, a different level of faith and a different driving factor.

"What would you attempt to do if you knew you could not fail?" is no longer a question that sends me on a quest for answers like it did in the beginning. There is no failure in my eyes now, because all results lead to personal growth and so even bad results are constructive and good.

I have replaced this coffee cup question with a quote I refer to earlier from Dr. Wayne Dyer, "Don't Die Wondering." This statement has taken on a deeper meaning for me, especially as I embark on a writing project with Doug (Chris's husband who has ALS). I never want to die wondering what it is like to truly live my life like each day might be my last, and to embrace mortality by learning to fully live in the NOW.

What will this look like? I don't have a clue. I could never have planned the book you hold in your hands. It just unfolded how it was supposed to, part by part, so I will let the next one do the same. Isn't the unknown a beautiful thing? As always, more will be revealed, and in God's time—not mine.

I do know how it will start though—by me returning to Portugal. With this in mind, I venture farther into full circle as I sell and store everything, yet again, and head overseas. My only dream is that my future books might help others, as I hope this one has.

As for love, I'm going with an open mind. It's a big world after all! Most importantly, I'm going with an open heart, which is the true key to love. It might have been the roughest part of my journey—the last twelve inches from my head to my heart—but I am there now, in my heart with God, and with God . . . *all things are possible!*

Acknowledgments

First, I want to acknowledge that this book would not have evolved into physical reality if I would not have evolved as a person. There were a lot of people who helped with *that* massive undertaking so my gratitude goes to them.

Karen Cleveland, you are my "all good things rolled into one" pillar of support. Not only does your guidance and love keep me on path, but it was your consistent message, "Baby, maybe it is not time for the book to be done yet. Maybe more is supposed to be revealed," that kept this dream alive with faith for so many years.

Christine Smith, my best friend and cheerleader, I could not have written this without you. You never let me give up and when I doubted myself, you refused to see me as anything but who I was meant to be. Even at the bitter end, you stuck by my side with words of truth.

Allen and Linda Bain, dad and mom, the two people who always tell me how proud you are of me, and who always keep faith in me through all my struggles. Thank you. Sunny and Lesa, same for you, my sisters of love and support. I am so glad part of this journey included all the Bain Girls.

Meg Burby, who is such a voice of reason and a fantastic editor. Thank you. The rush at the end was intense and I am so grateful you hung with me, and pushed me to dig deeper. I am also so happy you were with me through the revised edition so we could dig even deeper.

"Paul"—you know who you are. It was rough but your love made all the difference in who I am today. I am happy we are still friends from a distance, and will only ever want for your dreams to come true.

And God, thanks for allowing me to be a conduit. May this always continue as I grow in connection with You.

About the Author

MICHELLE BAIN is an author dedicated to using her personal life experiences, along with the wisdom of knowledgeable masters, to help improve the consciousness of people around the world. She resides in Los Angeles, CA and Albufeira, Portugal.

To learn more about additional books in the Laps of Life Series, please visit Michelle Bain's official Web site at www.michelle-bain.com.

www.ingramcontent.com/pod-product-compliance
Lightning Source LLC
Chambersburg PA
CBHW060148050426
42446CB00013B/2721